TRIBES AND TRIBULATIONS

TRIBES
& TRIBULATIONS

MISCONCEPTIONS ABOUT AMERICAN INDIANS AND THEIR HISTORIES

LAURENCE M. HAUPTMAN

University of New Mexico Press, Albuquerque

Library of Congress Cataloging-in-Publication Data

Hauptman, Laurence M.

Tribes and tribulations : misconceptions about American Indians
and their histories / Laurence M. Hauptman.

— 1st edition   p.   cm.

Includes bibliographical references and index.

ISBN 0-8263-1581-X (cl.). — ISBN 0-8263-1582-8 (pa.)

1. Indians of North America — Public opinion.

2. Indians of North America — History.

3. Indians of North America — Government relations.

4. Public opinion — United States.

5. Language and culture — United States.   I. Title

E98.P99H38   1995

970.004'97 — dc 20

CIP

Designed by Sue Niewiarowski

For my students in twenty-five years of teaching
and to two extraordinary teachers—
William T. Hagan and Jack Campisi

CONTENTS

ILLUSTRATIONS

PREFACE

*One false assumption . . .
and logic does the rest.*
—*Expression on sign at Gardiner, New York*

The following nine essays focus on some of the many misconceptions that Americans have about Native Americans and their histories. In the subtitle of this book, I have purposely used the word *misconceptions,* meaning erroneous conceptions, false opinions, wrong notions, or misunderstandings, rather than the word *myths.* The latter connotes stories which quite likely concern heroes or deities and attempt to explain a society's worldview or sense of identity. Although several chapters focus on the mythology of the frontier, the book, as the quotation at the beginning of the preface indicates, is largely about false assumptions, not all of which have taken mythic proportions, and which have restricted our understanding of Native Americans and their histories. Misconceptions are a product of many factors, including historical misconstruction, misinterpretation and omission, mythmaking and invented tradition, as well as stereotyping and racial bias.

To be sure, Native Americans are seriously affected by how Americans generally construct and define their nation's history. This framework has been labeled by Daniel J. Boorstin as the "Survival of the Victorious Point of View: The Success Bias." To Boorstin, much of the history of the United States is "hidden" because of this bias since a "dominant theme in the writing of American history has been the filling of the continent, the consolidating of a great nation. But the desire to secede, to move *away* from the larger political community might have become the leitmotif."[1]

As the primary resisters to American continental expansion from 1607 to 1890, Native Americans went against the majority of Americans' definition of "progress." Therefore, in Turner's model of frontier history, Native Americans had no place except as obstacles to be overcome. Michael Kammen has written that historians, the "ordained custodians of memory," as other Americans, "arouse and arrange our memories to suit our psychic needs." The "Winning of the West" was the great epic which largely defined American identity. Thus, when it came to "major episodes in the history of white–Indian relations," the truth was "simply repressed—sometimes deliberately and sometimes by apparent inadvertence." Even when first-rate academic training and cultural sensitivities were displayed, the result, according to Kammen, frequently produced the "same potent impact as the sun's ultraviolet rays upon vivid colors, exposing, bleaching, and diminishing."[2]

Thus, historians have themselves created or perpetuated certain misconceptions about Native Americans. In Chapter 1 I show that scholars have lacked an understanding about genocide in American Indian history, either denying it ever happened or categorizing every aspect of Indian–white relations as genocidal. I demonstrate in Chapter 2 that historians have often been unable to see the "underside" of the frontier, namely the violence as well as social deviance of the encounter. Recently scholars, as is shown in Chapter 3, have helped propagate myths about the United States Constitution and its intellectual origins. I argue in Chapter 4 that historians, by merely concentrating on the pronouncements of Andrew Jackson and Washington policymakers instead of the deeds of treaty negotiators, have failed to fully understand the comprehensiveness, and with it, the very nature of Indian removal policies. Both in the Jacksonian era and in later time periods, as is shown in Chapter 6, scholars have been misled by the paternalistic rhetoric of Washington officials about American Indians and American Indian policies.

Historians have also failed to focus enough attention on certain major aspects of Native American history, thereby contributing to misconceptions. The Civil War was a watershed for both Indians and non-Indians, affecting each well into the late nineteenth and early twentieth centuries. Native American participation—they served in the Union as well as Confederate war machines—was significant, one which is described in Chapter 5. In Chapter 9, I emphasize the legal struggles undertaken by contemporary Native American attorneys, largely out of the view of the American public or media, to maintain Indian existence.

All societies invent tradition, as Eric Hobsbaum has written, to create "a set of practices, normally governed by overtly or tacitly accepted rules and of a ritual or symbolic nature, which seek to inculcate certain values and norms of behavior by repetition, which automatically implies continuity with the past."[3] The myth of the frontier hero, treated in Chapter 2, is an invented tradition, rationalizing violence against Indians for a newly emerging society of colonists and their descendants. As Richard Slotkin has observed:

> the frontier hero stands between the opposed worlds of savagery and civilization, acting sometimes as mediator or interpreter between races and cultures but more often as civilization's most effective instrument

against savagery—a man who knows how to think and fight like an Indian, to turn their own methods against them.[4]

As is suggested in Chapter 2 the myth of the frontier at times obscured reality. In the case of Captain John Underhill, the hero of the Pequot War, killing Indians in the name of "progress" hides the darker side of his psychological makeup.

Native Americans also invent traditions. Despite having no basis in fact, the Six Nations Confederacy have evolved a tradition over the years, one most noticeable in the past decade, that the United States Constitution was the intellectual product of Iroquois leadership of the eighteenth century. This misconception/invented tradition is discussed in Chapter 3 by exploring the career of James Wilson, one key Founding Father who is frequently cited as having been influenced by Iroquois leaders and their ideas.

Racial stereotyping has also led to numerous misconceptions about Native Americans. Although stereotypes were created long before the establishment of major league sports franchises and Hollywood, both of these industries have perpetuated false assumptions about Native Americans and *still* do. Chapter 7 focuses on two extraordinary Native American talents—Louis Francis Sockalexis, one of the first Native Americans in major league baseball, and Jay Silverheels, the most famous Indian actor in Hollywood from 1940 to 1970, both of whom faced the institutional racism of their chosen professions.

Another misconception/stereotype, namely that all Indians today live west of the Mississippi River, is addressed in Chapter 8. Although 20–25 percent live in the East, many Americans, including some western Indians, associate Native America with the American West. In Chapter 8 I show the great resurgence of Indian pride in the East since the historic American Indian Chicago Conference of 1961, organized by anthropologist Sol Tax and his assistant Nancy Lurie.

The major underlying theme that connects these essays is that language affects our mental images and helps create and/or further misconceptions about American Indians. The book begins by focusing on whether the word *genocide* is a correct term to employ in American Indian history; it ends by analyzing how contemporary Native American attorneys fight to re-define the terminology of American law, which in the past and in the present have restricted Indian sovereignty, civil and treaty rights, and religious freedoms. Throughout, words define, restrict, and shape. Is the word *hero* applicable universally to Indian fighters? Did American Indians *influence* the drafting of the United States Constitution? What do we really mean by *Indian removal* in the Jacksonian Era? Were Indians simply recalcitrant *hostiles* resisting American Progress as depicted in old-style John Ford-directed westerns of the 1930s and 1940s? Can we characterize American Indian policies as *paternalistic?* Is there *Indian Country* east of the Mississippi? What do sports *lingo — tomahawk chops,* team mascots, and sales promotionalism — as well as Hollywood directors and screen writers do to our mental images of Native Americans? Why are certain Native American nations *federally recognized* and what does this term and the *federal acknowledgment process* mean?

Two caveats are in order. First, since my expertise is largely on the history of Native Americans of the Eastern Woodlands, much of the material presented in this book, but not all, has a distinct eastern focus. Second, this book does not claim to be the last word on the history of Indian–white relations and Native American history in general. My aim is simply twofold: to stimulate student interest in this important subject, one that too often has been marginalized in American history; and to raise the level of intellectual debate about Native Americans and their histories.

ACKNOWLEDGEMENTS

Tribes and Tribulations: Misconceptions about American Indians and Their Histories is a book that emanates from a quarter-century of classroom teaching about Native Americans. My students prompted these nine essays. Their initial assumptions upon entering class, their questions raised about the nature of the readings written by professional historians, and their reactions to guest lectures by Native American leaders led me to write these essays. As a result, I have dedicated this book to the more than five thousand students I have taught over the past twenty-five years.

I should also like to dedicate this book to two academics, both of whom I consider my own mentors over the past twenty-three years. For two decades, Professor William T. Hagan of the University of Oklahoma was my trusted colleague within the State University of New York system. He introduced me to the art of delivering an effective academic paper, shared with me his unique knowledge of Indian records at the National Archives and its branches, and amused me with stories about SUNY politics and about his graduate training at the University of Wisconsin. His many published writings are models of how to do effective American Indian historical research. Most importantly for me, he was an academic who first listened to my ideas and encouraged me to undertake primary research in Seneca history.

Professor Jack Campisi of Wellesley College has constantly prodded me to go beyond the literal interpretation of the document and see the nuances in Native American history. A trusted colleague within the SUNY system for many years, he urged me to go beyond "forensic history" and do fieldwork. Besides introducing me to the Oneida and Pequot Indian communities and their histories, he has shown me that history has legal applications to contemporary political and social issues from which academics cannot or should not shy away. Significantly, Campisi first coined the phrase "Tribes and Tribulations" for a conference that we directed together on federal recognition policies in 1982. He also opened up his research files on the Wintu Indians, which I employed in writing Chapter 1 of this book. Campisi has served as a valued sounding board for my research. I have benefited by coediting two books with him and by his friendship over the years.

Although the vast majority of material, over 80 percent, presented in these nine essays are original to this volume, two of the chapters appeared in full or in part in other forms: Chapter 2 as "John Underhill: A Psychological Portrait of an Indian Fighter, 1597–1672," *Hudson Valley Regional Review* 9 (September 1992): 101–11; and Chapter 8 as "The Voice of Eastern Indians: The American Indian Chicago Conference of 1961 and the Movement for Federal Recognition," *Proceedings* of the American Philosophical Society 132 (December 1988): 316–29 (coauthored by Jack Campisi). These writings are reprinted with permission of the two publishers as well as Jack Campisi.

The State University of New York contributed to this book in a variety of ways, including providing an internal grant and awarding me a sabbatical leave that facilitated the completion of this manuscript. The staff of the College at New Paltz's Sojourner Truth Library, especially its reference and interlibrary loan divisions, answered my persistent questions and helped me to obtain secondary and primary materials for my research. Joan Walker, the secretary of the History Department at the College at New Paltz, typed all of the numerous letters of inquiry required in my research. Other members of the college's History Department—Donald D'Elia, David Krikun, and Donald Roper—provided me with valuable bibliographic references. Moreover, Professor William A. Starna of the College at Oneonta read select chapters of this manuscript and gave me insightful criticism.

Two other friends helped make this project possible. I have had numerous conversations about the material presented in this book with David Jaman of Gardiner, New York, who provided me with the quotation I use at the beginning of the book's Preface. Roy Black of Esopus, New York tolerated my frequent ramblings about misconceptions in Native American history.

Finally, my wife and two children excused my work habits, which at times border on the compulsive. All three have no misconceptions about my intentions, realizing that they are at the center of my universe.

New Paltz, New York
January 1994

TRIBES AND TRIBULATIONS

1 GENOCIDE

Growing up in Brooklyn, New York, in the late 1940s and 1950s, I was surrounded by the haunting presence of the Holocaust. My barber—they were really called *barbers* in those days—was a Greek Jew named Moishe who had been taken away as a young man by the Nazis, but had, nevertheless, survived the horrors of the concentration-camp experience. The tattooed numbers on his arm and the emaciated and painful look of his face frightened me every time my father, his friend, took me to Moishe's barber shop in Coney Island. And there are other indelible memories. My boyhood friend's mother had survived the Warsaw Ghetto Uprising and periodically received a check, which she deemed "blood money," from the West German government. Moreover, both of my parents played a special part in inculcating the lessons of this horror into my psyche. On a regular basis, I was seated before the DuMont television set, a rather new device in those days, to watch the BBC documentaries about the liberation of the concentration camps. At my bar mitzvah, I remember asking my parents why so few of Dad's relatives were there when contrasted to the larger number of my mother's family. The reply to us was to the point: "They didn't survive Hitler."

I rarely reflected on these early life experiences until three decades later, largely as a result of discussions with Richard "Skip" Hayward, tribal chairman of the Mashantucket Pequot Indians. I can vividly recall one meeting held at a restaurant owned by these Indians, in which Chairman Hayward and noted ethnohistorian Jack Campisi were in attendance. After discussing a general outline for a conference on Pequot history as well as its educational aims, Chairman Hayward began to shift the conversation to talking about the English colonial army's burning of his tribe's Mystic Fort in 1637 and the near-total decimation of his people during the battle and the ensuing war. At the time when the contemporary Mashantucket Pequots were experiencing a tribal renaissance and achieving federal recognition, Chairman Hayward was sincerely concerned and inquisitive about the tragedy that befell his people nearly

350 years earlier. The three of us sat and reflected upon the Pequot historical experience, comparing and contrasting the events of 1637 with the all-too-numerous incidents of genocide in the twentieth century. Out of these discussions came a major historical conference, in October 1987 at the Mashantucket Pequot Reservation, as well as my continuing interest and research on group defamation and its impact on American Indians, which led to the publication of *The Pequots in Southern New England: The Fall and Rise of an American Indian Nation* (Norman: University of Oklahoma Press, 1990).

In October of 1988, I attended a Conference on Group Defamation and Genocide sponsored by Hofstra University and the Anti-Defamation League of B'nai B'rith. At that meeting, I delivered a paper entitled "Group Defamation and the Genocide of American Indians." At that extraordinary meeting, I had the privilege to hear Robert J. Lifton, Elie Wiesel, and many other outstanding scholars provide interdisciplinary as well as personal perspectives on genocide. The following article, which appears here for the first time, emanated from the Hofstra meeting.

In an article published during the Columbian Quincentenary, James Axtell, the noted historian of American Indians insisted that we use the word *genocide* with extreme care when describing the loss of Indian life in the colonial era. To Axtell, "Genocide, as distinguished from other forms of cruelty, oppression, and death, played a very small role in the European conquest of the New World." Axtell maintained that the word is too loosely used to apply wholesale to every Indian death in the colonial era in total disregard of its accepted definition, namely, its World War II origins. The historian from the College of William and Mary then added, "As you know, the word was coined in 1944 to describe the infamous Nazi attempts to annihilate the Jews, a religious and cultural group they chose to classify as a biological sub-species or race." Claiming that the word *genocide* is historically inaccurate if employed to describe the "vast majority of encounters between Europeans and Indians," Axtell contended that the word places an unfair "moral onus" on the European colonists by equating them with the Nazi S.S. He continued by maintaining that, since only a relatively few evil colonists or pernicious Nazis were guilty of atrocities, we have no right to "indict a whole nation." Consequently, in order to avoid "mental depth charges" which, if carelessly used, are capable of maiming their handlers, Axtell urged historians to avoid making sweeping moral judgments to avoid self-righteousness, the creation of new stereotypes, or the abdication of their responsibilities to write as complete a history as possible.[1]

Axtell's cautionary warning about moral judgments in history is a valid one. Historians have a responsibility to use words such as *genocide, holocaust, concentration camp,* or, more recently, *ethnic cleansing* in a careful manner.[2] As a Jew growing up in the post-Holocaust, I do not accept the trivialization of this horror by equating it with every instance of outrage in world history; however, Axtell appears to minimize the level of officially directed violence against American Indians in the colonial era and beyond. Nor is Axtell alone. Anthropologist James A. Clifton extends Axtell's disclaimer to the entire sweep of United States history: "In the over two hundred years it has existed as a nation, no U.S. administration from George Washington to Ronald Reagan has ever approved, tolerated, or abetted a policy aimed at the deliberate systematic extermination of Indians."[3]

Although epidemic diseases were the major reason for the significant depopulation of Indian societies over time, genocide was, nonetheless, a factor, albeit one that is extremely difficult to quantify with accuracy.[4] Genocide did occur sporadically in American Indian history. While the term *ethnocide* may be a more appropriate word to describe Indian policies over time, *genocide,* nevertheless, is a correct term to apply to specific times, places, and events in American Indian history. The present chapter focuses on two instances of genocide in American history: (1) what befell the Pequot Indians of southern New England during and after the so-called Pequot War of 1637; and (2) what befell the Indians of northern California after the discovery of gold in 1848. In each case, the actions had the sanctioning of government officials. Although other occurrences, such as removal policies inflicted upon the Cherokee, Creek, Winnebago, and other Indian nations in the 1820s and 1830s or the "Bosque Redondo Experiment" that the Navajo faced in the middle and late 1860s, could be cited, no clearer examples of genocide are to be found in all of North American history. In both instances, official policies cannot be rationalized away by simply suggesting that they were caused by paternalism that went astray or that the horrors were simply the result of bureaucratic mismanagement. Nor is my conclusion the result of presentism. Nineteenth-century historians such as John W. De Forest writing on the Pequot Indians and Hubert H. Bancroft writing on California Indians fully described the mass murders in each area.[5]

Part of our difficulty in acknowledging the reality of genocide in American history is due to the horrible pictures that the word connotes. There were no Nazi gas chambers in the American Indian experience; nevertheless, the same words of hate used by the S.S. were used periodically in American Indian history and resulted in extermination. Despite Axtell's contentions, American Indians, on occasion, were classified as a biological subspecies or "inferior" race, much like Jews were in Nazi Germany. At times, American Indians, like Jews, were characterized as subhuman, savage, satanic, vermin, or animal-like, making it "easier" to root them out.[6] "Manifestly westward the course of epithets took their way," historian Richard Drinnon has written. Indians were pictured as "consumptive wolves," "wild varmints," "nits," "lice," and "pests," and these labels became more disdainful as the frontier retreated westward.[7]

Scholars of genocide either employ a broadly based definition, stemming from the United Nations Convention on Genocide in 1948, or attempt to define the word in a more limited fashion. According to the 1948 convention:

> genocide means any of the following acts committed with intent to destroy, in whole or in part, a national, ethnical, racial or religious group, as such:
>
> (a) Killing members of the group;
>
> (b) Causing serious bodily or mental harm to members of the group;
>
> (c) Deliberately inflicting on the group conditions of life calculated to bring about its physical destruction in whole or in part;
>
> (d) Imposing measures intended to prevent births within the group;
>
> (e) Forcibly transferring children of the group to another group.[8]

In a recent scholarly study of genocide, Frank Chalk, a historian, and Kurt Jonassohn, a sociologist, define the term as "a form of one-sided mass killing in which a state or other authority intends to destroy a group, as that group and membership in it are defined by the perpetrator." To Chalk and Jonassohn, the "perpetrator has always had to first organize a campaign that redefined the victim group as worthless, outside the web of mutual obligations, a threat to people, immoral sinners, and/or subhuman." Chalk and Jonassohn also emphasize the "one-sided" nature of genocide, the "case in which there is no reciprocity; while the perpetrator intends to wipe out the victim group, the latter have no such plans." Although they exclude casualties of war, whether military or civilian from their definition, they include the victim-group that "has no organized military machinery" or through the very hopelessness of their resistance "underscores the one-sidedness of these mass killings." [9]

Despite the significant merit of Chalk and Jonassohn's work, which is accepted unquestionably by Axtell, the narrowness of their definition may even indeed exclude the recent process of "ethnic cleansing" in Bosnia simply because the horrors are occurring during a state of belligerency. Even Elie Wiesel, the Nobel laureate, philosopher, and survivor of the Holocaust, has equated the present suffering in the Balkans with Nazi genocide. Thus, any meaningful determination of genocide must fall somewhere between the United Nations' and Chalk's and Jonassohn's definitions of the term.[10]

What befell the Pequot Indians in 1637 and afterward clearly fits within this range. Axtell has judged the Pequot War of 1637 as an "unsuccessful" Puritan assault that does "not differ much in method or result from the Iroquois destruction of the Hurons in 1649." In fact, both wars were largely one-sided assaults of extermination that had genocidal elements; the horrors inflicted by the English in 1637 and Iroquois in 1649 were, despite Axtell's appraisal, quite successful in permanently weakening the power of these two Indian nations. The Pequot War was the first serious one between colonizers and the indigenous populations in New England. The war nearly exterminated one of the most powerful Indian groups in New England; opened southeastern Connecticut to English colonization, and established English hegemony over the Indians of southern New England; and allowed for future Puritan missionary endeavors in the region.[11]

In the early years of the seventeenth century, the Pequot Indians had fifteen villages in southeastern Connecticut, located along the coast between Niantic Bay and the Pawcatuck River and along the Thames and Mystic rivers. One of their two main villages was Mystic Fort, situated on the Mystic River; the other was two miles southwest at Fort Hill, overlooking Noank. At approximately the time of the initial European penetration of southern New England, the Pequot were also expanding their territory and their trade networks, as far west as present-day Hartford, to the coast between New Haven and Charlestown, Rhode Island, and to eastern Long Island and the environs of Block Island.

In 1632 the Pequot made their first recorded contact with Europeans, and, in the next five years, these Indians' lives were to be transformed beyond recognition. By 1633 both the English and the Dutch were already seeking trade advantages on the Connecticut River. During the winter of 1634–35, the English established Pyquag (now Wethersfield), and in 1635, they built Fort Saybrook at the mouth of the Connecticut River. In 1636, the inhabitants of three Massachusetts Bay towns migrated to the Connecticut Valley—Watertown to Wethersfield, Dorchester to Natianuck (Windsor), and Newtowne to Saukiog (Hartford). In the same year, Springfield was established as an English outpost on the Connecticut River. Importantly, in the mid-1630s the Pequot and Narragansett became involved in a war for the domination of southwestern New England, while, at approximately the same time, a major smallpox epidemic hit the same region.

A murder in 1634 was to cast a long shadow and set in motion a series of events that culminated in the Pequot War. Tatobem, a Pequot sachem, was captured and later killed by Dutch traders, even though the Indians had paid to ransom him. In retaliation, the Pequot attacked the Dutch trading post, The Hope, in the lower Connecticut Valley near modern-day Hartford. Soon after, John Stone, a Virginia trader, was murdered by Indians. In order to bring peace to the Connecticut Valley, Sassacus, the new Pequot chief sachem, worked out an accord with Massachusetts Bay officials. The Pequot agreed to hand over Stone's killers, to allow English purchases of land and settlement in the Connecticut Valley, and to pay a substantial indemnity of four hundred fathoms of wampum, forty beaver skins, and thirty otter skins. In return, the Puritans promised to send them a trader. John Oldham, the English trader sent, was subsequently murdered off the shores of Block Island. Although the Indians in the environs of Block Island were Eastern Niantics and Narragansetts, the English retribution for the murder of Oldham fell heaviest upon the Pequot.

In August 1636, John Endicott organized a punitive expedition against the Pequot, which soon became the first military attempt by the English to expand their power over the Indians of New England. Endicott sacked Block Island and then, with ninety volunteers, sailed into Pequot Harbor. He demanded that the Pequot hand over Stone's and Oldham's killers and that the Indians provide one thousand fathoms of wampum tribute, as well as Indian children to be held as hostages to ensure a future peace. After a brief skirmish and looting, the Puritan army departed for Massachusetts Bay, leaving the newly established English towns in the Connecticut Valley susceptible to the brunt of Pequot reprisals; nevertheless, the Pequot were weakened by an internal crisis and the political infighting between Sassacus and his rival, Uncas. The Mohegans, under Uncas's leadership, soon joined the newly formed anti-Pequot alliance of the English and the Narragansett.

On April 23, 1637, the Pequot attacked Wethersfield, destroying much property, killing nine English settlers, including three women, and taking two young girls as prisoners. This attack became the excuse for a full-scale Massachusetts Bay and Connecticut colonial war of extermination against the Pequot.

Just before dawn on May 26, 1637, an army of English soldiers led by captains John Mason and John Underhill, Mohegan–Pequot under Uncas, and a contingent of Narragansett and Eastern Niantic assaulted the Pequot's eastern fort on the Mystic River. This attack occurred while most of the Pequot men were away and resulted in the death of between three hundred and seven hundred noncombatants, women, children, and old men. Many of the Indians were killed when Mason ordered the wigwams burned. The English and their allied Indians surrounded the village and cut down those trying to flee. The massacre lasted less than an hour, and all but seven Pequot perished. Two English men were killed and twenty wounded, while twenty Indian allies were also wounded. The leaders of the expedition defended their actions as "God's will." [12] Even before the end of the war, Massachusetts Bay celebrated an official day of thanksgiving on June 15, 1637, "in all the churches for the victory obtained against the Pequods, and for other mercies."[13]

In addition to the sacking of Mystic Fort, this largely one-sided war, which spread into the swamps of southeastern Connecticut, had other dire consequences for the Pequot. Perhaps as many as fifteen hundred Pequot, 40 to 50 percent of their prewar population, were killed.[14] Many of the Pequot not in the fort during the conflagration were captured, killed in skirmishes, or executed in the months that followed by either the English or their Indian allies, including the Mohawk. Some Pequot prisoners of war were loaded on board the ship of Captain John Gallup, who subsequently threw them overboard to drown and/or be eaten by the fish. Others were enslaved, assigned to the "protection" of colonists or to Indian leaders—Uncas the Mohegan, Miantonomo the Narragansett, or Ninigret the Eastern Niantic—or sold into slavery and sent to Bermuda, the Bahamas, and the West Indies. The war formally ended in September 1638, when sachems for the remaining Pequot were forced to sign the Treaty of Hartford, also called the Tripartite Treaty. By the humiliating provisions of that accord, the Pequot nation was officially declared to be dissolved. Even the use of the designation "Pequot" was soon outlawed by colonial authorities, and no Indian settlement was allowed in their homeland until after 1650.[15]

Thus, the Pequot, viewed as aggressive, bellicose, blasphemous, and even satanic by the English in Connecticut and Massachusetts Bay colonies, were erased from history. According to a Puritan account of 1643, divine intervention had saved New England and had punished the Indian transgressors:

> And in the war, which we made against them [the Pequot], God's hand from heaven was so manifested that a very few of our men in a short time pursued through the wilderness, slew, and took prisoners about 1,400 of them, even all they could find, to great terror and amazement of all the Indians to this day; so that the name of the Pequots (as of Amalech) is blotted out from under heaven, there being not one that is, or (at least) dare call himself a Pequot.[16]

Two generations later, Cotton Mather, the venerable New England cleric, continued to rationalize his ancestors' actions against the Indians, declaring that "in a little more than one hour, five or six hundred of these barbarians were dismissed from a world that was burdened with them."[17]

The Pequot horror clearly fits the definition of genocide outlined by the United Nations Convention on Genocide in 1948. Even though the Pequot example challenges their narrow definition, Chalk and Jonassohn, nevertheless, describe the war of 1637 as genocide since they concluded the "Puritans murdered noncombatants, prisoners of war, and surrendering warriors."[18] The Pequot, in the words of Elie Wiesel referring to the Jewish experience in the Holocaust, became "disposable, dispensable creatures."[19] Sanctioned by officials of Massachusetts Bay Colony, the action against the Pequot became the first genocide of Indians in Anglo-American history.

Two centuries later, these genocidal actions were repeated on an even more horrible scale. The last great block of contiguous territory became part of the United States in 1848, with the signing of the Treaty of Guadalupe Hidalgo that ended the Mexican War. At the time of this treaty in which the United States received California, Arizona, New Mexico, and Utah, over 100,000 American Indians lived in California. With the discovery of gold at Sutter's Mill in 1848, nearly a quarter of a million settlers came to California within the next four years. What followed has been described by historian Hubert H. Bancroft as "one of the last human hunts of civilization, and the basest and most brutal of them all."[20] By 1860, only 35,000 Indians remained alive in the entire state. By the turn of the twentieth century, there were between 12,000 and 20,000 Indians who had survived the slaughter.[21] Moreover, these same Indians had been dispossessed without any compensation for more than 100,000 square miles "of the most beautiful and valuable country in the world."[22]

Many of these Indians were killed as the result of a systematic policy of extermination, although a significant number died as a result of disease, exposure, and starvation. Although the federal government began to create a series of Indian reservations in 1853, the natives were never adequately protected from marauding whites, nor were they fed, clothed, or housed. Conflicts over federal or state jurisdiction also restricted American military efforts in protection. Moreover, corrupt Indian agents frequently misappropriated federal funds that were set aside for the Indians' welfare.[23] California whites stereotyped the Indians as "ignorant, bestial savages who deserved no rights" and lobbied for total removal of the Indians from the state borders in order to do away with the "Indian menace."[24] Although Indians did kill whites and fight in organized campaigns, much of their violence seemed to be efforts in self-protection.

The rapid destruction of the state's Indian population was most evident in northern California. The Indians were denied access to ancestral lands to fish, hunt, or gather roots. The Hoopa, Nisenan, Shasta, Yana, Yuki, Yurok, Wintu, Wiyot, and others soon found themselves as starving refugees hiding out in the mountains. In order to survive, they periodically came down from the mountains, stole horses and cattle, or retaliated by killing their dispossessors, which only gave impetus to more organized "hunts" of the Indians. By the late summer of 1859, J. Y. McDuffie, superintendent of Indian affairs for California, reported that "the killing of Indians is a daily occurrence there." He continued in his report to the commissioner of Indian affairs: "If some means be not speedily devised, by which the unauthorized expeditions that are constantly out in search of them can be restrained, they will soon be exterminated." [25]

Brutal attacks occurred even after reservations were established to protect and feed the Indians. Most Indians remained outside the reservations for fear that they would be kidnapped and enslaved. Indian children and women were not safe even when they were on reservations. Historian Albert Hurtado clearly has shown that forced concubinage and the rape of Indian women by white men were common features of the violent youth subculture of the mines in California. The official "sanctioning" of these immoral activities stemmed from a California state statute of 1850 authorizing the indenture of Indians, a law which soon became a thinly disguised substitute for slavery, which had formally been abolished in the state in 1850. Kidnapping Indian children and women became an especially profitable trade in the 1850s.[26] As late as the fall of 1862, G. M. Hanson, the superintending agent of Indian affairs for the Northern District of California, blamed this indenture law "under cover of which all this trouble exists" and urged its repeal.[27]

Officials at every level of state government were directly or indirectly involved in this genocide. What befell the Yuki Indians was a case in point. In the 1850s, these northern California Indians were hunted down by William S. Jarboe and his Eel River Rangers, a motley assortment of Mendocino County ruffians. In a letter to the governor of California, Captain Jarboe stated that the "ukas [Yuki] are without doubt, the most degraded, filthy, miserable thieving lot of anything living that comes under the head of and rank of human being.... They are inferior in intelect [sic] so devoid of feeling." Despite evidence to the contrary, Jarboe rationalized a policy of "nothing short of extermination" because of these Indians' alleged thieving and murderous ways. In his subsequent depredations against the Indians, Jarboe received official authorization from the governor of California.[28]

J. Ross Browne, the special treasury agent who investigated the California situation in the late 1850s, reported that "a man named Jarboe now holds a commission from the governor of the state, in virtue of which he has raised a company, and has been engaged for some months past in a cruel and relentless pursuit of the Indians in this vicinity, slaughtering miscellaneously all with whom he comes in contact, without regard to age or sex." [29] Browne then graphically described the atrocities:

In the history of Indian races I have seen nothing so cruel and relentless as the treatment of these unhappy people by the authorities constituted by law for their protection. Instead of receiving aid and succor, they have been starved and driven away from the reservations, and then followed into their remote hiding places where they sought to die in peace, and cruelly slaughtered, till but few are left, and that few without hope.[30]

The special treasury agent suggested that "nothing short of military force could restrain the settlers" and save the Indians from destruction.[31]

At times the militia, not just the settlers, played a direct part in the genocide. In the early spring of 1853, Colonel E. A. Hitchcock of the Second United States Infantry reported to the adjutant general of the United States about the Indian war in northern California. A contingent of Indians was invited into the camp of Captain Ben Wright, under a white flag, to negotiate a peace; instead, the Indians were set upon and thirty-eight were killed in a planned trap. Wright took their scalps and later "was received with a general welcome by the local citizens of Yreka [Eureka]."[32]

The mass murder of Indians in this decade was well known in Washington, and it led to the federal "solution" of creating reservations in the region, including Nome Lackee (1854), Mendocino (1855), Klamath (1855), and Round Valley (1856). Yet only one of these reservations, Nome Lackee, had been properly surveyed. Violence against Indians actually intensified in the late 1850s. Unauthorized white-owned businesses were established on the reservations; these included a sawmill that adversely affected salmon fishing on the Mendocino reservation. At the Round Valley reservation, squatters literally overran the place, and, by the end of the decade, four-fifths of the reservation was in white hands.[33] By 1861, Commissioner of Indian Affairs William P. Dole, in his annual report about the events taking place in Humboldt and Mendocino counties, wrote that the "crimes that are committed in the wake" present "a picture of the perversion of power and of cruel wrong, from which humanity instinctively recoils." Dole continued: "This so-called 'Indian war' appears to be a war in which the whites alone are engaged. The Indians are hunted like wild and dangerous beasts of prey; the parents are 'murdered,' and the children 'kidnapped.'"[34]

Despite Commissioner Dole's concerns, Interior Department personnel were participants in the crimes taking place in northern California. A new level of graft was established by Colonel Thomas J. Henley, the postmaster of San Francisco, who was appointed superintendent of California Indians in 1854. Henley's disregard for his charges included selling off cattle herds intended to provide food for the starving Indians, allowing his sons and other partners to illegally establish businesses on the reservations at Nome Lackee and Mendocino, and permitting white squatters to overrun the Round Valley reservation.[35] In response to his actions, Henley insisted that the solution to the "Indian problem" was to refuse to allow any Indian off the reservation to be fed, an act he characterized "as injurious to the policy of colonization, as contemplated by the system now in operation."[36] Despite criticisms of his actions from 1855 onward, Henley retained his office, until the late spring of 1859, by backing up squatters' claims and by having powerful allies in Sacramento and Washington. Thus, those responsible for guarding Indian interests were themselves benefiting by defrauding the same Indians.[37]

Nor were underlings in the Interior and War departments alone in their involvement in the crimes. The top echelons of the United States government at times abdicated responsibility in keeping order. While atrocities were frequently reported to them, the United States Army's high command refused to budge, insisting that the federal government had no exclusive jurisdiction in the matter.[38] General John E. Wool, a hero of the Mexican War, insisted in 1856 that since "California is in no respect considered an Indian country," the military had no control over whites or Indians there. He maintained that California state laws applied even in the case where whites kidnapped "from the reserve one or more squaws, or one or more Indian children."[39]

By 1860, the conflicts over jurisdiction had begun to be resolved. California state militia, in cooperation with federal troops, forced many of the Indians onto nine temporary enclaves in the northern part of the state. Militia troops hunted down the Indians while federal troops guarded the prisoners, an understanding worked out by the Indian superintendent. Yet, even with this federal presence, Indian crops continued to be burned and Indian women continued to be kidnapped. Eventually, at the end of the Civil War, federal soldiers had the primary responsibility of subduing the Indians who were still off the reservations. It is also important to note that the United States Congress, which had never ratified eighteen treaties guaranteeing California Indian lands, later reimbursed the state for bonds that California issued in the hunting of Indians during the decade of the 1850s.[40]

Thus, the California experience clearly conforms to both the United Nations' Convention and to Chalk's and Jonassohn's definitions of genocide. The horror of the experience also clearly challenges James A. Clifton's insistence that no administration from Washington to Reagan "ever approved, tolerated, or even abetted" a policy of "systematic extermination" of American Indians.[41]

The two examples analyzed clearly show that genocide is an appropriate term to use in North American history, when applied carefully to specific case studies. Although official state-initiated genocide against American Indians,

as found in Puritan Connecticut in the 1630s or in northern California in the
1850s, has played itself out in the United States, it continues in other areas of
the Americas today. Despite commemorating the United Nations Year of Indigenous Peoples in 1993, it is important to realize that Indians are still victims
of sporadic genocide from Brazil to Guatemala. Reminiscent of the "hunt"
of northern California Indians by white settlers in the 1850s, a Brazilian gold
rush in recent times has prompted the massive settlement and ecological dev-
astation of the Amazon region, with its resulting disruption of indigenous life
through epidemics and the one-sided killing of Indians.[42]

Although depredations continue, a new era of world concern may be emerging.[43] In 1992, Rigoberta Menchu, a Quiché Indian from Guatemala who has
publicized the wholesale destruction of indigenous peoples in her country, was
awarded the Nobel Prize for Peace, the first Native American in history to be
so honored.[44] Perhaps we can avoid a further repetition of the Pequot and the
California Indian experiences as we approach the twenty-first century.

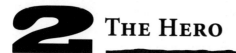

2 THE HERO

The conquest of the frontier, whether along the Atlantic coast in the seventeenth century or in the Far West of the nineteenth century, stands as the great American epic, one that defines the national identity. It serves the nation in the same way that the reconquest of the Iberian Peninsula does in Spain's history. Both experiences had "winners" who rationalized or romanticized the event and "losers" who were ostracized, deemed unworthy, and/or eradicated.

Historian Patricia Nelson Limerick has correctly observed, in her provocative study of *The Legacy of Conquest: The Unbroken Past of the American West* (1987): "Traditional frontier history flattened out Indians, rendering them insignificant both before and after the conquest" (p. 214). Until the last few decades, historians of the American frontier, fixed on the Turner model, presented history in linear fashion, as an inevitable dichotomy between pioneers and Indians, with "civilization" ultimately winning out over "savagery." America's idea of progress was emphasized, but usually at the expense and reputation of American Indians. At the center stage of this treatment was the frontier hero, admired for his courage, nobility, or exploits, especially in war. Unlike other misconceptions about American Indians, the Indian fighter as hero even took on mythic proportions, much like *The Cid* in Spanish literature and thought, often being presented as a superman in art, dime novels, wild West shows, and motion pictures.

On July 11, 1908, President Theodore Roosevelt dedicated a monument hailing the memory of Captain John Underhill. This monument, honoring the first professional Indian fighter in Anglo America, stands today in the Underhill Burying Ground at Locust Valley, New York, only a short distance from Roosevelt's own home at Oyster Bay, New York. It is located on the 150 acres of land deeded to Underhill by the Matinecock Indians in February 1667. In unveiling the monument, Roosevelt observed, "I thought it a good thing that the founder of what has become one of the distinctive Long Island families should have a Monument to his honor." Roosevelt, the author-historian of the multi-volume work *The Winning of the West,* added that Underhill was "a man who left his mark deep on the history of New England as well as New Holland, one of the men who in Colonial times helped to lay the foundation for the nation that was to be." (David Harris Underhill and Francis Jay Underhill, comp., *The Underhill Burying Ground* [New York: Hine Publishing Co., 1926], pp. 38–39).

In the following essay, which is reprinted with the permission of the *Hudson Valley Regional Review,* I explore the conquest of the Indians in the first half of the seventeenth century in southern New England and the Middle Atlantic colonies. By analyzing the career, motivations, and psychological makeup of John Underhill, the essay calls into question the criteria we use in designating someone as a "hero."

John Underhill is the archetype of the "Indian fighter." Although Kit Carson is better known in American history and Tom Quick more legendary in the annals of the Hudson and Delaware river valleys, Underhill, a professional soldier by training, was among the first to be commissioned to "pacify" the Indians in northeastern North America. As a successful commander of men, Underhill's actions against the Indians often took a violent course, and his campaigns resulted in the merciless slaughter of men, women, and children. Underhill engendered terror in Indian country from 1637 until his death thirty-five years later.

Officials in Boston and New Amsterdam viewed Underhill's campaigns against the Indians as the necessities of seventeenth-century frontier warfare; nevertheless, a careful study of his life suggests that Underhill was a truly disturbed individual. Although frequently lauded as a military hero in popular circles from New Hampshire to New Netherland and rewarded with a variety of political positions and lands, Underhill experienced difficulty in adjusting to civilian life and exhibited contrary behavior that continually led to trouble. Indeed, Underhill's combativeness fills the historical record. The obstinate Underhill took on all comers, from the Puritan founders of the Massachusetts Bay Colony to the Dutch director generals of New Netherland. As a result of his frequent penchant for challenging authority and inciting disorder, Underhill was eventually banished from three colonies—Massachusetts, New Hampshire, and New Netherland.

Underhill's actions suggest that he was a sociopath, or, in more correct psychological parlance, that he suffered from antisocial personality disorder. The American Psychiatric Association has listed ten patterns of behavior that indicate the presence of this disorder. Eight of these include: being "unable to sustain consistent work behavior"; failing "to conform to social norms with

John Underhill (courtesy Special Collections Office, New York Public Library).

respect to lawful behavior"; being "irritable and aggressive" outside of one's job; repeatedly failing "to honor financial obligations"; failing "to plan ahead" or being "impulsive"; having "no regard for the truth, as indicated by repeated lying, use of aliases, or 'conniving' others for personal profit or pleasure"; having difficulty sustaining a monogamous relationship; and lacking remorse after mistreating someone.[1] The colonial records of Massachusetts Bay, New

Hampshire, and New Netherland suggest that Underhill was afflicted with this disorder.

Underhill's military career was part of the larger American epic, namely, the "winning of the West." Because killing Indians, even en masse, was an "accepted" action at times in American history, Underhill's bizarre behavior has been conveniently overlooked and/or justified. The dedicatory tablet at a monument for Underhill at his grave in Locust Valley, New York, reads: "He became prominent in the government of the Colonies and achieved a high reputation as a soldier in the war with the Indians." [2]

Most of Underhill's life centered on soldiering. Born at Baginton, Warwickshire, England, in 1597, he was the son of Honor Pauley and John Underhill of Warwickshire. His father was a military adventurer in the Netherlands at a time when the Dutch were fighting for their independence against Spain. Indeed, the Netherlands was the center of military science in the first half of the seventeenth century. The younger Underhill lived in the Netherlands, where he married Helene de Hooch, a Dutch woman, and attended the famous military academy founded by Maurice of Nassau, Prince of Orange, the captain general of Holland and Zeeland. [3] This academy, which revolutionized warfare, emphasized systematic drills in loading and firing matchlocks as well as in regularized marching; stressed the importance of engineering, with soldiers fortifying their encampments by using their spades to construct makeshift ramparts, often by burrowing ditches; and advocated the employment of dividing an army into smaller tactical units that could react faster in combat, but would be tied to a hierarchical chain of command. According to one prominent historian, the academy's use of "drill made soldiers both more obedient and more efficient in battle." [4]

Underhill's chance to use his military training occurred in 1630, when he moved to Boston where the Puritan leadership appointed him captain of the militia of Massachusetts Bay Colony and allotted him land. Although a token Puritan from his days in the Netherlands, Underhill was not a man of deep religious convictions. At times during his life, he was associated with High Church Anglicanism, Puritanism, antinomianism, Anabaptism, and Quakerism. Most of his early years in Massachusetts Bay were devoted more to training a poorly supplied militia than to spiritual matters.

Underhill's reputation as a fighter of Indians began in 1637. On April 20, Massachusetts Bay Colony officials lent twenty men under the direction of Underhill to the garrison at Fort Saybrook, along the lower Connecticut River. There, they joined up with a larger contingent of Connecticut settlers headed by Captain John Mason, another veteran of military service in the Netherlands. Mason, even more than Underhill, was committed to a total war against

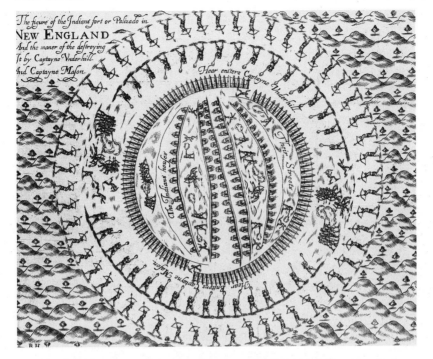

The attack on the Pequot Fort (courtesy Special Collections Office, New York Public Library).

the Pequot Indians, whom the English viewed as bellicose and as the "children of Satan."[5]

The Pequot War of 1637 is one of the most important events in early American history. The conflict was the first serious one between colonizers and the indigenous populations in New England. The war nearly exterminated one of the most powerful Indian groups in New England; opened southeastern Connecticut to English colonization and established English hegemony over the Indians of southern New England; and allowed for future Puritan missionary endeavors in the region.[6]

Just before dawn on May 26, 1637, an army of English soldiers commanded by Mason and Underhill, Mohegan–Pequots under their leader Uncas, and a contingent of Narragansetts and Eastern Niantics assaulted the Pequots' eastern fort on the Mystic River. This attack occurred while most of the Pequot men were away, and resulted in the death of between three hundred and seven hundred women, children, and old men. Many of the Indians were killed when Mason ordered the wigwams burned. The English and their Indian allies surrounded the village to cut down those trying to flee. The massacre lasted less than an hour and all but seven Pequots perished. Two English men were killed and twenty wounded, while twenty Indian allies were also wounded.[7]

Underhill's specific role in these events is well documented in the four major accounts of the battle. From his side of the fort, he started a fire with powder that met another one set by Mason at the other side of the fort. Underhill looked on as one Pequot prisoner was tied to a post and torn apart by twenty of his captors. Then Underhill shot the man with his pistol. To justify his and his men's brutal actions, Underhill dehumanized his victims in his own classic account of the war. He insisted that divine judgment allowed him to destroy the "wicked imps." Underhill also viewed the Indians as "roaring lions compassing all corners of the country for their prey." Underhill then further rationalized the massacre:

> Great and doleful was the bloody sight to the view of young soldiers that have never been in war, to see so many souls lie gasping on the ground, so thick in some places, that you could hardly pass along. It may be demanded, Why should you be so furious? (as some have said). Should not Christians have more mercy and compassion? But I would refer you to David's war. When a people [the Pequots] is grown to such a height of blood, and sin against God and man, and all confederates in the action, there he hath no respect to persons, but harrows them, and saws them, and puts them to the sword, and the most terriblest death that may be. Sometimes the Scripture declareth women and children must perish with their parents. Sometimes the case alters; but we will not dispute it now. *We had sufficient light from the word of God for our proceedings.*[8]
> [emphasis mine]

Many of the Pequots not in the fort during the conflagration were captured, killed in skirmishes, or executed in the months that followed. Others were enslaved, assigned to the "protection" of colonists or the Indian leaders—Uncas the Mohegan, Miantonomo the Narragansett, or Ninigret the Eastern Niantic —or sold into slavery and sent to Bermuda and the West Indies. The war formally ended in September 1638, when sachems for the remaining Pequots were forced to sign the Treaty of Hartford, also called the Tripartite Treaty. By the humiliating provisions of that accord, the Pequot nation was officially declared to be dissolved. Even the use of the designation *Pequot* was soon outlawed by colonial authorities.[9]

Historians have correctly observed that the Pequot War was rooted in the European military traditions of the time. Plunder, territorial aggrandizement, organized mayhem, and the dehumanization of one's enemies were all part of this tradition. In the era of the Europeans' Thirty Years War, 1618–48, the Pequot War was not all that distinct. In Europe, approximately 7.5 million Germans, one-third of the entire population, perished in these three decades. The intensity of the fighting led to the destruction of twenty thousand Swiss towns, and the suffering in Europe was unmatched since the days of the fall of the Roman Empire. Therefore, Underhill's actions in the Pequot War alone cannot simply lead to the conclusion that Underhill suffered from an antisocial personality disorder; nevertheless, Underhill's actions over the next two decades could lead one to that very conclusion.[10]

Underhill's career as an Indian fighter did not end with the Pequot War. In September 1643, Director General Willem Kieft of New Netherland recruited the professional soldier for service in a bloody Indian war raging in the lower Hudson Valley and Long Island. Governor Kieft's War, as it is known in history, was largely an outgrowth of increased European frontier expansion, Kieft's poor leadership and authoritarian style, and numerous cultural misunderstandings.[11] After taking an oath of allegiance to the Dutch, Underhill was given land in the colony.[12]

Underhill was one of the commanders in two major campaigns against Lenape Indian tribesmen in the early months of 1644. In February, he and his men advanced on an Indian village on Long Island, while a larger force proceeded toward the major concentration of Indians who were mostly Canarsee. In each instance, the Indians were set on by surprise in gruesome night attacks. In March, Underhill led a second expedition, this time against the Weequaesgeek. He was first sent to Stamford to gather information on the Indians of that region. After his return to New Amsterdam, Underhill and a contingent of 130 men set sail, disembarking near today's Greenwich, Connecticut. He then marched his troops northwestward over the snow-covered hills. After a day of slipping and sliding, he reached the Weequaesgeek Indian "castle" at Pound Ridge in Westchester County. His ensuing surprise attack under the full moon led to the killing of 180 Indians, followed by Underhill's torching of the bark wigwams.[13] One account, which was reminiscent of the Pequot War, described the massacre: "The Indians tried every means to escape, not succeeding in which they returned back to the flames preferring to perish by the fire than to die by our hands." Between three hundred and five hundred Indians were killed; only eight, three seriously wounded, escaped. The combined Dutch–English force lost one dead. Underhill and several others were wounded.[14]

Underhill's major role in Indian affairs continued well after the Pound Ridge massacre. On March 31, 1644, the chiefs of the lower Hudson Lenapes came to Stamford, "asking Captain Onderhil [sic] to appeal to the governor [the director general] of New Netherland for peace." They further agreed not to do "harm to either people, cattle, houses, or anything else within the territory of New Netherland." In return, the Dutch agreed "not to molest them" and allowed them to "cultivate their lands in peace."[15] Perhaps fearing Underhill's fury, the Indians of Long Island, primarily the Matinecock, entered into a similar peace pact in the summer of 1645 at Fort Amsterdam. Underhill was one of the commissioners representing the Dutch at this meeting.[16]

Although certain sources claim that Underhill was involved in another major conflict with the Indians of Long Island in the 1650s, no evidence has been found to confirm this interpretation.[17] By the time of renewed Indian wars in the 1650s and 1660s—the Peach War and the Esopus Wars—Underhill had already been banished from New Netherland by Director General Pieter Stuyvesant. After the English capture of the Dutch colony in 1664, which he actively promoted, Underhill and his new wife, Elizabeth Feake, moved to Oyster Bay, Long Island, establishing an estate of 150 acres ceded to him by the Matinecock Indians, his former enemies. According to one source, the old Indian fighter became the Indians' legal spokesman and protector when Hempstead settlers invaded Matinecock lands. More likely, these Indians remembered Underhill's earlier campaigns and attempted to appease this hardened soldier. Five years later, Underhill died at Locust Valley (Matinecock), Long Island.[18]

Underhill's civilian life was marked by conflict as well. As a man trained to be obedient and to serve authority, Underhill frequently found himself at odds with his nonmilitary political superiors. Perhaps the greatest thorn in his side was John Winthrop, governor of Massachusetts Bay Colony. Although for a time he called himself a Puritan, Underhill frequently found himself on the outs with the Puritan hierarchy. From 1636 to 1638, Underhill sided with the faction in Massachusetts Bay Colony that supported Anne Hutchinson, who was then challenging the Puritan orthodoxy of the time. These so-called antinomians eventually lost out when Hutchinson was placed on trial for heresy. After maintaining that she communicated directly with the Holy Spirit, the General Court banished Hutchinson to Rhode Island. She later moved to New Netherland, where she was killed by Indians in 1643.[19]

Underhill's adamant backing of the controversial Hutchinson took on aggressive proportions. The soldier "reputedly had such an unstable personality and fierce temper that opponents of Mrs. Hutchinson feared for their lives."[20] One historian has further maintained that Underhill's antinomianism was a sham, masking his "own flagrant immorality," which included adultery and smoking tobacco. During his trial by Puritan magistrates of the General Court, Underhill refused to admit his errant ways and/or to apologize for supporting antinomianism. Instead, the soldier insisted that he had "often spoken firmly to the Court of Nassau without suffering reproach." Because of his insolence and his conviction on charges of adultery, he was later dismissed from office, disenfranchised, excommunicated, and ostracized by being banished to New Hampshire.[21]

Underhill's actions in this and in other situations indicate that he experienced serious difficulty in telling the truth. Massachusetts Bay Colony officials viewed him as a licentious individual whose "acknowledgements of sin" and subsequent "professions of repentance were justly held in suspicion."[22] Winthrop and other leaders of the Massachusetts Bay Colony perceived him as cloaking his immorality, especially his adultery, by lying and/or hypocritically employing religion as a defense. Winthrop reflected on Underhill's flaws in his journal:

> The next Lord's day, the same Capt. Underhill, having been privately dealt with upon suspicion of incontinency with a neighbor's wife, and not harkening to it, was publicly questioned, and put under admonition. The matter was, for that the woman being young, and beautiful, and withal of a jovial spirit and behavior, he did daily frequent her house, the door being locked on the inside. He confessed it was ill, because it had an appearance of evil in it; but his excuse was, that the woman was in great trouble of mind, and sore temptations, and that he resorted to her to comfort her; and that when the door was found locked upon them, they were in private prayer together. But this practice was clearly condemned also by the elders, affirming, that it had not been of good report for any of them to have done the like, and that they ought, in such case, to have called in some brother or sister, and not to have locked the door, etc. They also declared, that once he procured them to go visit her, telling them that she was in great trouble of mind; but when they came to her, (taking her, it seems, upon the sudden,) they perceived no such thing.[23]

There is also no evidence to suggest that Underhill's adultery was limited to just this one incident or to one affair.[24]

After these romantic escapades, Underhill was exiled to New Hampshire. There, he secured the governorship; however, once again, he made himself *persona non grata*. At Dover, he helped to organize a church and hired as minister Hanserd Knolly, an unpopular Anabaptist cleric with antinomian sympathies. By 1640, the people of Dover rose up in protest against Knolly and revolted against Underhill's authoritarian behavior. Underhill was forced out as governor when an armed company of rebels established a rump court, found Underhill guilty of riot, fined him, and ordered him back to Massachusetts Bay.[25]

Eventually, Underhill was allowed to return to the Puritan colony only after he had admitted his transgressions and confessed to adultery. In the late spring of 1641, the General Court of Massachusetts Bay Colony repealed its sentence of banishment. On the surface, this action may appear to be inconsistent with the court's earlier action against Underhill. Aware of the onset of Governor Kieft's War in the nearby colony of New Netherland, the Puritan magistrates were undoubtedly swayed in pardoning Underhill by fears that the Indian conflict might spread into southern New England. Underhill's military skills as a commander most likely were seen once more as useful.

Underhill's life in New Netherland from 1642 to 1653 further suggests that he suffered from antisocial personality disorder. In March 1644, Nicolaes Coorn and three other men alleged, in a sworn statement, that Underhill and several other Englishmen disrupted a private party held at Philip Gerritssen's tavern in New Amsterdam. After starting the melee, Underhill allegedly knocked "to pieces all but three of the mugs which hung from the shelf" in the grog house. He drew his "sword in his right hand and his scabbard in the left" and made "cuts and hackings in the posts and doors." After making "unnecessary remarks" and battling with the landlady, he threatened violence. In a belligerent way, he insisted, "Clear out of here or I shall strike at random." Coorn indicated that those party guests present in the tavern heeded Underhill's warning. Coorn stated that in order to "prevent further and more serious mischief, yes, even bloodshed, we broke up our pleasant party."[26]

Underhill's bellicose behavior was also reflected in another arena, namely, in the law courts of New Netherland. He was involved in six legal proceedings, an unusually high number of cases, from 1644 to 1646. In May 1644, Phil Gerritsz, the fiscal (tax collector), won a judgment against him. In April 1646, Underhill sued one "Sergeant Huybert" for hiring Underhill's servant without his permission. The case ended in Huybert's favor when the court ordered Underhill to prove his assertion. In August of the same year, Underhill charged that Isaac Allerton, a highly influential member of the community, had forfeited on his promise to provide him with higher wages. In this apparent nuisance suit, Allerton won the case and Underhill agreed not to harass him. Only in December 1646 did Underhill receive a favorable decision in the courts of New Netherland, when he successfully sued Jan Hadduwe, who had impugned the virtue of Deborah Underhill, the captain's daughter.[27]

By the late 1640s, Underhill had secured lands and political plums on Long Island. He became a member of the Council for New Amsterdam and schout (sheriff) of Flushing. All this was to change with the appointment of Stuyvesant as the new director general of New Netherland in 1647 and the eruption of war between England and Holland in 1652. Underhill soon became a "militant defender" of English rights in the colony and "began to campaign openly against Dutch authority on Long Island." In 1653, he challenged Stuyvesant

Theodore Roosevelt dedicating a monument to John Underhill at Locust Valley, New York, 1908 (courtesy Special Collections Office, New York Public Library).

and Dutch rule by raising the English flag at Hempstead and Flushing. He then began to preach revolution against Dutch authority. As a result of his actions, Underhill found himself in exile for the third time in his stormy career. He fled to New England, where he offered his services to colonial officials in Rhode Island.[28] Later, he paid back Stuyvesant and Dutch authorities when he actively supported English efforts to seize New Netherland. After the English capture of the colony in 1664, he served as a surveyor of customs, high constable, and undersheriff on Long Island, until his retirement and subsequent death in 1672.

J. Franklin Jameson, the former president of the American Historical Association and one of the leading historians of the twentieth century, once characterized John Underhill as "this amusing reprobate."[29] Yet, with the exception of his testimony at his trial for adultery, there appears to be little that was amusing about him. The evidence suggests that he was a seriously disturbed individual who suffered from antisocial personality disorder. This brief survey of his life in and out of military service has shown that Underhill had an authoritarian personality that proved to be his undoing on numerous occasions; that he had difficulty with marital fidelity; that he was a litigious individual who perjured himself in court proceedings, on at least one occasion, to cover up his transgressions; that he had no core values and shifted his political and religious affiliations at the drop of a hat; and that he was a violent man whose overall aggressiveness was noted by officials in three colonies. In effect, what passed as "acceptable" actions in early colonial America—namely, Underhill's torching of Indian villages in Connecticut and New Netherland, and killing hundreds of Indian men, women, and children at a time—masked what appears to be deviance: antisocial personality disorder.

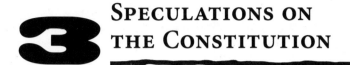

SPECULATIONS ON THE CONSTITUTION

Much has been written in recent days about how Native American ideas helped to shape the grand document of 1787, the United States Constitution. Over the past two decades, a new generation of academics and popular writers have propagated this old but questionable idea. According to one of these writers, historian Donald A. Grinde, Jr., "Indeed, the United States Constitution owes much of its emphasis on unity, federalism, and balance of power to Iroquois concepts" ("Iroquois Political Theory and the Roots of American Democracy," in *Exiled in the Land of the Free: Democracy, Indian Nations and the U.S. Constitution,* ed. Oren Lyons et al. [Santa Fe, N.M.: Clear Light Publishers, 1992], p. 240). Despite the highly speculative nature of the evidence, this misconception has become a shibboleth, one which has been given even the official imprimatur of the United States Senate (United States Congress, *Senate Resolution No. 76* [Washington, D.C.: U.S.G.P.O., 1988]).

The Iroquois have had a major influence in American history. Historians have long recognized their unique style of forest diplomacy and treaty making and their influence on the Euroamerican world. Because of their skills as diplomats and orators, the Iroquois remained a force, even after their power waned from the 1720s onward. The Oneida and Tuscarora played a major role on the American side during the American Revolution, one clearly recognized by the Founding Fathers. Moreover, the history of American anthropology owes much to the Seneca, most notably to the Parker family at Tonawanda, who opened their farmstead to Lewis Henry Morgan, the attorney who wrote *The League of the Ho-de-nau-sau-nee, or Iroquois.* Morgan's work, published in 1851, became the first ethnography ever written on a Native American nation.

The claim that the Iroquois influenced the Founding Fathers in drafting the United States Constitution in 1787 is speculative at best. The Iroquois themselves have long insisted that they taught American colonists democratic principles. (See, for example, Michael Kammen, *Mystic Chords of Memory: The Transformation of Tradition in American Culture* [New York: Alfred A. Knopf,

1991], p. 442n.) Native American and non-Indian educators constantly raise this idea in the numerous speaking engagements and workshops that I have conducted since 1987. I also know full well that tradition, once it is invented (as we have seen in Chapter 2) and as it is manifested in most cultures, is difficult if not impossible to dispel once it has been created. Motivated by constant queries about the Iroquois "contribution" to constitutional thought and perhaps by my own masochistic wish to be attacked as "Eurocentric," I finally decided to write down my own thoughts on this so-called accepted truth. I have purposefully chosen to focus on James Wilson, the United States congressman who signed the Declaration of Independence, one of the major theorists involved with the drafting of the United States Constitution, and an associate justice of the United States Supreme Court. According to Max Farrand, who edited the proceedings of the Constitutional Convention, Wilson was second only to James Madison in his influence at Philadelphia (*The Framing of the Constitution of the United States* [New Haven, Conn.: Yale University Press, 1913], p. 197).

I have selected Wilson for several reasons. First, I am more familiar with his published and unpublished writings, many of which are housed at the Historical Society of Pennsylvania. Second, the extent of his career and his involvement with Native Americans is most conducive to a brief article; unlike Franklin and Washington, one need not devote a lifetime to research before drawing conclusions about the influence of Native Americans on Wilson's intellect. Third, Wilson is a key person mentioned by those who cite the Iroquois contributions to the Constitution, since he was the major author of the preamble to the Constitution and was an especially active participant in the Philadelphia Convention of 1787.

Despite his importance in the early history of the Republic, few Americans are aware of James Wilson, one of the great minds who shaped the nation's government. Wilson was only one of six persons who signed both the Declaration of Independence and the Constitution of the United States. In 1787 at Philadelphia, as a member of the all-important Committee of Detail, he helped to formulate and promote several of the key features of the Constitution, including the theory of the separation of powers, a democratically elected chief executive, and the basic concept of the sovereignty of the people. Moreover, his oratory and overall Federalist leadership at the Pennsylvania State Convention of December 1787 contributed to the state's ratification of the United States Constitution. His influence continued well into both of George Washington's administrations. Wilson was appointed as associate justice of the United States Supreme Court in 1790, serving until his death on August 21, 1798. As a prominent Pennsylvania attorney and jurist, Wilson produced one of the most significant bodies of legal writings ever compiled in America, and, consequently, is considered by legal historians as one of the five greatest contributors to early American jurisprudence.[1]

Recently, Wilson and his ideas have been cited as proof that Native American antecedents helped to shape the Founding Fathers' ideas about democracy as well as the very nature and form of United States governmental institutions. Donald A. Grinde, Jr., and Bruce E. Johansen in *Exemplar of Liberty: Native America and the Evolution of Democracy* (1991) espouse this interpretation.[2] From their preface onward, the authors, who assume that Native Americans had true democracies in the Revolutionary era, insist: "Sympathetic Euro-Americans, such as Ben Franklin and James Wilson, wanted to institute a society and government that preserved the 'native rights' they had observed and experienced among Native American peoples."[3] To Grinde and Johansen, Wilson as well as other Founding Fathers turned to the Iroquois Confederacy for inspiration since they rejected European models and desired "unity with local freedom and autonomy, but with strong diplomatic and military leadership."[4] According to the authors:

> Franklin, Wilson, and John Rutledge and most of the people clearly perceived that the kinship state of the Iroquois could operate over vast geographic expanses and yet maintain human freedoms. So they borrowed some of the political structures of the Iroquois to create a nation-state (based on geographic identity) that balanced the personal freedoms and federalism of the kinship state with the coercive powers of European political systems. Thus Iroquois political theory and imagery should take its rightful place in American intellectual history as one of the theoretical and philosophical roots of American democracy.[5]

Throughout *Exemplar for Liberty,* the two authors attempt to make this case. In their discussion, they suggest that Wilson, in his desire to promote national unity, frequently used metaphors such as "chain imagery" in an allegedly Iroquoian manner of oratory and that he was present when, according to Grinde and Johansen, Iroquois leaders visited Philadelphia. They also assume that Wilson, as a result of his long contact with the Iroquois as a member of the Continental Congress's Committee on Indian Affairs and in his capacity as diplomat while serving as commissioner for the Middle Department at Fort Pitt, had sufficient exposure to Iroquoian ideas to absorb them into his thought.[6] In this book and in two subsequent articles by Grinde, grand conclusions are drawn from the notes made by the Founding Fathers at the Constitutional Convention, even though much of the note-taking was incomplete or cryptic by nature.[7]

Despite these contentions, Wilson was not a person who was significantly influenced by the Iroquois or had much respect for these Indians, their ideas, or their right to their homelands. Wilson was a product of the Enlightenment, especially influenced by the Scottish Common-Sense School of Thomas Reid; he was also influenced to an important degree by Montesquieu and Vattel. Moreover, his attitudes about American progress did not include Native Americans. His political and economic ties were to Americans intent upon dispossessing the Indians, including the Iroquois. Equally important, Wilson personally attempted to take advantage of Indian weakness after the American Revolution in at least one speculative land deal in the Upper Susquehanna region.

Born in Scotland in 1742, Wilson attended the University of St. Andrews and several other universities, where he was exposed to the ideas of the Enlightenment, including those of the Scot David Hume. Yet Wilson rejected Hume's ideas, especially his "speculative claims about certain fundamental matters of epistemology and human nature."[8] Instead, Wilson became a proponent of Thomas Reid, Hume's leading critic, and other members of the Scottish School of Common Sense, including Adam Ferguson, Lord Kames, William Robertson, Adam Smith, and Dugald Stewart. Wilson compared Reid to Francis Bacon and enthusiastically endorsed his ideas. He was influenced by Reid's appeal to moral science, which emphasized, among other points, free will, the perfectibility of human nature, and common-sense judgments. Moral sense, not reason, allowed for flexibility and for both individuals and societies to determine their ultimate ends, which, to Wilson, meant American republicanism.[9] According to Stephen Conrad, the leading scholar on Wilson's legal thought, his use of metaphor and figurative language were drawn from the Common-Sense School. Moreover, the "moralistic approach to republican theory led Wilson to emphasize the moral capability of 'the People' themselves as the 'real' foundation of any republic."[10] It is important to note that James Beattie's two-volume abridgement of Reid's *Elements of Moral Science* (1764) was essential reading for the educated elite in Philadelphia at the time of the Constitutional Convention.[11] Wilson recommended Reid's writings to his law students since he believed that the Scottish philosopher had cleared away "the rubbish, which during the long course of two thousand years, had concealed the foundations of philosophy."[12]

In 1765, after the death of his father William, a local farmer, Wilson decided to emigrate to America to seek his fame and fortune. Upon his arrival, he secured, because of his impressive education, a position as a tutor, teaching Greek and Latin and the natural-law doctrines of Hugo Grotius to young Philadelphians. In 1766, he was awarded an honorary degree by the College of Philadelphia. Eventually, he applied and was accepted to study law in the office of John Dickinson, the leading Pennsylvania conservative and Montesquieu-influenced theorist. There, Wilson was trained well in Blackstone and Coke and was admitted to the Pennsylvania bar in November 1767. After first setting up practice in Reading, he moved to Carlisle, where he became one of the most prominent attorneys in the colony by the early 1770s; he was eventually elected to the Second Continental Congress in 1775, serving until 1777.[13]

Wilson's extensive writings provide additional evidence that he was not especially influenced by the Iroquois or by other Native Americans. In an excellent two-volume collection of Wilson's writings published in 1967, only one paragraph out of a total of nearly eight hundred pages of text refers directly to American Indians. This paragraph is part of a larger essay entitled "On the History of Property." In it, Wilson mentions the Indians of Peru and their concepts of property, and he paraphrases from the eighteenth-century writer James Adair. He concludes by suggesting that "ideas and opinions of private and exclusive property are, as we have reason to believe, extending gradually among the Indians; though their uncultivated territory is still considered as the common property of the nation or tribe."[14] In sharp contrast, Greeks, Romans, and Saxons and their legal precedents are mentioned at least forty-seven times each. Bacon, Becarria, Cicero, Locke, Montesquieu, and Tacitus are each cited on at least fifteen separate occasions. Wilson refers to Blackstone eighty-five different times, while Coke is mentioned on sixty different occasions. Since Thomas Reid's name appears on only ten pages, this piece of evidence alone is not sufficient to properly judge Grinde and Johansen's contentions.[15]

Wilson formulated his unique views of the common law from reading Blackstone and Coke, even though he objected strongly to the centrality of their ideas. Wilson's writings emphasized popular sovereignty, the consensual basis of all legitimate political and legal obligations, and drew from sources as far back as ancient Greece and Rome for his inspiration. Since Blackstone emphasized the legality of Parliament and its rule over colonists, Wilson often used Blackstone as a foil since, to a degree, he saw the English legalist as an "apologist for despotism."[16] It is important to note that although he was influenced by Coke, he rejected both his and Blackstone's notion that English colonies were conquered areas and that colonists received their rights by acquiescing in the conquest. To Wilson, the colonists were conquerors and thereby had acquired the right to rule since "English theory applied only to aboriginal and infidel peoples, not to colonials."[17] Thus, to Wilson, colonists were not in the same category as Native Americans, whom he perceived as lowly, conquered peoples.

Wilson, it is clear, also drew from Montesquieu and Vattel. In fact, according to one contemporary observer, Montesquieu's works occupied a position of first importance in Wilson's library; he made a daily study of them.[18] Both Montesquieu and Vattel "had imagined a world of confederated states, freed from war."[19] Wilson drew not from the Iroquois Confederacy, but from Montesquieu when he insisted that the new union "consists in assembling distinct societies, which are consolidated into a new body capable of being increased by the addition of other members; an expanding quality peculiarly fitted to the circumstances of America."[20] Vattel wrote in the *Law of Nations:*

> The surest means of preserving a balance of power would be to bring it about that no state should be much superior to the others, that all the states, or at least the larger part, should be about equal in strength.... Confederations would be a sure means of preserving the balance of power and thus maintaining the liberty of Nations.[21]

Wilson and other conservatives, in wishing to escape the fate that had befallen Europe for centuries, feared disorder, anarchy, and a condition of warring states, which might lead to the return of tyranny. This intellectual leader of the Federalists believed that law "was the greatest preservative of society."[22]

Wilson, it is true, had ample opportunity to learn from the Indians. From 1775 to 1777, according to his major biographer Charles Page Smith, Wilson was "the most active and influential single delegate in laying down the general outline that governed the relations of Congress with the border tribes."[23] In the summer of 1775, he was appointed to the Committee on Indian Affairs with James Duane, Patrick Henry, Philip Livingston, and Philip Schuyler. This followed a New York plea to Congress in fear that hostile Indians would threaten the colony. He was soon sent off to Fort Pitt as one of the commissioners of the Middle Department.[24] There, Wilson observed the weakened power of the Iroquois, their rivalries with the Delaware, Shawnee, and Wyandot, and the growing independence and boldness of the Indians of the Ohio Valley. At Fort Pitt, he was not enamored of the Iroquois, and in fact, according to his major biographer, Wilson decided to try to use the Delawares as a counterforce to them.[25]

Grinde cites Wilson's speech of July 26, 1776, before the Continental Congress as evidence that the Pennsylvanian was influenced by the Iroquois, since Wilson stated that "Indians know the striking benefits of confederation" and "have an example of it in the union of the Six Nations."[26] Wilson's point is taken out of context, a frequent failing in the writings of Grinde and Johansen. If the Iroquois did have an influence on Wilson's thinking here, it was largely out of the necessity of keeping them at peace, not out of respect for their elders' wisdom. In this and in other speeches, Wilson repeatedly made references to the need for centralized authority and the uniform management of Indian affairs. Wilson was concerned with the need to control state rivalries

over western lands, which would antagonize the Indians and lead them to re-
taliate at a time of rebel weakness during the War of Independence.[27] Wilson's
point is clarified when his entire remarks of July 26, 1776, are quoted:

> We have no right over the Indians, whether within or without the real
> or pretended limits of any Colony. They will not allow themselves to be
> classed according to the bounds of Colonies. Grants made three thou-
> sand miles to the eastward, have no validity with the Indians. The trade
> of Pennsylvania has been more considerable with the Indians than that
> of the neighboring Colonies.
>
> No lasting peace will be [made] with the Indians, unless made by some
> one body. No such language as this ought to be held to the Indians. "We
> are stronger, we are better, we treat you better than another colony." No
> power ought to treat with the Indians, but the United States. Indians
> know the striking benefits of confederation; they have an example of it
> in the union of the Six Nations. The idea of the union of the Colonies
> struck them forcibly last year. None should trade with Indians without a
> license from Congress. A perpetual war would be unavoidable, if every-
> body was allowed to trade with them.[28]

Wilson's attitudes toward Native Americans are most revealing. When
American fortunes improved, he was not averse by 1777 to advocating a punitive expedition against the southern Indians to punish them for allying or
trading with the British.[29] After all, as a fervent proponent of westward expansion, he clearly believed that the Indians had to give way to the advancing
white man for the progress of civilization:

> If a nation establish itself, or extend its establishment in a country
> already inhabited by others, it ought to observe strict justice, in both in-
> stances, with the former inhabitants. This is a part of the law of nations
> that very nearly concerns the United States. It ought, therefore, to be
> well understood. The whole earth is allotted for the nourishment of its
> inhabitants, but it is not sufficient for this purpose, unless they aid it
> by labor and culture. The cultivation of the earth, therefore, is a duty
> incumbent on man by the order of nature. Those nations that live by
> hunting, and have more land than is necessary even for the purposes
> of hunting, should transfer it to those who will make a more advanta-
> geous use of it; those who will make this use of it ought to pay, for they
> can afford to pay, a reasonable equivalent. Even when the lands are no
> more than sufficient for the purposes of hunting, it is the duty of the
> new inhabitants, if advanced in society, to teach, and it is the duty of

the original inhabitants, if less advanced in society, to learn, the arts and uses of agriculture. This will enable the latter gradually to contract, and the former gradually to extend their settlements, till the science of agriculture is equally improved in both. By these means, these intentions of nature will be fulfilled; the old and the new inhabitants will be reciprocally useful; peace will be preserved; and justice will be done.[30]

Wilson carefully worked out his ideas for national control over Indian affairs as well as for planned frontier settlement. He feared that if states had jurisdiction over Indian affairs within their boundaries, it would exacerbate tensions with the Indians since state boundaries could cut across tribal areas.[31] To him, the establishment of Congress's authority over western lands was deemed necessary for the orderly development and security of the nation as a whole. In his most detailed writing on the frontier, "On the Improvement and Settlement of Lands in the United States," he foresaw planned frontier settlement as an outlet for massive European immigration. By encouraging and facilitating the migration of the best that Europe had to offer, America's greatness would be ensured. In effect, some of his ideas predicted those articulated a century later by historian Frederick Jackson Turner. In Wilson's scheme, American Indian interests were totally ignored.[32]

Indeed, the Iroquois were surrounded by similar sharks that were much more interested in their lands than in their ideas, or in what may have appeared to be their ideas. Eight of the delegates at the Constitutional Convention were "speculators on a grand scale." They were William Blount, Jonathan Dayton, Nathaniel Gorham, George Mason, Robert Morris, George Washington, and James Wilson.[33] It is essential to note that Gorham, Morris, Washington, and Wilson dabbled or were extensively involved in New York real estate, including that located in Iroquois country.[34] Strangely, recent writings on Native Americans' influence on the Constitution either ignore or minimize the Founding Fathers' roles as land-jobbers who sought to extinguish Indian title.[35]

Just as the Iroquois became entangled, much to their disservice, in the war of brothers between the colonists and Great Britain, the Indians became the victims of a battle within the American polity from 1774 onward. The contests between federal authority and states' rights and between states over each one's claim to western lands became major outside factors shaping the Iroquois world in the decade and a half after the war. The most prominent statesmen of the Revolutionary era fought major battles over these two issues.[36] Historian Reginald Horsman has correctly observed that land speculators were on both sides of the national control–states' rights debate: "Those speculators who hoped to profit by state-granted lands opposed cession to the central government, whereas the speculators who had not gained recognition by the state governments pressed enthusiastically for the land cessions, hoping to gain a more favorable hearing from Congress."[37] Those advocates of the states' rights position on Indian affairs in New York included the most famous and power-ful families, such as the Clintons and Livingstons, who stood to benefit most by Indian land-title extinguishment. On the other side were the likes of Morris and Wilson. Although the Constitutional Convention did not hinge merely on economic factors related to land speculation, as historian Forrest McDonald has correctly maintained, this issue did color the entire era from 1768 to 1797.[38]

As early as 1773, Wilson had caught the land-speculation fever. Some of his partners in these early ventures included George Croghan, Bernard and Michael Gratz, and David Franks. These same individuals had been among the "suffering traders" who had pushed for the Treaty of Fort Stanwix in 1768, in which Iroquois title to lands was extinguished east and south of a line drawn from today's Rome, New York, south to the Unadilla River; from there to the Delaware River near Hancock, New York; then westward to Owegy, southwest to the west branch of the Susquehanna near Williamsport, Pennsylvania, and along that river to its head; from there westward to Kittaning on the Allegheny, along that river and then the Ohio westward to the mouth of the Tennessee. The Indians received 10,460 British pounds worth of gifts and assurances that the treaty line would be respected and enforced by the British. The eminent historian Ray Allen Billington has called this Treaty of Fort Stanwix "one of the worst treaties in the history of Anglo-Indian relationships," largely because it promoted rather than limited "speculative fever" and encouraged a "new wave of land jobbing."[39]

Wilson's entrepreneurial activities burgeoned after he moved to Philadel-phia in 1778. His interest in acquiring more lands expanded; he also developed ironworks, engaged in the maritime trade, served as a legal advisor to the French government in commercial areas, and acted as Robert Morris's attorney in the formation of the Bank of Pennsylvania, becoming one of its directors soon afterward. His ties increased to some of the city's most successful invest-ment banking and trading houses run by the Franks, Gratz, Levy, and Lopez families. Wilson also became the most prominent attorney representing the political elite, including Charles Carroll, George Clymer, Silas Deane, William Duer, Thomas Mifflin, Arthur St. Clair, and, above all, Robert Morris.

Morris was economically, politically, and socially tied to Wilson. The two men were allies, part of Pennsylvania's conservative bloc. Morris also at-tempted to use his political influence to secure Wilson's appointment as at-torney general of the United States as well as an appointment to the United States Supreme Court. Both men were nationalists who pushed for a strong central union. Both joined in investments together, and interestingly, each in the end faced discreditation and financial ruin. Importantly, their wives were best friends as well.[40] The Morris connection was also evident in the so-called Fort Wilson incident of 1779. Since Wilson was viewed by some as less than patriotic because of his defense of loyalists and the perception that he was profiteering during the American Revolution, a mob of disgruntled militia attacked his home in Philadelphia, determined to expel him and his associates from the city. Although several deaths resulted, Wilson fled for safety to Robert Morris's country house, where he hid in the attic.[41]

In 1780, Wilson was elected president of the newly reorganized Illinois Company, by then known as the Illinois-Wabash Company, a vast enterprise that controlled some sixty million acres. Having been personally staked to one million acres of land, Wilson became the company's leading voice in and out of Congress throughout the decade of the 1780s. Soon Wilson's interests in land stretched well beyond Pennsylvania, to New York, Ohio, Virginia, Kentucky, and North Carolina, right to the Yazoo lands of Georgia. Despite sizable conflicts of interest, Wilson invested heavily in the lands within the so-called Connecticut claim to the Wyoming area of Pennsylvania, and he saw nothing wrong about lobbying in and out of Congress for Connecticut's relinquishment of its claim in return for the state's land exchange in the Western Reserve of Ohio. He challenged Virginia's claim to western lands, which state officials had insisted was guaranteed under their royal charter. Moreover, he was not averse to exploiting jurisdictional confusion to counter Virginia's head start in developing the trans-Appalachian frontier. He even suggested to Madison that his Illinois-Wabash Company had sufficient shares to bribe congressmen to get its way. Throughout the 1780s, he pushed for congressional control and organization of lands in the trans-Appalachian frontier, which he hoped would validate the Illinois-Wabash Company's previous and, in some instances, highly irregular purchases from the Indians. Although he eventually secured federal jurisdiction over these lands, he never succeeded in getting Congress to validate the claims of the Illinois-Wabash and other land companies.[42]

Incredibly, Wilson's speculative ventures brought him little permanent wealth since he invested his profits as well as the principal in even more grandiose land schemes. His actions snowballed and became a compulsive gambling sickness. According to Robert McCloskey, the editor of his writings: "Once on the accelerating treadmill of borrowing and postponed payments and more borrowings it was increasingly hard to keep pace with it, much less get off: his measures to survive became more and more desperate and less and less scrupulous."[43]

Even before the signatures on the Peace of Paris of 1783 were dry, Wilson was lusting after real estate in the Upper Susquehanna River Valley, in lands vacated by the Iroquois after the Sullivan–Clinton scorched-earth campaign of 1779. Along with William Bingham, a sometime partner of Robert Morris, Wilson organized the Canaan Company with the intention of purchasing sizable interest in lands (100,000 acres) on the Upper Susquehanna, in and around present-day Binghamton, New York, a city later named after Wilson's partner. These lands were part of the southern boundary of Oneida territory. Indian title to these lands was later extinguished in what the Oneida still claim was an illegal land transfer with New York State in the mid-1780s.[44]

By 1785, Wilson became involved with Dutch investors seeking to make their fortune in American lands. Although he offered to serve as their agent and subordinate his legal practice, nothing ever materialized until his dealings with Theophile Cazenove, a Dutch agent of several banking houses in the early 1790s. In the original contract signed in December 1790, the members of these banking houses had the right of selecting the choice property out of a million acres that Wilson had secured from the public land office; acreage not selected would revert to Wilson. The Dutch investors had to purchase 500,000 acres of Wilson's extensive Pennsylvania lands, with an option to buy an additional 200,000 acres. Wilson was paid 40 cents per acre, for a total of 280,000 dollars. In return, Wilson agreed to pay all expenses of warranting, surveying, and patenting. Wilson, however, was unable to fulfill his commitment because of insurmountable debts. In fact, five years after his death, Wilson's estate was still indebted to these Dutch capitalists, by then known as the "Hollandsche Land Compagnie"—the Holland Land Company—for $46,578.38.

When Wilson failed to carry out his obligations on these Pennsylvania lands, the Dutch investors turned to his friend Robert Morris, who offered them 1,300,000 acres of the choicest Genesee lands in western New York. Through alcohol and outright bribery, Robert Morris and his son, Thomas, subsequently swindled the Seneca out of most of their best lands at the Treaty of Big Tree in 1797, delivering his contractual obligation to the Dutch investors. Despite his diabolic skills at Big Tree, Robert Morris died in debtor's prison in 1803. Five years earlier, his friend, Justice James Wilson, had died at a seedy inn in Edenton, North Carolina, after fleeing from his own creditors.[45]

In conclusion, Wilson's innovative thinking was less a product of Iroquois Grand Councils than his own pragmatism. For the good of the country as well as for his and his associates' personal interests, he pushed for the ratification of the United States Constitution, for congressional authority over western lands, and for peaceful and orderly frontier settlement. As a leading conservative voice of his generation in Pennsylvania politics, he advocated popular sovereignty as well as a strong federal union to ward off social chaos and to ensure stability, which was needed to avoid a loss of American independence. What Wilson feared most was disorder—the urban rabble of Philadelphia, who had nearly killed him in 1779. As historian Henry May has demonstrated, Wilson was "educated rather than embittered by the attack on his house in 1779." The result was his advocacy of popular sovereignty.[46] Moreover, Wilson also feared state rivalries over western lands, which would intensify conflict with the Indians, threaten the loss of independence, and ruin his numerous schemes to amass a fortune.

Canasatego (Canassateego) and other Iroquois leaders were hardly part of Wilson's mind-set. Intellectually, Montesquieu, Reid, and Vattel appear to be at the central core of his thought. Wilson's highly materialistic side makes it unlikely that he drew inspiration from the Iroquois longhouse. Wilson's excessive acquisitiveness, which was self-destructive to him in the end, as well as his cultural-supremacist attitude toward Indians indicate that they had little, if any, influence on him. As an individual with a compulsive gambling obsession for land, he was more interested in the Indians' estate than in their intellect. To Wilson as well as to most Founding Fathers, peace with the Indians was a preferable goal since the fledgling nation was struggling, financially insecure, and still surrounded by English and Indian enemies. To most of this generation of American leaders, Indians, in effect, had to be controlled or manipulated out of their lands for America's national advancement and/or for individual, company, or states' economic benefit.

THE MISSIONARY
FROM HELL

Historians of American Indian policies have focused on the age of Jackson, 1815–40, more than on any other era. In this period, American Indians faced dispossession and death as a result of forced removals and/or wars of conquest. Although statistics vary, 10,138 more Cherokees alone "would have been alive in 1840" if removal to the West had not taken place (Russell Thornton, *The Cherokees: A Population History* [Lincoln: University of Nebraska Press, 1990], p. 76). Long before the current moral indictment of Euroamericans during the Columbian Quincentennary, historian William T. Hagan rightly determined that, at their worst, the removal of the Cherokee and other members of the Five Civilized Tribes approached the "horrors created by the Nazi handling of subject peoples" (*American Indians,* 1st ed. [Chicago: University of Chicago Press, 1961], p. 77).

As is demonstrated in the following chapter, Indian removal did not affect only the Cherokee and other members of the Five Civilized Tribes, but had an impact across sections. Indeed, Indian removal was the linchpin that helped build the Democratic party and tie the northern and southern wings of the party together after Jackson's election in 1828. According to historian Richard B. Latner, in *The Presidency of Andrew Jackson: White House Politics, 1829–1837* (1979), "the Indian question was more than a sectional one. It was also a 'party question' and support for Indian removal became a distinguishing feature of the emerging Democratic Party" (pp. 97–98). Unable to agree or even discuss the slave issue, southern Democrats and Van Buren men — the Bucktails or Albany Regency, as they were called — coalesced on Indian removal and increased state jurisdiction over Indian affairs, both of which were symbolized by the national hero, Andrew Jackson. Thus, during the Jackson and Van Buren presidencies, a political consensus on state predominance in Indian affairs permeated the Democratic party, leading to Indian removals in New York, the Midwest, and the Southeast (Richard Ellis, *The Union at Risk: Jacksonian Democracy, States' Rights and the Nullification Crisis* [New York:

Oxford University Press, 1987], pp. 25–31; Ronald N. Satz, *American Indian Policy in the Jacksonian Era* [Lincoln: University of Nebraska Press, 1975], p. 25). Even in Jackson's first annual address to Congress, the president made reference to Maine, New York, and Ohio, as well as to Alabama and Georgia and their need to establish jurisdiction over the Indians within their borders (James D. Richardson, ed., *A Compilation of the Messages and Papers of the Presidents, 1789–1897* [Washington, D.C.: U.S.G.P.O., 1900], 2: 457–458).

Unfortunately, many historians have been misled by focusing on the paternalistic rhetoric of the era and not seeing that American Indians of almost every region were affected by policies as well as the tone set in Washington during the Jackson–Van Buren presidencies, from 1829 to 1841. One such historian is Robert V. Remini, the foremost scholar of the Jacksonian era. To Remini, Jackson did not intentionally attempt to destroy Indians and their culture, but believed that removal was for their own good. Instead of ignoring the "Indian problem," as his predecessors in the White House had done, Jackson, according to Remini, took the issue head-on, following the dictates of humanity in efforts to save the Indians.

Historians rightly teach their students to look for nuances and to show disdain for the "we" versus "they" approach to history; however, as I note in the following essay, some policies such as Indian removal of the 1830s had conspiratorial elements. I focus on the career of John Freeman Schermerhorn to show the comprehensiveness and planned nature of Indian removal policy, one that affected widely separate Native American communities across regions of the United States.

Since the late 1950s, Robert V. Remini, Professor of History and Distinguished Professor of the Humanities at the University of Illinois at Chicago Circle, has almost singlehandedly reshaped the historiography of the Jacksonian era by his numerous writings. In the past decade, Remini has attempted to defend President Jackson and exorcise him of any personal guilt for the disaster of Indian removal, the policy that invites the sharpest criticism of Old Hickory. Although other distinguished scholars such as Francis Paul Prucha have found a more favorable side of Jackson and his Indian policy, no contemporary historian has gone as far or reached as wide an audience in the president's defense as has Remini.[1]

In the final volume of his Jackson biography, *Andrew Jackson and the Course of American Democracy, 1833–1845* (1984), Remini recognized Indian removal as a "total violation of American principles of justice and law," one that led to the loss of 100 million acres of the Indians' estate and contributed to countless deaths of Indian men, women, and children. Remini conceded that Jackson was "shot through with ethnocentrism and paternalism that allowed little regard or appreciation of Indian culture and civilization." Nevertheless, he concluded that Jackson had accomplished his "humanitarian" goal of removing thousands of Indians to what "he considered a safe haven west of the Mississippi River."[2] Three years later, in an abridgement of his three-volume biography of Jackson, Remini further cemented a favorable view of Jackson's Indian policy in the popular mind.[3]

In 1988, Louisiana State University Press published Remini's Walter Lynwood Fleming Lectures. In one of these essays, Remini insisted that Jackson has been "condemned virtually out of hand for the horrors" of Indian removal. The Jacksonian scholar maintained that the president's policy of removal went haywire when it was put in place by less capable and less honest men, who subverted the generally benevolent but paternalistic intentions of the president. Remini claimed that Jackson personally saw "removal as a humanitarian means of preserving Native American life and culture" in the Trans-Mississippi West, where they would not "constitute a threat to the safety of the Union" or be a "bother to the greed, arrogance and racism of whites." He credited Jackson with undertaking to solve "a problem that no previous president had dared to tackle." Despite his own admission of a degree of bias in favor of Jackson, Remini stated that he was providing a "more balanced statement" than most other historians, whom he accused of being unwilling "to grant any other motive for removal than greed, psychological trauma, political opportunism, or some other base intention." In conclusion, Remini asserted that even "the best intentions in the world can sometimes end in human misery and death."[4]

The next year, Remini added to his defense of Jackson by reaching an undergraduate audience. In a chapter in a college-level textbook, he went well beyond the need to plead the president's innocence. Unabashedly, Remini insisted that Jackson was responsible for the overall survival of those tribes removed to the west, "whereas other tribes in the east disappeared."[5] Despite Remini's contentions of a "vanishing race" and no thanks to Jacksonian policies, between 20 and 25 percent of the Native American population survive today east of the Mississippi!

The career of John Freeman Schermerhorn calls into question many of Remini's judgments about the Indian removal policies of the 1830s. Perhaps next to Andrew Jackson and Martin Van Buren themselves, no figure had more direct involvement in carrying out Indian policies in the 1830s than did Schermerhorn. He was involved in treaty negotiations with twenty different Indian nations, resulting in the removal of thousands of Indians from their homelands, "many of whom died or were killed as they were marched westward beyond the Mississippi River." The cleric was, according to his biographer James Van Hoeven, "indirectly responsible for provoking the Seminole War" as well as for factional conflicts within several Indian nations, including the Cherokee and the Seneca. In fact, his machinations extended into the Van Buren administration and were still felt well after the clergyman's death in 1841. Van Hoeven has stated that "no appointed government official did more to implement Jackson's program of Indian removal in the field" than did Schermerhorn during the Jackson era.[6]

Schermerhorn's career also shows the wholeness of Indian policy in this time period and the relationship of removal negotiations taking place in the Southeast, Northeast, and Midwest. More importantly for a discussion of the "Remini thesis," Jackson, despite Schermerhorn's questionable methods of opportunism and strong will, rewarded his chief negotiator in the field with new sinecures for his loyal service. Schermerhorn was also seen as "Jackson's man" by the Indians themselves. The Oneida, forced by Jacksonian policies to emigrate to Green Bay from New York, complained to Cherokee Chief John Ross "bitterly of Schermerhorn's past conduct towards them also," and Ross insisted that "*they feel as we* [the Cherokee] *do,* in regard to Indian affairs generally" [Ross's emphasis].[7] Less than a year later, the young Seneca chief Maris Pierce referred to Schermerhorn sarcastically as that "certain notorious minister who preaches General Jackson's *humane* policy for the removal of the Indians now east of the Mississippi" [Pierce's emphasis].[8]

Schermerhorn was a prominent Dutch Reformed minister from Schenectady and Utica, New York. He was a descendant of one of the founders of Schenectady. The cleric had been a longtime admirer and supporter of Andrew Jackson, whom he had first met during the War of 1812. He was less tied to Martin Van Buren and the rising Democratic party until General Jackson's election to the presidency in 1828; nevertheless, it should be noted that Schermerhorn and Van Buren were both members of the Dutch Reformed Church in the capital district and that Van Buren was an uncle to one of Schermerhorn's close ministerial colleagues.[9] According to his biographer, "drawing on these relationships, the prestigious legacy of his own family name in the Schenectady–Albany area, and his 'friendship' with Jackson, Schermerhorn apparently was able to gain *entree* into the select circles of New York politicians."[10]

Schermerhorn's fanatical religiosity obscured other sides to his character. Dogmatically judgmental and uncompromising, the New York minister fervently backed Jacksonian removal policies and viewed its political opponents as morally inept. Schermerhorn was also a slimy supplicant constantly badgering his political supporters for appointments to office. While serving as

Jackson's ear to the missionary societies, he frequently sought his due rewards, not final judgment. Although his elaborate plan for the emigrant Indians included provisions for eventual statehood and Indian representation in Congress, Schermerhorn, with a strange sense of ministerial ethics, was always careful to provide for his own financial needs at every turn. He speculated in Wisconsin lands while serving as a commissioner dealing with the Indians in the West, and he lobbied successfully for a two-thousand-dollar reimbursement in Article 8 of the Treaty of Buffalo Creek with the New York Indians, three months after he had been relieved of his negotiating duties![11]

Schermerhorn kept Jackson informed about the activities of the American Board of Commissioners for Foreign Missions, the Boston-based proselytizing society that opposed the president's Indian removal policies. He also transmitted news of the Indian Board for the Emigration, Preservation, and Improvement of the Aborigines of America, founded in 1829, whose "exclusive object" was to promote the federal government's Indian removal policies. Although Schermerhorn was not in the leadership of the New York Indian Welfare Board, as it became known, his own Dutch Reformed Church was the driving force in this organization.[12] Sincere humanitarian zeal, not the Schermerhorn variety, calling for Indian removal to the West to isolate the natives from the greed, arrogance, and racism of the East has masked the crass intentions and harsh political realities of policymakers during this period. Although there were undoubtedly sincere, good men associated with the cause of removal, it is clear that the Jackson and Van Buren administrations used them for their own political advantage.[13]

Because of his constant political badgering, Schermerhorn was eventually appointed to the Stokes Commission in 1832, as one of three commissioners who were required to examine the western region in an effort to obtain the necessary information to draft legislation to ameliorate existing tribal disputes over boundary lines and treaty obligations. In reality, this Stokes Commission had as its chief aim the facilitation of further tribal removal to Indian Territory. It was to make recommendations for a plan for the improvement, government, and security of the Indians to the War Department, a plan intended to quiet critics of removal.

In 1832 and 1833, the three commissioners held councils and negotiated with the Cherokee, Chippewa, Creek, Miami, Osage, Ottawa, Potawatomi, Quapaw, Seminole and Seneca-Shawnee.[14] It is important to note that Schermerhorn was judged by the Indians as well as by his fellow commissioners as the "least compromising" of the three men, and his "manner and rhetoric was pedantic and less polite than his colleagues."[15] Although there were successes in convincing Indians to remove west, the Seminole, for one tribe, refused to accept the commission's findings, and soon the Florida frontier erupted in a full-scale bloody conflict known in history as the Second Seminole War, 1835–42. The conflict resulted in the loss of more than fifteen hundred white soldiers and probably a greater number of Indian lives.[16] Significantly, during his tenure as commissioner, Schermerhorn visited Buffalo Creek reservation, in March 1835, to discuss the possibilities of Seneca exploration of the West.[17] While being apprised of the situation in New York in 1835–36, the minister had another major responsibility to undertake for his commander in chief, Jackson, namely, the removal of the Cherokee Indians.

Schermerhorn's notoriety in history stems from being Jackson's emissary, the chief federal negotiator of the fraudulent New Echota Treaty of 1835. Threatening the Cherokees with reprisals if they rejected the treaty, Schermerhorn consciously played up divisions in Cherokee society, with little concern for Indian cultural sensitivities. He saw John Ross in cosmic dimensions as the "Devil in Hell." Despite the Cherokee leadership's rejection of a removal treaty on previous occasions, Schermerhorn called a national council referendum. Although several hundred people attended and there were thousands of eligible voters in the Cherokee Nation, the vote at New Echota was only 75 to 7 in favor of emigration. Native Americans frequently showed their displeasure by boycotting referenda and other elections, but Schermerhorn fanatically defended the propriety of this questionable action and pushed for the treaty until its final ratification by the United States Senate in May 1836.[18] Gary Moulton, the editor of the John Ross Papers, has suggested that "Schermerhorn's desire for success was prompted by his hope of attaining a personal reward from the Jackson administration, perhaps a government position in the future Indian state."[19]

What Schermerhorn had aided and abetted in 1835 had horrific results by 1838. In the summer of that year, federal troops began rounding up and imprisoning the recalcitrant Cherokees, burning cabins and crops in their sweep of Indian villages. Unable to prepare for their removal and with their property confiscated, the Indians were not provided with enough food or water after the roundup and disease took its toll as well. The removed Indians faced starvation, inclement weather, several different epidemics, as well as jackal-like whites who murdered, burned, and looted as the Cherokees moved westward. Reflecting on Cherokee removal years later, John G. Burnett, a soldier-interpreter in the United States Army and an eyewitness to Cherokee suffering, observed:

> I was sent as interpreter into the Smoky Mountain Country [where I] witnessed the execution of the most brutal order in the history of American warfare. I saw the helpless Cherokees arrested and dragged from

their homes and driven at the bayonet point into the stockades. And in the chill of a drizzling rain on an October morning I saw them loaded like cattle or sheep into six hundred and forty-five wagons and headed for the West.... The trail of the exiles was a trail of death. They had to sleep in the wagons and on the ground without fire. I have known as many as 22 of them to die in one night of pneumonia due to ill treatment, cold and exposure.[20]

In his third volume of Jackson's biography, Remini described Schermerhorn as an "ambitious cleric" who used "chicanery pure and simple" in getting the Cherokee to "ratify" the Treaty of New Echota in 1835. Remini readily admitted that Schermerhorn, with "the zealousness of a religious fanatic, including a fire-and-brimstone harangue," forced the treaty down the Cherokees' throats. Despite these actions, Remini failed to mention that the New York clergyman was rewarded for his "success" with the Cherokee by being appointed by Jackson, his benefactor, to serve as the commissioner to make a treaty of removal with the New York Indians. This appointment was especially significant since the Indians in the Empire State were one of the last major eastern indigenous populations that remained largely untouched by Jacksonian policies, and they continued as a thorn for Washington policymakers.[21]

Schermerhorn's third major chance to serve Jackson came in May 1836, when he was appointed by the president as a commissioner to treat with the New York Indians. Yet, by 1836, he had a political albatross around his neck, namely, the fact that he was associated more than any other individual, outside of Jackson himself, with Indian removal policies. Political opponents of Jackson, such as Whig senators Henry Clay and Hugh Lawson White, frequently sniped at Jackson by attacking his special emissary Schermerhorn.[22]

Two weeks before the Senate vote on the New Echota Treaty in 1836, Schermerhorn was already lobbying to secure a position to negotiate a treaty for removal of the Six Nations from New York. In fact, Schermerhorn had also been corresponding with members of the Seneca Indian emigration party! By July, he had calculated how many Indians he had to remove from New York.[23] Writing to his benefactor Andrew Jackson in the early fall of 1836, Schermerhorn referred to his past experience with the Cherokee, but pointed to obstacles in his way in New York, where he maintained that the majority of Indians were opposed to removal; nevertheless, he reassured Jackson about his commitment to secure the removal of the New York tribes.[24] Nine days later, he wrote the commissioner of Indian affairs that he had "laid the foundations for the ultimate and speedy removal of the whole of the New York Indians, both those who reside at Green Bay and those who are still within this state."[25] What he had resolved was his strategy to isolate and divide the tribesmen by negotiating separately with each group. First, he was going to finalize agreements with the Oneida, Mohawk, and Tuscarora, then the Stockbridge and Munsee, and finally the remaining New York tribes.[26]

In the spring of 1837, the New York zealot, now serving the new Van Buren presidency, announced that he was set to solve the thorny problem of the Ogden Company and their preemptive right to the lands occupied by the Senecas. What Schermerhorn had apparently done was to further exacerbate Indian division by personally picking all of the members of an Indian exploring party, thus bypassing the general councils of the Iroquois nations. When the exploring party, composed of pro-emigration Indians on the payroll of the federal government, Ogden Land Company, or the negotiators, filed their reports from August 1837 onward, it was little surprise that they defended their appointments as delegates. Although Schermerhorn had apparently even offended some of the pro-removal party by showing them only certain western lands, they, nevertheless, largely defended the minister: "He [Schermerhorn] did not consider it necessary to hold a general council on the subject in as much as the very object in view might be defeated by delay."[27]

Schermerhorn and James Stryker, the corrupt subagent for the New York Indians, worked in tandem in the grand design to drive the Indians out of the Empire State.[28] After the return of a Schermerhorn-directed exploring party to the West in August 1837, Stryker conveyed the pro-removal report to Secretary of War Joel Poinsett in most flattering terms. Stryker maintained that the pro-emigration party included "the most respectable and enlightened portion of our chiefs" and that removal was the most "liberal action of the government in behalf of their people." The subagent falsely conveyed the impression that the selection of the delegates by the Indians was based upon merit and not upon Schermerhorn's and his own dealings, and claimed that treaty opponents were diminishing in number.[29] At the same time, he indicated that there was an increased stirring up of trouble by anti-emigration forces. It is also clear that by that time, Stryker and the Ogden Land Company were collaborating, even at times suggesting the same names to the Indian office, to aid in the negotiations with the Indians.[30]

In October 1837, in three separate memorials, Seneca, Oneida, and Onondaga chiefs protested Schermerhorn's actions. The Seneca protest argued that the minister had selected the exploring party himself and that these Indians "did not have any desire of again exploring the western country" since they wished to remain on their lands. They further insisted that Schermerhorn had violated the Pickering Treaty of 1794 and that negotiations between the United States and the Indians could only be transacted in "open council" with the Seneca leadership.[31] Because of increasing congressional criticisms of the minister and the powerful Democratic senator Silas Wright's desire to reward a protégé, Schermerhorn was "cut loose" by the Van Buren administration and replaced by former congressman Ransom H. Gillet as commissioner in late 1837.

Just before his dismissal, Schermerhorn had secured agreements from some of the Oneida, Mohawk, Tuscarora, and Stockbridge-Munsee, by repeating his Cherokee formula, namely, by promoting internal chaos. Angered by War Department officials' refusal to compensate him for negotiations with the Indians at Green Bay and for "expenses" incurred on one of the exploring parties to Indian Territory, Schermerhorn inserted the following provision into the Buffalo Creek Treaty:

> It is stipulated and agreed that the accounts of the Commissioner, and expenses incurred by him in holding a council with the New York Indians, and concluding treaties at Green Bay and Duck Creek, in Wisconsin, and in the State of New York, in 1836, and those for the exploring party of the New York Indians in 1837, and also the expenses of the present treaty, shall be allowed and settled according to former precedents.[32]

Through Gillet and Stryker's help, the New York cleric later received two thousand dollars under this provision, Article 8 of the treaty.[33]

When Schermerhorn was replaced by Gillet as primary negotiator of the Treaty of Buffalo Creek in late 1837, tribal discord had already been intensified, leading subagent Stryker to suggest that Seneca support for removal "has undoubtedly gathered strength since the return of the delegates."[34] Schermerhorn, on being replaced by Gillet, defended his actions, insisting that he was a party loyalist faithful to the removal policy, and that Indians opposed to emigration as well as his anti-Jackson opponents were responsible for his fall from grace.[35] Gillet never criticized Schermerhorn or Stryker before the treaty was concluded in January 1838, and he even had high praise for the negotiations. After the exposures of fraud, coercion, and bribery in securing the treaty, ratification of the agreement was put on hold until April 4, 1840, when President Martin Van Buren finally promulgated the treaty.[36]

Besides the loss of the Seneca's Buffalo Creek reservation, the center of Iroquois traditional life after the American Revolution, the treaty led to the removal of many Indians from the state. Under this fraudulent treaty, the Seneca ceded all of their remaining New York lands to the Ogden Land Company and relinquished their rights to Menominee lands in Wisconsin, which had been purchased for them by the United States. In return, the Indians accepted a 1,824,000-acre Kansas reservation that had been set aside by the federal government for all of the six Iroquois nations as well as for the Stockbridge-Munsee. The Indian nations had to occupy these Kansas lands within five years

reservation. For a total of 102,069 acres in New York, the Indians
ve 202,000 dollars, 100,000 dollars of which was to be invested
by the president of the United States; the income earned was to
o the Indians. The United States was to also provide a modest
sum to facilitate removal, establish schools, and purchase farm equipment and
livestock for the Indians' use.[37]

The treaty had other far-reaching results. As in the Cherokee "Trail of
Tears," members of the New York tribes died, en route to or in Indian Territory, of cholera, exposure to the elements, or starvation. In addition, the bitter
in-fighting in tribal politics after the treaty's consummation eventually led to
the creation of a new political entity, the Seneca Nation of Indians, in 1848.
Moreover, the treaty led to a Quaker-directed campaign to restore the Indian
landbase in New York, resulting in the United States Senate's ratification of a
"compromise treaty" in 1842. The Seneca regained the Allegany, Cattaraugus,
and Oil Springs reservations, but not the Buffalo Creek and Tonawanda reservations. Only in 1856 was the Tonawanda Band of Senecas finally "allowed"
to buy back a small part of its reservation from the Ogden Land Company.
This land purchase, as well as the confirmation of federal reservation status,
was acknowledged by the United States and the Tonawanda Band of Senecas
in a treaty concluded the following year. American Indian claims under the
Treaty of 1838 were not settled until the 1890s, in a major United States Court
of Claims award. In effect, the Buffalo Creek Treaty was the basis of much of
federal–Iroquois relations throughout the nineteenth century.[38]

In 1831, Alexis de Tocqueville wrote that the "expulsion of the Indians often
takes place at the present day in a regular, and, as it were a legal manner....
Half convinced and half compelled, they go to inhabit a new desert, where the
importunate whites will not let them remain ten years in peace. In this manner do the Americans obtain, at a very low price, whole provinces, which the
richest sovereigns of Europe could not purchase." [39] Although hardly sympathetic to the Indians, the perspicacious Tocqueville saw removal correctly as a
planned policy to secure Indian land in the cheapest manner. He clearly saw
through the paternalistic rhetoric of the age, which has masked reality and
blinded historians to the conspiratorial nature of Indian removal. From the
evidence, it is clear that Schermerhorn and Jackson were tied together in the
singlehanded mission to rid the East of indigenous peoples. By placing the bur-
den of guilt on Jackson's underlings, historians such as Remini have largely
whitewashed Jackson of any direct responsibility for the tragedy that befell
Indians during his presidency. At the very least, the president was responsible
for the criminally negligent homicide of thousands of American Indians during his tenure in office by rewarding political loyalists such as Schermerhorn
and tolerating their misdeeds.

 # HOSTILES

From the earliest days of Euroamerican settlement, American Indians were usually pictured as the instigators of conflict. By the nineteenth century, they were often deemed as hostiles and/or renegades intent on "savage war." In reality, as Richard Slotkin has brilliantly written, the "accusation is better understood as an act of psychological projection that made the Indians scapegoats for the morally troubling side of American expansion." It became "a basic ideological convention of a culture that was itself increasingly devoted to the extermination or appropriation of the Indians...." (Richard Slotkin, *Gunfighter Nation: The Myth of the Frontier in Twentieth-Century America* [New York: Atheneum, 1992], pp. 12–13). Viewing Indians as hostile enemies ignores a major reality, namely that, from the earliest colonial era onward, Native Americans were also allies of the Euroamerican world.

At least twenty thousand American Indians were in military service during the Civil War. Yet, Native Americans are an important but neglected area of Civil War historiography. From Annie Heloise Abel's three-volume classic written between 1915 and 1925 to more modern treatments such as Alvin M. Josephy, Jr.'s *The Civil War in the West* (1991), historians have almost exclusively focused on the Five Civilized Tribes—the Cherokee, Chickasaw, Choctaw, Creek, and Seminole—and their military role in Indian Territory and environs; however, the war was a much larger reality for American Indians, affecting communities east as well as west of the Mississippi River.

Bell I. Wiley, the noted military historian, in his two-volume study on the "common soldier" of the Civil War, quickly dismissed the role of Native Americans. Although acknowledging their helpful service as scouts and in raiding, he concluded that their contributions to the Confederate States of America "was admittedly insignificant and marked by large-scale defection." While recognizing Indian gallantry in combat for the Union, Wiley insisted that the Indians "were often slovenly in dress, careless of equipment, neglectful of camp duties and indifferent to prescribed routine...." Wiley added: "They also seemed inclined at times to support the side which appeared in strongest force among

Gen. Ulysses S. Grant's military staff, late spring 1864, with Ely S. Parker (Seneca) seated at the far right (courtesy Buffalo and Erie County Historical Society).

them" (*The Life of Johnny Reb: The Common Soldier of the Confederacy* [Baton Rouge, La.: Louisiana State University Press, 1943; paperback edition, 1992], pp. 326–327; *The Life of Billy Yank: The Common Soldier of the Union* [Baton Rouge, La.: Louisiana State University Press, 1952; paperback edition, 1992], p. 318).

American Indians played a more significant role in the Civil War than Wiley's conclusions suggest. While some American Indians tried to survive by avoiding participation in the war, many others contributed to Union and Confederate causes on both land and sea, as "grunts" in the trenches, and even as commissioned and non-commissioned officers. Two of their number—Ely S. Parker, a Seneca sachem and Union general, and Stand Watie, a Cherokee chief and Confederate general—were among the most distinguished commissioned officers of the war. Indeed, American Indians had diverse reasons for volunteering and quite varied experiences during the war itself.

The following essay focuses on several Native American communities during the Civil War. Their diverse histories illustrate the different ways that

Native American communities coped with, participated in, or were affected by the Civil War. It also calls into question the misconception that Indians were simply hostiles resisting American progress in the nineteenth century.

The Civil War is the great dividing line in the history of the United States. Every major American history textbook begins or ends with this momentous event which claimed 618,000 soldiers' and sailors' lives, nearly 2 percent of the nation's population. As one of the defining moments in the nation's experience, the war affected every community in the United States, including those of American Indians.[1]

Despite the uniqueness of their enlistment, American Indians faced similar battlefield horrors as their white and black counterparts. Two-thirds of Union deaths have been attributed to poor field sanitation, improper medical care, poor diet, and disease. The Civil War records of the Town of Salamanca, New York revealed another grotesque aspect of the war. Next to an entry of one Samuel Patterson, a Seneca Indian, a clerk penciled in: "starved to death on Belle Isle and to starve an Indian is a hard task yet the hounds were equal to it."[2] Captured Union Indians were also sent to Andersonville while Confederate Indian prisoners-of-war were sent to a similar hell-hole at Elmira, New York.

Most Native Americans who served in the Civil War were proud of their military service. A walk through most nineteenth-century Native American cemeteries reflects this fact. Tombstones frequently indicate the Indian's regiment, be it in Confederate or Union service, much like their non-Indian counterparts.[3] Yet, there were also abuses in the recruitment of Native Americans. As a result of a sharp drop in enlistments caused by the intensity of fighting after the Battles of Shiloh and Antietam in 1862, Congress passed the Enrollment Act in March, 1863. Before and especially after the bloodbath at Gettysburg in early July, 1863, desperate recruiters and mercenary bounty brokers began to entice underage or desperately poor Indians to join military service. Among the Seneca, forty-three volunteers were either underage and/or were not paid their requisite bounty payment, leading to a formal protest to President Abraham Lincoln. The Indians eventually achieved a hearing and a partial rectification of the situation.[4]

The irony that Native Americans participated at all in the war effort is clearly apparent. In the decade just before the outbreak of the conflict, American Indian communities faced a perilous existence and even tribal destruction. As we have seen, over one hundred thousand California Indians had to contend with enslavement, kidnappings, and a genocidal war of extermination sanctioned by federal, state, and county officials after the discovery of gold along the American River in 1848, and, with it, the flood of a quarter of a million

(above) Tombstone of Pvt. Austin George (Pequot), Mashantucket Pequot Indian Reservation (photograph by the author).

(above right) Pvt. Jacob Winnie (Winney), a Mohawk Indian, in his Civil War uniform (courtesy Barney Waterman).

(right) Pvt. Winnie's tombstone on the Cattaraugus Indian Reservation of the Seneca Nation (courtesy Barney Waterman). Note that Pvt. Winnie was in his fifties when he served the Union.

non-Indians to the state by 1852. Delaware, Shawnee, and other Indian nations, who had earlier been removed to the West, found themselves in the mid-1850s the victims of lawless sectional violence known as "Bleeding Kansas," which was largely an excuse to take their Indian lands in eastern Kansas. As late as the 1850s, Seminole Indians in Florida fought efforts at their removal to the

West. Even as Confederate artillery pieces were aimed at Fort Sumter during the secession crisis of 1860–1861, Washington officials discussed or made plans for other Indian removals as an option to solve the so-called Indian Problem.[5]

The question arises as to why American Indians, the most victimized of all groups within the United States, chose to serve in what was mostly a blood-bath between non-Indians? The answer goes well beyond one simple reason. To be sure, poverty induced enlistment. Despite their separate nationhoods, some Indian communities had by 1861 also been integrated into the region that surrounded them, and thus were dependent on the non-Indian world for economic and political survival. Participating in the Civil War was also somewhat motivated by Indian wanderlust and search for adventure. In other instances, it was also based upon past alliances, treaty obligations, and earlier military experiences. Participation in war validated tribal leadership and status within one's community. Moreover, Native Americans had their own views about slavery, leading at times to internal disputes since some Indians were slave-holders and others were opposed to the "peculiar institution." At times the reasons for volunteering were not for lofty ideals, but the result of persuasive and well-respected community leaders who were committed to joining the war efforts of North or South.

One of the more extraordinary fighting units was Company K of the 1st Michigan Sharpshooters, a complete company of Indians in the Union Army that saw action against the Confederacy east of the Mississippi.[6] Company K was largely recruited by Garrett G. Gravaraet, an Ottawa who was a talented artist, musician, and teacher. Because of his prestige and influence, Gravaraet was able to recruit approximately one hundred Ojibwa, Ottawa, and Pota-watomi Indians from both sides of the United States–Canadian international boundary. The unit was mustered into service on January 12, 1863, originally serving at Camp Douglas, Illinois as guards for Confederate prisoners of war. In March, 1864, the entire regiment was transferred, ordered to join the Army of the Potomac in Virginia.[7] From May onward, Company K served with distinction at the Battles of the Wilderness, Spotsylvania Court House, and at the assault on Petersburg. At the Battle of Spotsylvania alone, twelve in the company were killed. From early May 1864 onward, nine others were taken prisoner and shipped off to the Confederate prison at Andersonville, where they perished. Lieutenant Gravaraet was seriously wounded during the first Union assault against the Confederate citadel at Petersburg on June 17, 1864; two weeks later, Gravaraet died of his wounds.[8]

On July 30, 1864, the Union army attempted to breach the Confederate lines at Petersburg by blasting four tons of black powder in a mine run below and beyond the southern fortifications. Although the mine was successfully sprung, the Union efforts to take Petersburg ended in fiasco because of poor overall planning, incompetent battlefield leadership, and the ensuing chaos which resulted after the mine's detonation. The Battle of the Crater, as it is known in history, ended in heavy Union casualties and was a major Union defeat.[9] Despite the setback, Indians in Company K were cited for their heroism. One young private, Antoine Scott, an Ottawa, "deliberately drew the enemy fire" so his comrades-in-arms could escape being pinned down by the Confederate advance.[10] Union soldiers, in defenseless positions in the crater formed after the mine was triggered, waited to die at the hands of the Confederate enemy. In one of the more remarkable accounts of the battle, Lieutenant Freeman S. Bowley described the Indians of Company K and their actions. According to Bowley, a few of the Indians "did splendid work. Some of them were mortally wounded, and drawing their blouses over their faces, they chanted a death song and died—four of them in a group."[11] In the end, at least two of the Indians perished, two were missing in action, and two were taken by the Confederates as prisoners of war.[12]

The Indians of Company K were not the only Indians at the battle. At least two other Union regiments contained Indian recruits. Eight Iroquois, mostly Seneca from the Cattaraugus Indian Reservation, were in Company D of the 14th New York Heavy Artillery. These same Indians were battle-tested veterans and had been cited for heroism at the Battle of Spotsylvania, after they captured a nest of Confederate snipers.[13] In Company F of the 31st United States Colored Infantry of the Army of the Potomac during the battle were at least two other Indians: Private Austin George, a Mashantucket Pequot Indian from Ledyard, Connecticut, who was seriously wounded in the battle; and Private Clinton Mountpleasant, an Iroquois Indian (Tuscarora) from Lewiston, New York, who was killed in action in the battle.[14] It should be noted that historians have incorrectly assumed that the United States Colored Troops, as they were designated, were all African Americans; yet, some Indians in southern New England and a few others from New York were represented in these regiments. Because of racist perceptions in the region, Native Americans and African Americans were grouped together as "men of color" and sent off to war.[15]

Ironically, within the Confederate ranks at Petersburg on July 30 were Catawba Indians as well. Confederate Catawba Indians served in the 5th, 12th and 17th South Carolina Volunteer Infantry. Nelson George, William and Frank Canty, James and John Harris, and Alexander Timms [Tims] were all privates in Captain Cadwallader Jones' famed company of the 12th, "that had one of the most brilliant records of any in the war."[16] At least nineteen Catawba in all served the South in the war, including at Antietam and Gettysburg. Since some Catawba had been removed in the 1840s and lived in the environs of Cherokee Country in western North Carolina by the time of the Civil War, these tribesmen may have also represented in the ranks of William Holland Thomas' famed four companies of North Carolina Cherokees, the so-called Thomas Legion, which operated as units in the Confederate army in the mountainous country of western North Carolina and eastern Tennessee.[17]

Those Indians in the Thomas Legion had joined the Confederate war effort as a result of Thomas' persistent coaxing and pro-Confederate stance. Thomas was an extraordinary white man who emerged as an adopted Cherokee, benefactor, chief, and spokesman largely after Cherokee removal of the 1830s.[18] But what about the Catawba tribesmen who remained in their homeland and joined the three South Carolina infantry regiments? Decades after the Civil War era, Catawba told anthropologist Frank Speck that the Indians were threatened by Ferguson Barber, a white man who lived near their South Carolina homeland, who demanded that the Indians "would have to enlist or the whites would come down and kill them."[19] Although South Carolina–Catawba relations were often tense and the state frequently attempted to remove the Indians, the explanation given to Speck appears to be a concocted postwar rationale for Catawba involvement in the Confederate cause. The Catawba had an outstanding Confederate military record, one that cannot be simply rationalized by their "impressment" into the South's military service. Although these Indians were generally not slaveholders and were dirt poor by 1860, they had been involved in catching runaway slaves in the eighteenth century and were increasingly dependent on their white neighbors for economic survival in the decades prior to the Civil War.[20]

Other Native American communities, North and South, had their own specific reasons for their involvement in the Civil War. In 1861, the Seneca of western New York saw the Confederate firing on Fort Sumter in terms of their treaties with the federal government. As staunch allies of Washington since the Pickering Treaty of 1794, they now saw their ally in peril facing an internal rebellion. Moreover, Seneca young men, as warriors in the past, viewed the Civil War as an opportunity to rise in rank and status and/or validate their leadership, much like their ancestors had done in the wars out of Niagara of the eighteenth century and in the American Revolution. Other Seneca leaders such as Young King and Farmer's Brother had served the Americans in distinguished fashion during the War of 1812.[21]

The Seneca of western New York, two separate nations by 1860—the Tonawanda Band of Seneca Indians and the Seneca Nation of Indians—were among the most loyal troops to the Union war effort, excelling at New Bern, Petersburg, and Spotsylvania. Besides their capture of a Confederate nest of sharpshooters at Spotsylvania, other Iroquois troops, including a majority of Seneca, were cited for heroism in the War Department's Official Record because of their courageous stand holding a bridge at the skirmish at Batchelder's Creek in the winter of 1864 in North Carolina.[22]

In sharp contrast to the Seneca experience, most, but not all, of the Choctaw of Mississippi saw military service on the side of the South.[23] Yet, the Choctaw had much in common with the Seneca. Their greatest chief, Pushmataha, had served the Americans in the War of 1812. Both Indian nations had been disastrously affected in the age of Indian removal. Andrew Jackson–Martin Van Buren Indian policies had contributed to dispossession of the Seneca from their Buffalo Creek Reservation, the present-day city of Buffalo, in 1838.[24] Much like the Seneca, the emissaries of Andrew Jackson, the Choctaw's ally in the War of 1812, had forced these Southern Indians to agree to the devastating Treaty of Dancing Rabbit Creek in 1830. As a result of this treaty as well as the actions of corrupt federal Indian agents' actions in administering the agreement, the Choctaw were dispossessed of most of their lands in Mississippi. In order to survive, most of the Choctaw retreated deeper into the hills and swamps of east central Mississippi.[25]

For the majority of Choctaw of Mississippi, their pro-Confederate position, which did not run deep, was largely determined, as in the Catawba case, by being surrounded by overwhelming numbers of Southern sympathizers and being dependent on these same whites. At least some of these Confederate Choctaw were apparently conscripted by local officials in Mississippi against their will. By the spring of 1863, a sizable contingent of Choctaw were already serving in the 1st Choctaw Battalion, Mississippi Cavalry, spending much of the year tracking down Confederate deserters in the swamps. Many of these Choctaws, under the command of Major J.W. Pierce, deserted en masse later that spring after Confederate officials were late in paying them and after General John Pemberton ordered them to be relocated from their central Mississippi homeland to another battlefront in order to counter Union activities in the lower Mississippi River Valley. Fourteen of the remaining Choctaws in this regiment were later captured during the Vicksburg Campaign and sent off as Union prisoners of war to Fort Columbus, Governor's Island, in New York harbor.[26]

The Pequot and Mohegan Indians of southeastern Connecticut had a far different experience during the Civil War. Both of these coastal Algonkian peoples had common histories, at least through the early colonial era. The Mohegans and Pequots of southeastern Connecticut are two related but rival Indian communities separated since the bloody Pequot War of 1637. The Mohegan and Pequot Indians were largely centered on lands from Norwich to New London, Connecticut. Their communities had been largely associated with the whaling trade since the seventeenth century. They and their Massachusetts neighbors, the Wampanoags, had inspired Herman Melville's Indian characterizations in *Moby Dick*.[27]

These two historically related small Indian nations provided soldiers for the Union war effort. Many of their ancestors had served with distinction in the French and Indian War as well as in the American Revolution. Mohegan Indians—Uncas, Ashpow, Quocheets, and Wyox—built ships and served in the crews of the fledgling American navy during the War for Independence. These coastal Algonkian communities had also served in the War of 1812.[28]

Yet, the Pequot and Mohegan Indians were reluctant volunteers in the Civil War. Local military officials even began to try to conscript Connecticut Indians into Union military service. On July 25, 1863, only a brief time after the Battle of Gettysburg and the Draft Riots, the Mohegan Indians sent an official protest to the United States Provost General about the conscription of Indians into Union service, arguing that Norwich and Montville local agents "have taken the liberty to enroll some of the said Mohegan tribe for the present draft and without our consent." The protest cited the Constitution of the United States' Article I, section 2, clause 3, in noting that the Mohegan, a small community "already reduced by war and other pestilence," were legally exempt for the draft.[29]

No evidence has been found of any Indian being drafted in southeastern Connecticut. Less than a year after the protest, several Indians from the region, including Austin George, were in Union military service. The reasons for enlistment appear to be largely motivated by economic factors. By the time of the Civil War, the minuscule Indian landbases in southeastern Connecticut could not provide enough sustenance since they had been reduced considerably in size. Despite tribal protests, a Connecticut law was passed allowing the auctioning off of six hundred acres of Mashantucket Pequot lands on January 1, 1856. A Mohegan "land distribution" act was passed five years later. Moreover, as a result of the authoritarian and corrupt Connecticut overseer system, both communities were denied benefits and monies due them.[30]

To make matters worse for both Indian communities, their livelihood as whalers had largely come to an end by the Civil War years. The southeastern Connecticut whaling industry, already in decline since 1849, suffered considerably in the Civil War and went out of existence soon after. As part of the North Atlantic Blockading Squadron, the Union navy purchased much of New London's great whaling fleet, filled them with stone, and sank the vessels in the channels of major southern ports in order to strangle the Confederate war machine.[31]

By 1864, local, state, and federal officials were desperate in their recruitment of soldiers for the war. By the time some Pequots and Mohegans enlisted in 1864, local towns were paying bounties of $150 and the State of Connecticut $600 to any recruit who signed up. To desperately poor Indians with no economic livelihood at sea, the Union war machine was a more appealing way out of their dire economic predicament than shipbuilding at the great yards in and around Mystic, Connecticut, which were flourishing by serving the Union navy's needs. For a whaler, factory work in textiles and arms, which also boomed in southeastern Connecticut during the Civil War, was equally unappealing.[32]

The Indians of Virginia faced an even greater threat to their survival than the Indians of southeastern Connecticut. These Indians—the Chickahominy, Mattaponi, Nansemond, Pamunkey, and Rappahannock—found themselves at the center of the fighting. Their territories were invaded by Confederate and Union armies who foraged, stole, or exacted labor in their efforts to destroy their enemies. These Virginia Indians, descendants of the great Powhatan Empire, one which had faced off with English settlers at Jamestown in bloody wars of the first half of the seventeenth century, once again found themselves in a desperate struggle for survival.[33] As early as the First Battle of Bull Run in July 1861, the Indians of Virginia found their homeland in the midst of the heaviest fighting of the Civil War. For almost four years, the immense Union and Confederate war machines—the Army of the Potomac and the Army of Northern Virginia—tore each other apart in bloodletting unsurpassed in the history of the Western Hemisphere. Many of the major battles of the war—First and Second Bull Run, Chancellorsville, Cold Harbor, Fredericksburg, the Peninsula Campaign, Petersburg, Spotsylvania—were all fought in and around Indian country.

The Indians of Virginia were technically neutral during the Civil War, but clandestinely served the Union. Classified by the white society of the Tidewater as "Free Persons of Color," a label they resisted, the Indians had been forced into a legal "twilight zone." In the white supremacist society of antebellum Virginia, there were only two races—white and black. Because of the violent repercussions against both blacks and Indians following the failed Nat Turner slave rebellion of 1831, the Indians had survived in the three decades prior to the Civil War by distancing themselves from the African American experience. In these years, Virginia Indians played an "accommodationist" strategy of survival with the white power structure in Richmond; at the same time, they became more restrictive about tribal enrollment, forbidding intermarriage with blacks, "fully aware of the importance of 'blood' in proving their Indianness to outsiders." In the Civil War, at least five Indians from Virginia served as land guides and/or river pilots for Union gunboats; others fled as far north as Canada to save themselves and to avoid Confederate conscription.[34]

Despite resenting the South much more than the North because of past treatment in Virginia, most, although not all, chose no outward tribal alliance with either because of fears of reprisals.[35]

No Native American community was more disastrously affected by the Civil War than the Cherokee Nation of Indian Territory. Although some Cherokee of Indian Territory were slaveholders and others opposed the "peculiar institution," Cherokee participation in the Civil War was not merely an ideological struggle conditioned by moral or economic factors. Cherokee involvement was to a large extent an internal power struggle between two major divisions within the Indian nation's polity, intratribal warfare rooted in their existence since the 1830s. As a result of five years of desolation—Civil War fighting, smallpox and other epidemics, and impoverishment and starvation caused by refugee status—the Western Cherokee population declined from 21,000 to 15,000 people.[36] Perhaps even more devastating to tribal fortunes, the Cherokee in Indian Territory faced a civil war within the Civil War.

In the fall of 1861, Chief John Ross signed a treaty with General Albert Pike of the Confederate States of America at Tahlequah, the capital of the Cherokee Nation in the West. Two separate contingents of Cherokee from Indian Territory, one commanded by John Drew and the other by Stand Watie, soon entered the Civil War on the side of the Confederacy. Drew was a nephew by marriage to Chief Ross, Stand Watie's political enemy since the 1830s. Despite service to the Confederate cause at the Battle of Pea Ridge, most of Drew's regiment had little sympathy for the South. Some of his soldiers were members of the Keetoowahs, an Indian secret society opposed to secession and slavery which blamed the South for Cherokee removal from their homeland in Alabama, Georgia, Kentucky, North Carolina, and Tennessee. Drew's regiment eventually lost almost its entire membership through desertion to the Union ranks.[37] In sharp contrast, Stand Watie and his Cherokee followers were essential cogs in the Confederate war effort in the Trans-Mississippi West.

Watie and other members of his family had signed the Treaty of New Echota in 1835, which acceded to Cherokee removal from the East. Two of his brothers, Elias Boudinot and Thomas Watie, his uncle Major Ridge, and his cousin John Ridge had been assassinated by the anti-removal party of Cherokee during and after the removal. The assassins had been the son and followers of Ross, who remained Watie's major rival even during the Civil War.[38]

Watie preyed on the nearly seven thousand Cherokee who remained loyal to the Union. At the same time, he and his Confederate battalion, which included a smattering of tribesmen from all of the Five Civilized Tribes, attacked Union forces with abandon throughout Indian Territory. Even after the surrender at Appomattox, Watie was a devotee to the "Lost Cause."[39]

Gen. Stand Watie of the Confederate States of America (courtesy Western Historical Collection, University of Oklahoma).

Although most Cherokee leaned toward the Confederacy and three thousand served in the Confederate army, many others remained loyal or sought refuge with the Union army at Fort Gibson. By 1863, there was virtually two Cherokee nations in Indian Territory, the "Southern" and "Northern" Cherokee. In that year, the Northern Cherokee, mostly followers of Ross, abrogated the treaty of 1861 made with the Confederacy. They also abolished slavery. Thus, in effect, the Cherokee of Indian Territory faced two civil wars between 1861 and 1865.[40]

These Native American experiences provide only a representative sampling of the American Indian experience during the Civil War era. While these Indians served, other communities not involved in the conflict experienced a different fate. In 1862, Santee of Minnesota were defeated in the "Great Sioux Uprising"; thirty-eight of their leaders were subsequently executed. Two years later, Navajo Indians were forced on their "Long Walk" and relocated, for a four-year incarceration, at a concentration camp, the Bosque Redondo, at Fort Sumner, New Mexico. In the same year, Colonel John Chivington, a crazed religious fanatic, and the troops of the 1st and 3rd Colorado Cavalry, attacked a peaceful camp of mostly Cheyenne Indians along the Sand Creek, killing about 150 men, women, and children and mutilating their bodies. American Indian life in the West was transformed in other ways during the Civil War. The Transcontinental Railroad Act, passed by Congress in 1862, led to the disruption of traditional Plains Indian life, resulted in the extermination of bison

Grand Army of the Republic reunion, 1907, at Gowanda, New York, with Jimmy Cornplanter (Seneca) standing in back row, fourth from the left (courtesy Seneca-Iroquois National Museum).

herds, brought massive non-Indian population westward, increased Indian–white tension and conflicts, and led to reservation existence and overall Indian dependence.[41]

For Native Americans, wartime experiences were not soon forgotten. Indian veterans were buried with military as well as with Indian honors well into the 1920s. Those luckier ones who survived participated in the pageantry of postwar reunions, erected Confederate and Union monuments in their communities to honor their regiments, or paraded with veterans' associations such as the Grand Army of the Republic every Memorial Day. Union Indian veterans and their heirs sought Civil War pensions from the federal government well into the 1930s.

The impact of war was especially noticeable in small tight-knit Indian communities. As participants in the bloodiest fighting from the Napoleonic Wars to World War I, many veterans came back disabled. Amputees and psychologically scarred veterans were a common feature of every community in the United States, including those of Native Americans. The war also created a disproportionate number of widows and orphans, leading to further Indian dependence and poverty and to the establishment of numerous orphanages and asylums in Indian country.

In many ways, the Civil War was even more devastating to Indians than to non-Indians. Unlike their white counterparts, Indian communities who lost men in combat were not replenished by massive immigration from Europe. Unlike their black counterparts who fought a war, overcame slavery, and theoretically had legal standing under the 13th, 14th, and 15th Amendments to the Constitution passed during Reconstruction, American Indians were still in legal limbo as "domestic dependent nations."

The image of "hostile" that pervades America's popular culture does not take into account Native Americans and their roles in the Civil War. Unlike Bell I. Wiley's generalized assessment, the Indians' role was not insignificant nor were they indifferent to routine. Although some were loyal to the side which appeared strongest in their territory and some were reluctant belligerents, they did make their mark as allies to both sides in this tragic conflict. Attendance at a modern-day pow-wow, which poignantly begins with the flag ceremony dedicated to all veterans, Indian as well as non-Indian, clearly shows how Native Americans value military service in the United States Armed Forces; it also provides a strong counterweight to the popular conceptions that Indians were merely the "obstacles to frontier settlement and progress."

 **PATERNALISM**

This as well as previous chapters call into question the misconception that American Indian policies were paternalistic by nature. As early as 1867, after insisting that the Indian nations were headed for extinction and that Americans had to make use of land vacated by the Indians, the commissioner of Indian affairs wrote, in his annual report, that "this benevolent and bounteous [United States] government has from the onset accorded to them rights and possessions, and extended over them a paternal care which is most simply and admirably acknowledged in their appellation which styles the government 'the great father'" (United States Department of the Interior, Commissioner of Indian Affairs, *Annual Report on Indian Affairs, 1867* [Washington, D.C.: U.S.G.P.O., 1867], p. 145). More recently, the prominent historian Francis Paul Prucha has reinforced this overall conclusion about Washington-directed policies. In the preface to his monumental two-volume work, *The Great Father: The United States Government and the American Indian,* Prucha argued:

> Cries for extermination of the Indians occasionally sounded by aggressive frontiersmen and exasperated frontier commanders were rejected by United States officials responsible for Indian affairs. These officials instead sought to treat Indians honorably, even though they acted within a set of circumstances that rested on the premise that white society would prevail. The best term for this persistent attitude is *paternalism,* a determination to do what was best for the Indians according to white norms, which translated into protection, subsistence of the destitute, punishment of the unruly, and eventually taking the Indians by the hand and leading them along the path to white civilization and Christianity. ([Lincoln: University of Nebraska Press, 1984], I: xxviii.)

As I show in the following chapter, Native Americans faced constant threats to their survival on the road to their present status of dual citizenship. Although benevolence rather than butchery was more valued by Washington officials, it was hardly paternalism that determined what was good for the Indians. Throughout much of United States history, Indian affairs had low priority. More often than not, cost-conscious congressmen and bureaucrats determined the fate of American Indians. Moreover, Washington officials rationalized taking Indians' land in numerous public works projects for the nation's progress and security. (See, for example, Laurence M. Hauptman, "General John S. Bragdon, the Office of Public Works Planning, and the Decision to Build Pennsylvania's Kinzua Dam," *Pennsylvania History* 53 [July 1986]: 181–200.) Hence, as a result of American policymakers defining and redefining their status, the Indians had to wend their way through political and legal minefields.

Most Americans, including state and federal officials, have misconceptions about American Indians and their status under American law. At a news conference at Moscow State University in May 1988, President Ronald Reagan, who was attending a summit meeting at that time, was totally unaware that American Indians were/are in fact citizens of the United States ("Remarks on 'Humoring' Indians Bring Protest from Tribal Leaders," *New York Times,* June 1, 1988, p. 13A). In the classroom, I am asked, "Why is there so much legal history in the course?" I answer by insisting that American Indians' status is like no other in the United States. They have numerous treaties with the federal government, and at the same time, they are citizens of the United States with rights to sue to protect their lands, their resources, their civil rights, and so on. The student then responds by asking how Native Americans can have separate Indian nationhood guaranteed by treaties, and, at the same time, United States citizenship? I then recount how and why this legal "twilight zone" developed.

An earlier version of this essay was originally written for an Indian Rights Association conference on the United States Constitution in October 1987. I have now expanded and updated it in order to answer these perplexing questions about Native Americans' legal status. This chapter also calls into question whether it is correct to label American Indian policies over time as "paternalistic."

For American Indians, both the Constitution and its development over the past two centuries represent a mixed blessing. The development of United States citizenship for American Indians is a case study illustrating this point. In the process of securing United States citizenship, a meaningful and important achievement, American Indians had to pass through minefields triggered to destroy Indian tribalism and identity.

Nowhere does the Constitution provide for United States citizenship for American Indians. In fact, the Constitution, as ratified in 1788, only mentions

American Indians twice.[1] In 1868, the states ratified the Fourteenth Amendment, the only other reference to American Indians in the Constitution. "Indians not taxed" are excluded by both Article I and the Fourteenth Amendment from being counted in the apportionment of taxes and representatives to Congress from the states.[2] The so-called commerce clause, also in Article I, is the only grant of power that specifically mentions American Indians: Congress is authorized to "regulate commerce with foreign nations, and among the several states, and with the Indian tribes."[3] American Indian policies, including the development of United States citizenship for Indians, have also been affected by the so-called treaty clause of the Constitution, which granted exclusive authority to the national government to enter into treaties.[4] Congress enacted many laws relating to or implementing treaties. Although federal–Indian treaty making was discontinued by Congress in 1871, many Indian treaties remain in force.

Today, American Indians are entitled to the same benefits and privileges that other United States citizens receive. They are guaranteed equality by the "Equal Protection Clause" of the Fourteenth Amendment. Yet racial discrimination against American Indians persists on many levels. Frequently, American Indians have to enter federal courts to maintain services that other United States citizens receive.[5] Federal statutes and constitutional amendments since 1948 removing barriers to voting, of course, have affected and benefited American Indians. State constitutions have been amended to remove distinct categories, such as "Indians not taxed," that were used for decades to limit the Indian's civil rights. Thus American Indians are less frequently denied rights or benefits based on their separate status as was commonly true before the historic *Harrison* v. *Laveen* decision of 1948.[6]

The development of Indian citizenship and with it civil rights, not provided in the grand document of 1787, have become a reality. Yet the Indian's path to United States citizenship and its resulting rights and privileges was lined with minefields. Not all of the American Indians and Indian nations survived the battle unscathed. Some, such as the Iroquois traditionalists in New York, rejected going down the path at all and saw their future solely in Indian moccasins, rejecting the white man's road to citizenship. Others, a majority of American Indians in the United States, viewed dual citizenship as the only viable option.

United States citizenship for American Indians was first extended through federal Indian treaties. Throughout the nineteenth century, the offer of citizenship was tied to assimilationist values, to individual Indian land allotments of the tribal estate, and even to the total destruction of tribal organization and government. United States treaties with the Cherokees in 1817 and 1819 provided for individual allotments of tribal lands to heads of families "who may wish to become citizens of the United States."[7] In 1830, the federal Treaty of Dancing Rabbit Creek with the Choctaws clearly specified that "each Choctaw head of a family being desirous to remain and become a citizen of the States, shall be permitted to do so, by signifying his intention to the agent within six months from the ratification of this treaty."[8] Individual Indians, in each of these treaties, had to choose between tribal membership and removal or land allotments and United States citizenship. It is important to note that when Indians chose the latter, they were often denied the rights and guarantees of United States citizenship.[9]

Other Indian nations were faced with more direct threats to their tribal existence through the extension of citizenship. The Stockbridge Indians of Wisconsin, in federal treaties from 1843 to 1864, "vacillated between dissolving the tribe and admitting all members or retaining the separate organization and allowing individuals to choose either citizenship or tribal membership."[10] Federal treaties with the Wyandots and Ottawas in 1855 and 1862 required relinquishment of tribal government in exchange for allotment and the rights of United States citizenship.[11] By the 1860s, certain treaties with Indian nations gave the president and the federal courts the power to determine Indian competency to warrant admission to United States citizenship. Despite these coercive efforts, the commissioner of Indian affairs reported in 1891 that only 3,072 Indians had been admitted to United States citizenship before the (Dawes) General Allotment Act of 1887![12]

Washington policymakers throughout much of the nineteenth century adhered to the belief that the Indians' continued insistence on and maintenance of tribal organization was proof positive against extending United States citizenship to American Indians. Despite attempts at extending citizenship, many leading legal scholars and jurists in the United States saw Indians as members of nations apart and not capable of United States citizenship. Chancellor James Kent in the New York Court of Errors insisted that individual Indians did not qualify as United States citizens because of their own tribal allegiance. In a case involving an Oneida Indian in 1823, Kent observed:

> Though born within our territorial limits, the *Indians* [Kent's emphasis] are considered as born under the jurisdiction of their tribes. They are not our subjects born within the purview of the law, because they are not born in obedience to us. They belong, by birth, to their own tribes, and these tribes are placed under our protection and dependent upon us; but we still recognize them as national communities.[13]

Six years later, the South Carolina Court of Appeals rejected the appeal by a Pamunkey Indian to allow him to vote. The Pamunkey was a veteran of the

Continental army, who had taken an oath of allegiance and received a federal pension. The judge insisted that the Indian was not a citizen, but belonged to a "race of people, who have always been considered as a separate and distinct class, never having been incorporated into the body politic."[14]

The American Indians of the Southeast faced other problems that affected the development and/or retention of United States citizenship. In 1835, Indians in North Carolina were legislated out of existence with the adoption of a state constitution that designated them as "free persons of color." Moreover, from 1826 onward, restrictive laws, the "Free Negro Code," were passed that led to Indians being denied the right to vote, legally bear arms without a license, or serve in the militia. Similar racist restrictions on Indian citizenship occurred from Virginia to Louisiana and were a feature of southern life well into the twentieth century. State agencies such as Virginia's Bureau of Vital Statistics waged a relentless campaign attempting to deny a continued Indian identity that affected Indian political and civil liberties until the civil rights revolution of the 1950s and 1960s![15]

The United States Supreme Court, in the 1830s, also put obstacles in the way of United States citizenship for Indians. Chief Justice John Marshall, in *Cherokee Nation v. Georgia* (1831), defined Indian tribes within the United States as "domestic dependent nations" occupying a "state of pupilage," with respect to the United States, resembling the relationship "of a ward to a guardian."[16] More significantly, in *Worcester v. Georgia* (1832), Marshall insisted that the relation of the Cherokees to the federal government "was that of a nation claiming and receiving the protection of one more powerful: not that of individuals abandoning their national character, and submitting as subjects to the laws of a master."[17] To Marshall, American Indian nations were not nations such as Great Britain or France, but were sovereign enough to demand loyalty from tribal members. Regardless of their dependency on the United States, they were aliens holding quasi-sovereign status. Thus, the Marshall court helped to create a "twilight zone" status for American Indians in the United States, and laid more mines in the waters. Since Indian nations remained separate no matter how dependent or limited their sovereignty, their individual members could not successfully claim to be American citizens by birthright. According to prominent legal scholar James Kettner, the Marshall court's decisions "ultimately served the purposes of those who wished to maintain control over Indians without fully incorporating them into the community of citizens.[18] Kettner added: "Because the tribes were 'domestic' and 'dependent,' white laws could be extended over them. Yet, such extension did not constitute the kind of protection that elicited allegiance and sustained citizenship as long as political and judicial authorities considered the tribes, in some sense, 'nations' whose members were aliens." [19] Kettner concluded: "The logic of combining dependency and wardship with the idea of a separate allegiance and nationality was perhaps inconsistent; but it sufficed to exclude the Native Americans from the status and the privileges of American citizenship." [20]

At times, American Indians were also barred from achieving United States citizenship through the naturalization process because that procedure was often restricted to "free white aliens." In 1856, Attorney General Caleb Cushing outlined his theory on the Indian's status:

> In fact, therefore, that Indians are born in the country does not make them citizens of the United States. The simple truth is plain, that the Indians are the *subjects* of the United States, and therefore are not, in mere right of home-birth, citizens of the United States. But they cannot become citizens by naturalization under existing general acts of Congress. Those acts apply only to *foreigners,* subjects of another allegiance. The Indians are not foreigners, and they are in our allegiance, without being *citizens* of the United States. Moreover, those acts only apply to "white" men. Indians, of course, can be made citizens of the United States only by some competent act of the General Government, either a treaty or an act of Congress. [21]

Despite Cushing's official opinion, the Congress, after the ratification of the Fourteenth Amendment, passed specific naturalization acts affecting certain American Indian nations. In 1870, the Congress allowed Winnebago male Indians considered aliens to apply for citizenship from the federal district court in Minnesota, provided they could prove that they were sufficiently intelligent and prudent in the administration of their affairs, had adopted the "civilized" life, and were self-supporting of themselves and their family. If proven worthy of United States citizenship, the Indian would be awarded a certificate that would then allow the secretary of the interior to issue a patent in fee simple title with powers of alienation as well as a share in his tribal estate. His award of United States citizenship would mean that he would cease to be a member of his tribe and his land would be subject to taxation like that of other citizens. Hence, once again, the protection of United States citizenship was tied to the assimilationist values of the dominant white society. Thus, the "statutory formula," as Felix Cohen observed in 1942, was based on the "assumed incompatibility between tribal membership and United States citizenship." [22]

A major result of attempts to make Indians citizens was factionalism. By the mid-nineteenth century, several Indian nations fractionated into "citizens" parties advocating United States citizenship and "Indian" parties opposed to such a course of action. Vine Deloria, Jr., and Clifford Lytle have correctly noted: "Today when we survey the list of federally recognized Indian tribes and find a 'Citizen's Potawatomi' or an 'Absolute Shawnee' tribe, we find the remnants of a disastrous congressional policy concerning citizenship that somehow went astray from its original intentions." [23]

In the civil rights ferment of Reconstruction in the late 1860s came the Fourteenth Amendment of the United States Constitution. Section 1 of this amendment stipulates that "all persons born or naturalized in the United States, and subject to the jurisdiction thereof, are citizens of the United States." [24] Even members of the United States Congress were unclear about the Indian's status under section 1 since Indians were not specifically excluded. When Congress began debating the merits of ending the Indian treaty system in the late 1860s, questions were raised concerning the effect of the Fourteenth Amendment on Indian treaties. As one historian has correctly observed: "Obviously, if the amendment had collectively made them [Indians] citizens, this could have an impact as a country does not sign a treaty with its citizens." [25] The Senate Committee on the Judiciary studied this problem and concluded that, indeed, the Fourteenth Amendment had not made Indians citizens. According to the committee's report, the tribes had "never been subject to the jurisdiction of the United States, in the sense in which the term *jurisdiction* is employed in the fourteenth amendment to the Constitution." The tribes were domestic dependent nations, and the United States had always dealt with them "in their collective capacity as a state." The United States had jurisdiction over individual Indians, but only when "such members were separated from the tribe to which they belong." [26] Thus, once again, the criteria of detribalization was attached to the Indians' road to United States citizenship. Later, in *McKay* v. *Campbell* (1871), a federal district court in Oregon declared that the Fourteenth Amendment had not made Indians citizens. According to the decision, Indian tribes were "distinct and independent communities, retaining the right of self-government," and therefore their members were sufficiently outside the jurisdiction required by the United States to make them natural-born citizens under the Fourteenth Amendment. [27]

The (Dawes) General Allotment Act of 1887 was the first congressional statute providing for citizenship for American Indians. Section 6 of the act of February 8, 1887, awarded citizenship to American Indians accepting allotments and adopting the "civilized life."

> That upon the completion of said allotments and the patenting of the lands to said allottees, each and every member of the respective bands or tribes of Indians to whom allotments have been made shall have the benefit of and be subject to the laws, both civil and criminal, of the State

or Territory in which they may reside; and no Territory shall pass or en-
force any law denying any such Indian within its jurisdiction the equal
protection of the law. And every Indian born within the territorial limits
of the United States to whom allotments shall have been made under
the provisions of this act, or under any law or treaty, and every Indian
born within the territorial limits of the United States who has voluntarily taken up, within said limits, his residence separate and apart from
any tribe of Indians therein, and has adopted the habits of civilized life,
is hereby declared to be a citizen of the United States, and is entitled to
all the rights, privileges, and immunities of such citizens, whether said
Indian has been or not, by birth or otherwise, a member of any tribe of
Indians within the territorial limits of the United States without in any
manner impairing or otherwise affecting the right of any such Indian to
tribal or other property.[28]

The Dawes Act did not give citizenship outright to American Indians. It merely
gave the president of the United States discretionary power to allot reservation
lands in severalty and thereby extend United States citizenship. The act excluded many members of tribes occupying Indian territory as well as the New
York reservations of Senecas and extended exclusion "to that strip of territory
in State of Nebraska adjoining the Sioux Nation on the south added by executive order." [29] Although during the debate over the Dawes Act, there was much
congressional dissent about extending United States citizenship to American
Indians, an amendment to strike out this provision was rejected largely because Congress saw Indian citizenship as both humanitarian and the basis for
sound economic policies that might even eliminate expensive subsidies and
annuity programs.[30]

    This act was the culmination of lobbying by eastern reform groups, such as
the Indian Rights Association, the Women's National Indian Association, and
the Lake Mohonk Conference of Friends of the Indian. To the reform mind
of the late nineteenth century, American Indians had to be transformed for
their own good. American Indians could not endure much longer as separate
enclaves in the dominant white world and must learn to cope with the larger
society. Reformers believed in bringing "civilization" to the Indians in order to
absorb them into American society through a four-pronged formula of forced
assimilation. This "Americanization" process included the proselytizing activities of Christian missionaries on reservations in order to stamp out "pagan-
ism"; the exposure of the Indian to the white Americans' way through compul-
sory education and boarding schools; the breakup of tribal lands and allotment
to individual Indians to instill personal initiative, allegedly required by the free

enterprise system; and finally, in return for accepting land-in-severalty, the reward of United States citizenship.[31] To Henry S. Pancoast, one of the founders
of the Indian Rights Association, American Indians had to be educated and
prepared for United States citizenship. Writing in 1884, Pancoast added:

> Nothing [besides United States citizenship] will so effectively do away
> with contempt for the Indian and prejudice against him, as placing him
> on a political equality. *Nothing will so tend to assimilate the Indian and
> break up his narrow tribal allegiance,* as making him feel that he has a
> distinct right and voice in the white man's nation [emphasis mine].[32]

To the bill's author, Henry L. Dawes of Massachusetts, United States citizenship
was an enticement for the Indian to turn his back upon the "savage" life.[33] Thus,
the Dawes Act extended United States citizenship to American Indians at the
expense of sacrificing the Indians' wishes to retain his separate tribal identity.

Another important aim of the Dawes Act was to overturn the United States
Supreme Court's decision in *Elk* v. *Wilkins* (1884), one that had been viewed as
an outrage by eastern reformers. John Elk, an Indian who voluntarily severed
his connection with his tribe, had attempted to register and vote in a municipal
election in Omaha, Nebraska. Charles Wilkins, the registrar in the city, refused
to register him since he was an Indian and therefore not a citizen of the United
States. Elk, with financial and legal support from eastern reformers, appealed
to the United States Supreme Court, insisting that Wilkins' action violated his
rights under section 1 of the Fourteenth Amendment. Wilkins defended his
action by insisting that Elk was not a naturalized citizen, was untaxed, and
was not even recognized as a citizen either by the United States or by the state,
within the meaning of the Fourteenth Amendment of the United States Constitution. Justice Horace Gray of the United States Supreme Court wrote the
opinion, agreeing with Wilkins's contention:

> Indians born within the territorial limits of the United States, mem-
> bers of, and owing immediate allegiance to, one of the Indian tribes (an
> alien, though dependent, power), although in a geographical sense born
> in the United States, are no more "born in the United States and subject
> to the jurisdiction thereof," within the meaning of the first section of
> the Fourteenth Amendment, than the children of subjects of any foreign
> government, or the children born within the United States, of ambassa-
> dors, or other public ministers of foreign nations.[34]

Thus, Gray declared Indian tribes to be "alien nations" since an Indian owed
immediate allegiance to his tribe and not to the people of the United States.
To Gray, an Indian could not become a United States citizen unless the federal

government consents to it by treaty or by naturalization.[35] Since federal–Indian treaty making had ended in 1871, the Indian had only the route of naturalization open to him if he desired to become a United States citizen. In the twilight zone of Indian existence, the Elk decision literally made the Indian a legal alien in his native land! Although the majority supported Justice Gray's logic, Justice Harlan provided an eloquent dissent exposing the dilemma of Indians who sought United States citizenship:

> Born, therefore, in the territory under the dominion, and within the jurisdictional limits of the United States, plaintiff has acquired, as was his undoubted right, a residence in one of the States, with her consent, and is subject to taxation and to all other burdens imposed by her upon residents of every race. If he did not acquire national citizenship on abandoning his tribe and becoming, by residence in one of the States, subject to the complete jurisdiction of the United States, then the Fourteenth Amendment has wholly failed to accomplish, in respect of the Indian race, what, we think, was intended by it; and there is still in this country a despised and rejected class of persons, with no nationality whatever; who, born in our territory, owing no allegiance to any foreign power, and subject, as residents of the United States, to all the burdens of government, are yet not members of any political community nor entitled to any of the rights, privileges, or immunities of citizens of the United States.[36]

The Dawes Act, which was partly a response to Elk v. Wilkins, was soon followed by the congressional passage of the Indian Territory Naturalization Act of 1890. According to this most important piece of federal legislation, any member of an Indian tribe in Indian Territory could become a United States citizen by formally applying for such status in federal courts. Quite significantly, the act maintained that the Indian did not lose his tribal citizenship or the right to share in tribal assets if and when he accepted United States citizenship.[37] Thus, this statute is the basis of much of Oklahoma Indians' concept of citizenship, namely, that they hold dual citizenship or could do so by an appearance in a federal court.[38]

In 1906, Congressman Charles H. Burke of South Dakota introduced an amendment to the Dawes Act, delaying the granting of United States citizenship to Indian allottees until the end of the twenty-five-year trust period in order to safeguard the Indians' personal welfare; however, the act, which passed in May of that year, did not affect those Indians who had received their allotments prior to that date and who were already considered citizens.[39] Thus, although the Burke Act was intended to clarify the Dawes Act, it instead compounded an already complicated situation. It, in effect, put the Indians into two categories: (1) those who received land allotments prior to 1906, who were citizens and subject to no more federal authority than white citizens except in the matter of their land; (2) and those who received allotments after that date, who were subject to federal authority and were wards, not citizens, until they acquired land patents in fee at the expiration of the trust period.[40]

In 1911, the Society of American Indians, the first national Indian organization, was formed by some of the most prominent and highly educated American Indians in the United States, including Charles Eastman, Arthur C. Parker, Carlos Montezuma, and Thomas Sloan. Although divided over leadership and the organization's relationship to the Bureau of Indian Affairs, the Society was the major advocate of the extension of United States citizenship to American Indians. Until the organization's demise in the 1920s, the Society promoted this goal. In October 1919, the Society's annual meeting in Minneapolis had as its slogan, "American Citizenship for the Indians."[41] After rebuking an earlier speaker for only advocating the extension of United States citizenship to certain Indians, such as World War I veterans who had shown themselves "capable or equal to certain requirements," Thomas Sloan, the noted Omaha Indian attorney, insisted:

> The Indian is a native of this country and it is a universal rule of civilization that a person shall be a citizen of the country of which he is native. The Indian is a subject of the United States Government, a native, and of right is or ought to be a citizen.... The backward subject Indian needs citizenship more than the advanced Indian.[42]

Thus, by the era of World War I, many educated American Indians saw the need for all Indians to come under the constitutional umbrella, to guarantee Indian civil liberties in America.

On November 6, 1919, Congress passed an act allowing Indians who served in the army or navy during World War I and received an honorable discharge to become United States citizens. In order to receive citizenship, Indians had to apply to "courts of competent jurisdiction." Although approximately nine thousand Indians participated in the American Expeditionary Forces during World War I, few sought this route to United States citizenship.[43] Despite the legal protections associated with acquiring citizenship, few Indians refused to turn their back on their heritage or to go through the demeaning process of being declared "competent." One hundred years after the Cherokee Treaty of 1817, many Indians, although not all, associated acquisition of United States citizenship with their own detribalization. Having survived the minefields for a century, the Indians, already suspicious, saw white officials continually tying

United States citizenship to the removal of trust restrictions on Indian lands. As Vine Deloria, Jr., and Clifford Lytle have perceptively observed: "This requirement actually meant that citizenship, which is supposed to be a personal right of the individual, was really a function of the status of whatever real estate the Indian might possess."[44] Thus, to certain American Indians such as the Iroquois traditionalists in New York, United States citizenship was always, then and now, viewed as the first step toward taxation and the loss of the tribal estate.[45]

The culmination of congressional efforts to extend United States citizenship to American Indians occurred on June 2, 1924, when President Calvin Coolidge signed the Indian Citizenship Act: "That all non-citizen Indians born within the territorial limits of the United States be, and they are hereby, declared to be citizens of the United States."[46] The act added an important disclaimer: "That the granting of such citizenship shall not in any manner impair or otherwise affect the right of any Indian to tribal or other property."[47] Despite decades of lobbying, this act was the creation of the lingering Progressive reform spirit of the 1920s. Senate Progressives, seeking to protect Indians from the rapacious and unscrupulous politicians of the Harding era, pushed for regulations to control the scandal-riddled Interior Department, an agency beset by lingering memories of Teapot Dome and the Bursum Pueblo Land Bill. Historian Gary Stein has observed that the Progressives hoped that granting

> automatic citizenship to all Indians would prevent anyone in the Interior Department or the Bureau of Indian Affairs from profiting as a result of unjust citizenship regulations, would hopefully reduce bureaucratic inefficiency, and might even cause some embarrassment to the administration should the House refuse to accept the Senate amendments.[48]

Major western Progressives Robert M. LaFollette, Burton K. Wheeler, Lynn Frazier, Charles McNary, Henry Ashurst, C. C. Dill, and Robert Owen, a Cherokee Indian, all of whom had attended the Progressive conference of 1922, were all on the Senate Committee on Indian Affairs in 1924. They "forged an act to strike a blow at big bureaucracy in the way earlier Progressive legislation had struck at big business."[49] Thus, the act of 1924 was in the spirit of the gospel of efficiency and reform advocated by the Progressives since the period prior to World War I.

One irony was that New York Congressman Homer P. Snyder introduced the bill, despite the opposition to it by most New York tribes.[50] The Iroquois in New York formally protested the passage of the Indian Citizenship Act and repeatedly challenged its application over the next half-century. According to the late Tuscarora chief Clinton Rickard:

The Citizenship Act did pass in 1924 despite our strong opposition. By its provisions all Indians were automatically made United States citizens whether they wanted to be so or not. This was a violation of our sovereignty. Our citizenship was in our own nations. We had a great attachment to our style of government. We wished to remain treaty Indians and reserve our ancient rights. There was no great rush among my people to go out and vote in white man's elections. Anyone who did so was denied the privilege of becoming a chief or a clan mother in our nation.[51]

For certain Indian nations, the Indian Citizenship Act proved to be a major thorn in their side and was openly challenged in the federal courts. A crisis of monumental proportions was to occur after the passage of the United States' Selective Service Act of 1940, an act that was challenged by Iroquois in New York and Seminoles in Florida, as well as by other Indians. Despite Indian willingness to participate actively in the war effort, the Iroquois in New York were uniformly against the application of the act to them. For the first time since the Civil War, the federal government conscripted Indians against their will into the armed services. These Iroquois, following their own views of sovereignty, insisted that the Selective Service Act and the earlier Indian Citizenship Act did not apply to them since they had never accepted the 1924 law and considered themselves foreign nationals, not United States citizens. Both laws, they maintained, had been promulgated unilaterally by Congress and without their consent; thus, the Iroquois rejected the doctrine of plenary power or federal supremacy over Indians and Indian affairs, insisting they were Six Nations citizens, not United States citizens. Even though many willingly enlisted to help the war effort, a significant number of Indians, clinging to traditional beliefs about sovereignty, were arrested and some were prosecuted as draft evaders.[52]

Subsequently, to test their status, the Iroquois brought a case, *Ex Parte Green* (1941), to federal court. The United States Court of Appeals for the Second Circuit rejected Iroquois contentions and upheld the application of the Selective Service Act to these Indians.[53] In two later draft cases, *United States v. Claus* (1944) and *Albany v. United States* (1945), involving Mohawk Indians from the Six Nations and Caughnawaga reserves, the federal courts went even further, holding that the Selective Service Act was applicable to Indian noncitizen aliens from Canada residing in the United States. The courts rejected arguments by the Mohawks that, since Canada did not conscript Indians during World War II, the United States had no right to draft Canadian Indians. The courts dismissed the Mohawks' contention that the Jay Treaty, granting the right of free passage back and forth across the international boundary, exempted them from being drafted into military service in the United States.[54]

In spite of the Iroquois failure to gain recognition for their views on conscription and United States citizenship, these legal appeals reinforced the separate Indian belief about their sovereignty and nationhood at a time when the dominant white society was beginning to talk about absorbing the Indian into the mainstream. In response to the continued jailing of young Indians under the act, Iroquois leaders urged their tribesmen to enlist before being faced with the issue of conscription. In addition, in order to counter the unfavorable effects of media coverage of Iroquois draft resistance, which was largely misunderstood by the American public at large, a group of six well-known Iroquois, without formal approval of most of the Six Nations, "declared war" against the Axis on the Capitol steps in Washington, D.C., on June 11, 1942.[55]

World War II had a dramatic impact on the extension of civil rights in the United States. It must be pointed out that a higher percentage of Indians fought in World War II than any other ethnic or minority group. Indian servicemen were awarded a total of sixty-one air medals, fifty-one silver stars, forty-seven bronze stars, and two congressional medals of honor. Navajo "Code Talkers" delivered strategic messages in the Pacific in their native language and helped to ensure success in the American war effort against Japan.[56] Yet Indian veterans returned after World War II to the most extreme poverty in the United States, to severe racial discrimination, and to limited political rights. In New Mexico and Arizona, two states that contained one-quarter of the total Indian population, Indians were denied the right to vote. For more than a decade after the passage of the Social Security Act of 1935, these two states discriminated against American Indians by refusing to allow Indians to receive benefits for their aged, their blind, and their dependent children.[57]

The Indian Citizenship Act of 1924 had "naturalized" approximately 125,000 American Indians, while approximately two-thirds of the Native American population had previously acquired United States citizenship.[58] Despite the extension of United States citizenship, the states still held the power to establish qualifications for voting, which affected Indian suffrage. State constitutions, especially in the West in areas with large Indian populations, prevented Indians from voting. The state constitutions of New Mexico, Idaho, and Washington defined "Indians not taxed" as meaning that Indians were not citizens of their states.[59] The North Dakota Constitution went so far as to require an American Indian to end his/her connection to his/her tribe before the granting of suffrage. It extended suffrage only "to civilized persons of Indian descent who shall have severed their tribal relations two years next preceding such election." [60] Minnesota's Constitution required full-blooded Indians to be adjudged by a court to be competent before being awarded the rights of citizenship. The constitutions of Colorado, North Dakota, and Arizona also denied the franchise to any person under guardianship, which restricted Indian rights of citizenship.[61]

In 1928, two Pima Indians in Arizona had attempted to register and vote in the United States presidential election of that year. Their request for a ballot was denied since the Arizona Constitution stated: "No person under guardianship, *non compos mentis*, or insane shall be qualified to vote at any election." The Indians then brought suit, arguing that they were both residents of their reservation and the state of Arizona and that the Arizona Enabling Act prevented abridging suffrage on account of race, color, or previous condition of servitude. Despite these arguments, the Arizona Supreme Court, in *Porter* v. *Hall*, concluded that Indians in the state of Arizona were within the meaning of the state's constitutional provision—"persons under guardianship"—and, thus, were not entitled to vote.[62] For twenty years, this court decision remained unchallenged.

In one of the most important cases in American Indian legal history, the Arizona Supreme Court overturned the *Porter* v. *Hall* decision in 1948. Frank Harrison and Harry Austin—one a veteran of World War II and both members of the Mohave-Apache Indian tribe residing on the Fort McDowell Indian Reservation—sought to register to vote in Scottsdale, Maricopa County, Arizona. Roger G. Laveen, the county recorder, refused to permit the Indians to register. What followed was a major test case brought on behalf of Indian voting rights, largely orchestrated by legal scholar Felix S. Cohen, the National Congress of American Indians, and the American Civil Liberties Union. The plaintiffs and their attorneys argued that the Indians attempting to register possessed all of the qualifications for suffrage set forth in the constitution and laws of the state of Arizona, and insisted that their rights as citizens, as guaranteed under the Arizona and United States constitutions, had been violated. The Arizona Supreme Court specifically overturned *Porter* v. *Hall* and held for the plaintiffs. The court interpreted the phrase "person under guardianship" in the state constitution as having no application to Indians "or to the Federal status of Indians in Arizona as a class." It specifically cited Felix S. Cohen's writing as well as *The Report of the President's Committee on Civil Rights* (1947), which had branded the decision in *Porter* v. *Hall* as discriminatory and had urged that it be overturned.[63]

Harrison v. *Laveen* was a landmark decision; however, while individual American Indians in the postwar era were making strides in achieving protection of their civil rights, American Indian nations were facing new threats to their tribal existence. The postwar Indian policy of termination disastrously affected the Native American world. The termination legislation of the Truman and Eisenhower administrations ended federally recognized status for 109 Indian groups, totaling 13,263 individuals owning 1,365,801 acres of land; removed restrictions on Indian trust lands to allow for easier leasing and sale; shifted Indian health responsibilities from the BIA to the Department of Health, Education and Welfare; and established relocation programs to encourage Indian out-migrations from reservations to urban areas. Even the creation of the Indian Claims Commission in 1946 became tied in with congressional efforts at "getting the United States out of the Indian business." [64]

Most importantly, in the twenty years following World War II, American Indians lost significant acreage in federal power development, flood control, navigation projects, and water programs largely sponsored by the Bureau of Reclamation and/or the Army Corps of Engineers. The Pick–Sloan Plan led to the construction of six massive dams in the Missouri River Valley, including the building of two of the largest earthen dams in the world. The six dams destroyed 550 square miles of Indian land and displaced nine hundred Indian families. The Standing Rock and Cheyenne River reservations lost 160,000 acres; while the construction of the Garrison Dam on the Fort Berthold reservation inundated 152,000 acres of tribal lands. Much of the reservation timber land and wild game on five Sioux reservations was also destroyed in the process, and the gathering of traditional plants for medicinal and ceremonial purposes was disrupted and seriously affected by these changes. Tribal relocation led to the uprooting of entire communities, including religious shrines and even the graves of ancestors. [65]

Other Indian nations faced similar, although somewhat less, land loss. The Senecas fought unsuccessfully from 1957 to 1966 to save their last remaining Indian lands in Pennsylvania. The Kinzua Dam flooded over nine thousand acres of their tribal lands, including the entire Cornplanter Tract. In the same period, the Tuscaroras lost one-eighth of their reservation near Niagara Falls to Robert Moses's grandiose plans for the New York Power Authority's Niagara Power Project. [66] Federal and state policymakers of the late 1940s and 1950s unilaterally broke treaties and took Indian lands for massive public works projects. In the Kinzua Dam instance, the federal courts extended the Doctrine of Plenary Power to interpret that a one-million-dollar rider to a federal appropriations bill showed sufficient congressional intent to justify the breaking of the Canadaigua (Pickering) Treaty of 1794 with the Senecas, one of the oldest federal–Indian treaties. [67]

Despite this reversion to the "Dark Ages" and the erosion of the Indian landbase in the immediate postwar era, American Indians and Indian nationhood have survived. Today, American Indians are entitled to all of the rights and privileges of other American citizens, even when the Indians such as the Iroquois view themselves as citizens of their own Indian nations and not of

the United States. Over the past several decades, court decisions have repeatedly upheld the Indians' right to vote, serve on juries, hold state public offices,
serve on school boards, be counted in legislative apportionment, receive state-
supported welfare benefits, and attend state-supported public schools, as well
as to enjoy many other rights.[68] The federal Civil Rights Act of 1968 contained
six titles focusing on Indian matters.[69] The federal Indian Self-Determination
and Education Act of 1975 declared that tribal self-government and tribal self-
determination, not Indian assimilation, was national Indian policy.[70]

While the passage of the American Indian Religious Freedom Act of 1978
has not been effective in guaranteeing First Amendment freedoms with respect
to peyote use by members of the Native American Church or in protecting
sacred sites from California loggers, other legislative actions have been more
favorable. For example, the Indian Child Welfare Act, passed in 1978, also extended and broadened civil rights for American Indians.[71] Although the battle
is still being waged, as will be shown in Chapter 9, American Indians today,
much more than in the past, experience less pressure to renounce their cultural,
religious, and political heritage and their separate allegiance and ties to their
Indian nations in order to acquire equal protection under the Constitution
of the United States. This partial "victory" was not the result of government
"paternalism" but was due more to Native American courage and persistence
in the face of threats to their survival.

7 PLAYING INDIAN

Misconceptions are frequently the result of imagery. Sports caricatures and film portrayals of the "Indian," as will be demonstrated in this chapter, have little or nothing to do with the realities of Native American life. False images of the "Indian," whether demeaning or not, are usually simplistic and generally classify the great diversity of Native America into a single entity, obscuring the textures as well as the complexities of the past or present, whether because of convenience, economics, or other reasons. Although professional sports and Hollywood did not invent the imagery of the "Indian," both industries furthered misconceptions and have profited financially by propagating stereotypes.

Explored in this chapter are the lives of two remarkable persons—Louis Francis Sockalexis and Jay Silverheels—who were associated with and deeply affected by stereotyping. Both men possessed extraordinary talents, but because of the prejudices of their times and the institutional racism of their professions, as well as a general lack of understanding about Native Americans and their cultures, they were denigrated to playing the white man's Indian. Sockalexis, a Penobscot, played major league baseball—one of the first Native Americans to do so—in Cleveland from 1897 to 1899; during World War I, his former team was renamed the Cleveland Indians, supposedly to "honor" his memory. Jay Silverheels, a Mohawk, was the foremost Native American actor in Hollywood working between 1940 and 1970. His indelible image-stereotype of the "Indian" is well ingrained in the American psyche for those over the age of forty-five as a result of Silverheels' costarring role of "Tonto," the Lone Ranger's trusted Indian sidekick, on television and in two full-length motion pictures.

Native Americans increasingly have shown their displeasure with the "Indian" image used by amateur and professional sports as well as by Hollywood. Despite these protests, the Atlanta Braves continued to use their fans' "war chants" and "tomahawk chops" to fuel their pennant drives and get them into the World Series in 1991 and 1992. In the same period, the Washington Redskins, a perennial professional football powerhouse, faced similar pressures to change its name; their owner, Jack Kent Cooke, refused to do so, insisting, however strangely, that his team's name was not demeaning to Indians. On the college athletic scene, Dartmouth, Siena, and Stanford, among others, have all changed their school nicknames and/or mascots to ones deemed to be less offensive. Despite the age of political correctness on campuses throughout the United States, Florida State University, nicknamed the "Seminoles," still has a student armed with a makeshift lance in "Indian garb and war paint," riding a horse on the sidelines urging his football team downfield to victory; the University of Illinois is resisting efforts to change its symbol and mascot, the "Fighting Illini"; and Miami University of Ohio still proudly refers to itself as the "Redskins."

After describing National Congress of American Indians efforts to counter these images, Tim Giago, the editor-in-chief of the *Lakota Times,* wrote during "Superbowl Week" in 1992: "Our complaint: very simply, Indians are people, not mascots." In the same article, William Means of the International Indian Treaty Council insisted: "If we can't get white America to understand the basic issue of human respect, how can we get them to understand more substantive issues like sovereignty, treaty rights and water rights?" (Tim Giago, "I Hope the Redskins Lose," *Newsweek* 119, Jan. 27, 1992, 8).

Hollywood has provided more employment opportunities for Native American actors and actresses in recent times and has finally allowed them to emerge from behind the shadows. From Chief Dan George's achievement in *Little Big Man* in 1970, Native American performers such as Graham Greene (*Dances with Wolves*), Will Sampson (*One Flew Over the Cuckoo's Nest*), and Sheila Tousey (*Thunderheart*) have received starring or costarring roles as well as critical acclaim in major Hollywood productions. Despite these individual successes, Hollywood's most profitable films involving Native Americans are still either remakes of James Fenimore Cooper (*Last of the Mohicans*) or stories of whites who become "Indian" (*Dances with Wolves*), much like Hawkeye in Cooper's *Leatherstocking Tales.* Thus, Hollywood, as the noted Native American writer Michael Dorris has correctly observed, still places "Indians in aspic," by reworking older, simplistic, familiar, and financially successful themes (Michael Dorris, "Indians in Aspic," *New York Times,* Feb. 24, 1991, sec. 1, 28: 3). Moreover, the previous images of the "Indian"—attacking western stagecoaches or forts; rarely speaking, or talking in broken phrases and stereotyped ways; as childlike victims of frontier and Great Father whims; as "half-breeds" or white captives caught between two cultures; and as the faithful companion to the white man in his search for truth, justice, and the American way—are repeated on cable television reruns of Hollywood's movie classics.

Most Americans who follow baseball are quite familiar with the Cleveland Indians, the often hapless baseball team that until 1993 played the "summer game" in the largest of all baseball palaces, decrepit Municipal Stadium (Cleveland Stadium) which borders Lake Erie. The franchise has a long and sad history. Since the dream year of 1954, when they won 111 games and the American League pennant with one of the finest pitching staffs ever assembled, the Cleveland Indians' fortunes have gone downhill. In the past quarter of a century, they have rarely finished as high as third place. They have faced numerous last-place finishes and, as a result, have borne the brunt of frequent jibes. In 1989, they were the centerpiece of a Hollywood satire entitled *Major Leagues,* a successful commercial film. On August 24, 1992, Hurricane Andrew seriously damaged the Cleveland Indians' brand-new spring training complex at Homestead, Florida, after they had recently moved from Arizona. In spring training of 1993, at a time when it appeared that there was a strong chance for a team turnaround, two of the team's relief pitchers, Steve Olin and Tim Crews, were killed in a tragic boating accident. In 1994, when the Cleveland Indians were finally challenging for the pennant, major league baseball cancelled its season! To many of its faithful following, who dream of the likes of another Lou Boudreau, Larry Doby, Bob Feller, Napoleon Lajoie, and Early Wynn, the franchise is viewed as "jinxed."

Baseball fans are quite familiar with the team's nickname as well as its famous insignia. The team is affectionately referred to by sportswriter as "the tribe." Chief Wahoo, a dark red caricature of an "Indian" with a wide-mouth set of teeth, is the symbol that appears on every team member's hat. In the cavernous surroundings of Municipal Stadium, which was often underpopulated because of the poor showing of "the tribe," one could frequently hear the drums of a "tom-tom" played by long-suffering fans who still rooted and hoped to see their team win another American League pennant, or at least reach higher than third place!

This Indian "imagery" was there almost from the earliest days of baseball in Cleveland. In 1897, the city's baseball franchise, then known as the Cleveland Spiders and playing in the National League, hired a straping six-foot, left-handed hitting, right-handed throwing outfielder named Louis Francis Sockalexis. Born on the reservation at Indian Island, Old Town, Maine in October 1871, Sockalexis was a Penobscot Indian. He came from a family of athletes. His cousin Andrew ran the marathon at the Olympic Games in Stockholm in

1912. Francis was to become one of the first Native Americans to play major league baseball. Many other Indians were to follow later in his footsteps, including Hall of Fame pitcher Charles A. "Chief" Bender (Chippewa); John T. "Chief" Meyers (Cahuilla), the "iron man" catcher of Christy Matthewson; the legendary Jim Thorpe (Sac and Fox and Potawatomi), infielder and outfielder; and the noted Yankee pitching star Allie Reynolds (Creek).

In ninety-four major league games from 1897 through 1899, Sockalexis had a lifetime batting average of .313.[1] To John McGraw, the extraordinary manager of the New York Giants, he was the greatest natural athlete he had ever seen in baseball.[2] Unfortunately, because of the racism of the era, the lack of understanding of Native Americans and their cultures and Sockalexis's own emotional and psychological problems, his baseball career, and his life as a whole, were marked by tragedy.

Sockalexis's early life portended great accomplishments to come. As a youth in Maine, he excelled in track, skating, and baseball. Unlike most Indians of the time, he was not sent off to an all-Indian boarding school such as Carlisle Institute. Instead, he attended Catholic schools and eventually was admitted to college, matriculating at both Notre Dame and Holy Cross. At Worcester, Massachusetts, he immediately became the star pitcher and outfielder of Holy Cross's college baseball team, pitching three no-hitters and hitting an incredible .436 in 1895 and .444 in 1896.[3] Sockalexis has been described as a man of "pride and intelligence" and a man of "trusting nature."[4] Despite these admirable qualities, he was totally unprepared for what he was to experience on his arrival in the major leagues in 1897.

Sockalexis's college baseball exploits soon came to the attention of Patsy Tebeau, the hard-boiled manager of the Cleveland Spiders. Tebeau eventually signed the budding star to a contract with the team. Sockalexis's first year in Cleveland, in 1897, showed the promise of McGraw's evaluation. In his first major league appearance, he hit home runs in his first two at-bats. Before injuring himself that year and missing two months of the season, the Penobscot was hitting as high as .413. In 1897, he was part of one of the best hitting outfield trios of all time, which included Jesse Burkett, who hit .383, and Ollie Pickering, who hit .352. Few pitchers were able to throw their fastballs past Sockalexis. Despite his prolonged appearance on the disabled list, he still stole sixteen bases and hit a respectable .338 that season.[5]

According to historian David Q. Voight, baseball reflected the social Darwinism of the age in America. Those "players of distinct ethnic origins were faced with the cruelest of jibes." Native Americans in baseball did not face the same restrictions as African Americans did. They did not have to "pass" as Cubans or break the "color line." They did not need a Jack Roosevelt Robinson

Louis Francis Sockalexis (Penobscot) in his major league baseball uniform (courtesy Cleveland Indians Baseball Club).

to blaze the trail of fairness for them. Nevertheless, Native Americans in baseball, as reflected in Sockalexis's personal travails, were hardly accepted with open arms, faced frequent racial slurs, and suffered cruel indignities. Voight has even insisted: "Perhaps no group suffered taunts so mercilessly as did native American Indians."[6]

As a result of Sockalexis's quick success, the Cleveland Spider franchise as well as sportswriters across the nation began to cultivate his image, exploiting his Indian background to sell tickets as well as newspapers. He became the most talked about person in Cleveland. Soon the Cleveland Spiders were being referred to as the "Indian's team." Since sports nicknames were a necessary requirement of this and later years, his teammates dubbed him the "chief," a designation that continued to be applied to Native American players from Charles Bender's era through that of Allie Reynolds in the 1950s. One sportswriter wrote a poem in his honor, titling it "Sockalexis, Chief of Sockem." Tabloids proclaimed him a direct descendant of Sitting Bull, even though he had never been west of Chicago in his life. Another far-fetched story had Sockalexis's father paddling his canoe from Maine to Washington to ask the Great White Father to make Louis chief of the tribe. Sports cartoonists pictured him in newspapers with a large war club in hand and a headdress with feathers.[7]

Stirred up by this disgraceful journalism, baseball fans began to shower the Penobscot with racial indignities. Every time Sockalexis came to bat, fans did ear-splitting war whoops. They parodied Indian dances, "rain" and "war" dances allegedly performed in his "honor." Although there were some objections from some sportswriters, the taunts continued and even intensified. Whenever the Cleveland Spiders went on the road to play in an opponent's ballpark, he was abused to an even worse degree. Fans actually started calling for his "scalp." He became the focus of opposing fans' venom, not only because of his Native American ancestry, but also because the Cleveland Spiders, a rowdy team of hard-nosed players, were strongly disliked. He was constantly insulted and even faced personal threats and racial epithets. Opponents on the diamond, seeing the advantage of "ragging," taunted him throughout his brief career.[8] Citing the case of "Chief" Sockalexis, the noted sports historian Benjamin Rader has observed: "The psychological warfare of the players was developed into a brutal art." Rader added: "Verbal and physical harassment drove more than one player out of the league." [9]

The decline of Sockalexis's career is part of the folklore of America's pastime. In July of 1897, he is alleged to have badly injured his leg while jumping out of the second floor window of a brothel. His skills further deteriorated with alcoholism. Newspaper writers exploited his substance dependence to sell newspapers in moralistic crusades against the evils of the demon rum. Consequently, Sockalexis's tragedy reaffirmed the stereotyped drunken Indian image in the American popular mind. His problems with alcohol steadily worsened, and ultimately his skills faded. His batting average plummeted downward and his fielding skills, already suspect—he made sixteen errors alone in sixty-six games in 1897—diminished further.

When his team finished in fifth place in 1897, Sockalexis was sent down to the minor leagues after the season, although he managed to return for brief major league appearances in both the 1898 and 1899 seasons. Despite promises of total abstinence, his alcoholism grew worse. Because of his drinking problem, he missed trains taking the Spiders to the next city; he was also arrested for being disorderly in front of a Cleveland bar. By the end of the 1899 season, Lave Cross, Cleveland's new manager, sent Sockalexis packing. After failed attempts at a comeback in the minor leagues at Lowell, Massachusetts, and at Hartford, Connecticut, Sockalexis returned to live out his remaining days in Maine. He was employed as a ferryman, logger, and baseball barnstormer giving batting and throwing exhibitions, as well as a part-time baseball coach. Much of the time, he was a drifter and unemployed because of his inability to cope with his alcoholism. Sockalexis died on Christmas eve in 1913 at Burlington, Maine, of chronic heart disease at the age of forty-two.[10] His tombstone on Indian Island reads: "In memory of Louis Sockalexis, whose athletic achievements while at Holy Cross and later with the Cleveland major league baseball team won for him national fame."[11]

In 1915, James Dunn, one of the new owners of the Cleveland baseball team, which had switched into the American League in 1901, had a major dilemma. After the 1914 season, the franchise, then known as the Cleveland Naps and in desperate need for cash, traded Napoleon Lajoie to Connie Mack's Philadelphia Athletics. No longer could Dunn's team be referred to as the "Naps," in honor of their gallant Frenchman, the future Hall of Fame star player-manager Lajoie. The trade to the much-hated Athletics, a rival team, was also one of the least popular moves in the history of baseball. In order to remedy this public-relations disaster, a newspaper contest was held in Cleveland in 1915 to suggest a new name for the team and to generate continued fan interest in the franchise. As a result of this contest, the name "Indians" was selected, the same nickname associated with the Cleveland Spiders of Sockalexis's day. As part of the lore of baseball in Cleveland, the name was suggested by a fan and chosen by the franchise to supposedly honor Sockalexis's memory, since he had died only a year and a half earlier. Long after the tragedy of Sockalexis's life faded from memory, the Cleveland Indians invented Chief Wahoo to once again merchandise the franchise to a public suffering from historical amnesia about the original Cleveland Indian.[12]

Although less tragic, Jay Silverheels's long experiences as a Hollywood Indian have much in common with Louis Francis Sockalexis's brief but noteworthy career in baseball. Both of these remarkable men played the white man's stereotypic "Indian," suffering humiliation for it.

Jay Silverheels was born Harry (Harold Jay) Smith on the Six Nations Indian Reserve near Brantford, Ontario, Canada. The date of his birth is usually cited as May 26, 1919, although it appears to be more likely May 26, 1912. A Mohawk Indian whose family is still prominent as artists on the reserve, Smith was the son of Captain A. G. E. Smith, the most decorated Canadian Indian soldier of World War I. Little is known about his mother or her family. Smith, along with nine brothers and sisters, was raised on his family's farm on the reserve. As a youth, he excelled in sports, including lacrosse, hockey, and horsemanship. He attended the Brantford Collegiate Institute until the age of seventeen, when he quit school to play professional lacrosse in Toronto.[13]

For the next decade, Smith was to become one of the leading professional athletes in Canada as well as in western New York State. By 1933, he was already a star in the professional lacrosse leagues that were popular in that day. Along with Seneca legends Arleigh Hill and Francis Kettle, Smith achieved kudos for his brilliant play in the violent world of professional lacrosse. As a result of his participation in the sport, Harry Smith soon became "Silverheels." Doc

Morris, his team's manager, bestowed the name upon him because the Mohawk lacrosse player always ran on the balls of his feet with his heels up, painted his footgear silver, and had blinding speed, easily dodging opponents' checks. To his Iroquois teammates and to lacrosse devotees, he became "Silverheels" since all anyone could see was his silver-painted footgear as he whizzed by. Thus, he acquired the stage name that he used throughout his acting career. Later, nine years before his death, he legally changed his name from Smith to Silverheels.[14]

Besides his legendary skills in lacrosse, Silverheels was also a semiprofessional hockey player; a football, track, and wrestling star; and winner of the Eastern States Middleweight Golden Gloves Boxing Championship in the United States in 1937. He was also an accomplished horseman as well, a skill which later proved beneficial in his acting career.[15]

In 1938, Silverheels was "discovered" by Joe E. Brown, the prominent comic actor, during a lacrosse match. Brown served as his mentor, promoting Silverheels's slow rise to fame by introducing him to the people and the workings of the Hollywood film industry. Silverheels became a member of the Screen Actors' Guild and, soon after, found himself working as an "extra" making $16.50 per day falling off horses in battle scenes in Hollywood westerns. For nearly ten years, he struggled to make a living as an extra in "B westerns," and in memorable motion pictures such as *Drums Along the Mohawk* (1939).[16]

In all, Silverheels performed in 32 westerns and in 221 episodes of *The Lone Ranger*. He received the biggest "breaks" in his acting career in 1947 and 1948. In 1947, he received his first major screen role as the Aztec Indian named Coatl, playing opposite Tyrone Power's Pedro de Vargas, Cesar Romero's Cortez, Lee J. Cobb's Juan Garcia, and Jean Peters' Cataña in Darryl Zanuck's Hollywood version of the encounter, entitled *Captain from Castile*. The next year, he filtered back into the shadows, playing (along with Indian actor Rodd Redwing) one of the Osceola brothers, killed by mistake by the sheriff in John Huston's classic *Key Largo*. Nevertheless, his stage presence and his handsome features had finally been noticed by the Hollywood establishment. By the latter year, he had become *the* Indian in the film industry.[17]

Because of these two roles, his extensive film credits, and his horsemanship skills, Silverheels was selected to costar as Tonto in *The Lone Ranger,* opposite actors John Hart and Clayton Moore. This highly successful ABC weekly television program, thirty minutes in length, aired for the first time on September 15, 1949. The show was a spin-off of the famous radio program created by Fran Striker and George W. Trendle in 1933. The television program continued uninterrupted until September 12, 1957. Even though no new episodes were made after 1961, the western has been widely syndicated in reruns around the world since its final episode.[18] Americans of all ages anxiously awaited

Jay Silverheels (Mohawk), right, as Tonto and Clayton Moore, left, as the Lone Ranger in the 1950s (courtesy Collection of Laurence M. Hauptman).

weekly installments of *The Lone Ranger,* which was set to the music of Rossini's "William Tell Overture." Announcer Fred Foy would open each show the same way each week:

A fiery horse with the speed of light, a cloud of dust and a hearty hi-yo Silver! The Lone Ranger! With his faithful Indian companion, Tonto, the daring and resourceful masked rider of the plains led the fight for law and order in the early West. Return with us now to those thrilling days of yesteryear, the Lone Ranger rides again![19]

Unlike his forceful and articulate counterpart, the Lone Ranger, Tonto had no mask, no silver bullets, rode a brown horse named Scout, and spoke in butchered English. Tonto's speech, in a clipped monosyllabic fashion, was the perfect foil for the Lone Ranger. Unlike Tonto, the Lone Ranger spoke easily understandable English with a mellow voice reminiscent of the 1940s and 1950s crooner Vaughan Monroe. According to film historian Donald L. Kaufmann, Tonto knew his "linguistic place." Kaufmann added: "Whatever the Lone Ranger was, Tonto was less—less fast, less a sharpshooter, less domineering."[20]

As the friendly and loyal Indian companion of "Kemo-sabe," Tonto, nevertheless, was presented as a decent man of innate wisdom who could track down "bad hombres" such as the Butch Cavendish gang with the best of them. Although in Spanish *tonto* means "numbskull" or "fool," Striker and later television scriptwriters did not intend the name to be interpreted in Spanish.[21] No matter, Tonto was still an Indian in the shadows. In his perceptive study of stereotyping, Raymond Stedman has observed:

What, for example, do we know of Tonto that is not a function of his relationship to the Lone Ranger? Riding beside a driven wrong-righter, did he have any aspiration but that of following? Did he ever long to see his homeland? Was there a lost love? Did he revere a father? Did he ever wish to suggest the next trail? Did he despair of his hopeless grammar?[22]

Much like the portraits of African Americans and Asian Americans in the same period, Tonto, according to Vine Deloria, Jr., "represented a silent subservient subspecies of Anglo-Saxon whose duty was to do the bidding of the all-wise white hero." Yet Deloria points out correctly:

But Tonto also had another quality about him. Although inarticulate to a fault, he occasionally called upon his primitive wisdom to get the Lone Ranger out of a tight spot. Tonto had some indefinable aboriginal knowledge that operated *deus ex machina* in certain situations. It was almost as if the Lone Ranger had some tragic flaw with respect to the mysterious in nature which Tonto could easily handle and understand.

In those crises where Tonto had to extricate the Lone Ranger by some impossibly Indian trick, a glimmer of hope was planted in the subconscious of the Indian that someday he would come into his own. Few whites realized what this was, or that it existed; but to Indians it was an affirmation of the old Indian way. In an undefined sense, Tonto was able to universalize Indianness for Indians and lay the groundwork for the eventual rejection of the white man and his strange ways.[23]

During and after Silverheels's success in *The Lone Ranger* series, he was in great demand as Hollywood's leading Indian. His major film credits included playing Geronimo in *Broken Arrow* (1950); costarring in *The Lone Ranger* (1956) and *The Lone Ranger and the Lost City of Gold* (1958); and performing in *Brave Warrior* (1952, *Saskatchewan* (1954), *True Grit* (1970), and *The Man Who Loved Cat Dancing* (1973). He also appeared in numerous television episodes, including *Cade County* and *Love American Style*, as well as in television commercials. Besides Clayton Moore and Tyrone Power, he worked with many major Hollywood actors, including Lauren Bacall, Lionel Barrymore, Humphrey Bogart, Errol Flynn, Henry Fonda, Burt Reynolds, Edward G. Robinson, James Stewart, Elizabeth Taylor, and John Wayne.[24]

Silverheels was well aware of the limitations on Indians in the Hollywood of his era and worked to open up the studio system to Native American performers. In the age of the Hollywood blacklist, any agitation or protest could lead to the undoing of actor—white, black, Indian, or Asian. Despite being criticized by many political active Indians for playing this clearly subservient role, Silverheels's character was the first major fictional Indian film hero and paved the way for other Native American actors. Until Silverheels, Indian actors, with the exception of Will Rogers (who played cowboys), had largely been relegated to the roles of foils in western epics. In 1960, Silverheels protested the way that Native Americans were portrayed in films, sending letters to President Eisenhower, Vice President Nixon, and the executives of the three television networks. He also assisted aspiring actors and, in the mid-1960s, founded the Indian Actors Guild as well as the Indian Actors Workshop in Hollywood, working later with Jonathan Winters and Buffy Sainte-Marie in this endeavor. He taught acting skills to Native Americans and promoted the use of Native people in "Indian" roles, rather than relying on white actors such as Sal Mineo, Jeff Chandler, Chuck Connors, and others. As a result of his reputation in the film industry, he became the first American Indian to have his star set in the famous Walk of Fame, along Hollywood Boulevard, at what is today Mann's Chinese Theatre.[25]

During the last years of his life, Silverheels obtained a license to work as a harness-racing driver and raced competitively around the country with his horse Tribal Dance, as well as with other horses. His racing days ended when he suffered a stroke that caused paralysis. After being treated for a heart condition, he died in the Motion Picture and Television Country House at Woodland Hills, California, on March 5, 1980, of complications from pneumonia. Silverheels was survived by Mary Di Roma, his wife of three decades, and their four children—Marilyn, Pamela, Karen, and Jay Anthony.[26]

Silverheels, much like Sockalexis earlier, was caught by the institutional racism of his time and the phenomenal success of his portrayals of "Indians." He was only offered certain parts, namely, as Indians in westerns. Yet his success in playing these roles furthered his career and ironically perpetuated the Hollywood image of the "Indian." Unlike Sockalexis, Silverheels's career was a long one and did not end in tragedy. Importantly, unlike Sockalexis, Silverheels's legacy appears to be positive and to be focused on two areas: (1) Although his roles as a Hollywood Indian are commemorated in a display case in the Woodland Indian Centre at his home on the Six Nations Reserve, many elders among his people fondly remember him as much for his lacrosse exploits; and (2) despite the restrictions of his acting career to what appear today as subservient roles, he did open the door, however so slightly, for future actors, including Chief Dan George, Graham Greene, Will Sampson, and Wes Studi.

8 THERE ARE NO INDIANS EAST OF THE MISSISSIPPI

The following chapter, coauthored by Jack Campisi and re-printed with permission of the *Proceedings* of the American Philosophical Society, focuses on one of the most damaging as well as widely held misconceptions, namely, that American Indians live only in isolated areas in the Trans-Mississippi West. I have frequently encountered this false assumption both in classroom teaching and in lecturing to community groups. Even respected non-Indian historians such as Robert V. Remini, as described in Chapter 4, have perpetuated this misconception. Prominent Native American scholars have also helped to reinforce this view. In 1984, Alfonso Ortiz, a Pueblo and a nationally acclaimed anthropologist at the University of New Mexico, in his otherwise fine coauthored collection of American Indian myths and legends, wrote unequivocably: "The Pequod, or Destroyers, once a much-dreaded Algonquian people, were originally part of the Mohegan tribe.... They are now considered completely exterminated" (Richard Erdoes and Alfonso Ortiz, eds., *American Indian Myths and Legends* [New York: Pantheon Books, 1984], p. 514). To the contemporary Mashantucket Pequot Tribe of Connecticut, fed-erally recognized in 1983 and undergoing a tribal renaissance since the 1970s, this comment, although troubling, is hardly surprising since they face similar views every day.

From 20 to 25 percent of all American Indians live east of the Mississippi, and most Indians in the East as well as in the West live in metropolitan areas such as Chicago, Denver, Los Angeles, Minneapolis, New York, Phoenix, and Seattle. Eastern Native Americans such as the Iroquois have had federal recog-nition through treaties with Washington since the 1780s and 1790; however, as the following chapter shows, many other eastern Native Americans have long sought federal recognition, the "outcome of a process that establishes a government relationship between an Indian Tribe and the United States gov-ernment" (Native American Rights Fund, *Federal Recognition Briefing Paper*, 1992 [Boulder, Colo.: NARF, 1992]).

Much of the modern impetus for federal recognition among eastern Native American communities emanated from the American Indian Chicago Conference of June 1961 and its preliminary meetings. Organized by Sol Tax, this convocation, described in this chapter, was designed to provide a forum for all Native American communities, East and West, federally and nonfederally recognized, concerning a wide variety of issues affecting Indian affairs in the United States.

Today, federal recognition can be achieved in three ways: (1) a Native American tribe may take action in court to force the United States to recognize its trust responsibilities; (2) it may be deemed a federally recognized tribe by congressional legislation; or (3) it may follow a bureaucratic and often convoluted process established by the Department of the Interior. To long-neglected Indian communities, attaining federally recognized status fosters community pride and allows eastern Native Americans to gain a more equal footing in the Native American world. In most cases, it provides them with access to federal Indian programs and allows these newly recognized Indian nations the right to sue for land in federal court as well as to seek other federal protections against the willful actions of states. In more recent times, federally recognized status often, but not in all cases, allows Indian nations to put purchased lands into trust, with the secretary of the interior's approval, giving special tax advantages to them. This strategy has been used effectively in more recent years by Indian nations intent on entrepreneurial activities such as gaming.

As of January 1994, seven criteria had to be "satisfied" in the petition for federal recognition sent to the Federal Acknowledgment Branch of the Bureau of Indian Affairs:

a. establish that they have been identified from historical times to the present on a substantially continuous basis as American Indian or aboriginal;

b. establish that a substantial portion of the group inhabits a specific area or lives in a community viewed as American Indian, distinct from other populations in the area...;

c. furnish a statement of facts which establishes that the group has maintained tribal political influence or other authority over its members as an autonomous entity throughout history until the present;

d. furnish a copy of the group's present governing document... describing in full the membership criteria and the procedures through which the group currently governs its affairs and its members;

e. furnish a list of all known current members...based on the group's own defined criteria. The membership must consist of individuals who have established, using evidence acceptable to the Secretary of the Interior, descendancy from a tribe which existed historically or from historical tribes which combined and functioned as a single autonomous entity;

f. establish that the membership of the group is composed principally of persons who are not members of any other North American Indian tribe;

g. [demonstrate] that the group or its members are not the subject of congressional legislation which has expressly terminated or forbidden the Federal Relationship. (25 CFR 83.7)

The petition route through the Department of the Interior was established in 1978. Seven eastern Native American communities have won recognition—the Grand Traverse Band of Ottawa and Chippewa; the Tunica-Biloxi Indian Tribe of Louisiana; the Narragansett Indian Tribe; the Poarch Band of Creeks; the Wampanoag Tribe of Gay Head; the Micmac Tribe of Maine; and the Mohegan Tribe of Connecticut. An eighth eastern Native American community, the Mashantucket Pequot Tribe of Connecticut, achieved federal recognition through congressional legislation.

In the East as well as in the West, many Native American communities have not yet been able to secure federal recognition because it is a time-consuming, expensive, and politically charged, as well as demeaning, process. Congressional politics and budget cutting, BIA stonewalling, and racist perceptions described in this chapter are all roadblocks on the route to federal recognition. Moreover, certain Native American leaders themselves do not want Washington to recognize more Indian communities, such as the populous but nonfederally recognized Lumbee of North Carolina, since they fear the further shrinking of the federal pie to Indian communities.

The American Indian Chicago Conference (AICC) was a major watershed in the history of contemporary Native peoples. Between June 13 and 20, 1961, 467 American Indians from ninety separate communities met at the University of Chicago, at a convocation organized by anthropologist Sol Tax, to voice their opinions about a wide variety of concerns affecting Indian affairs in the United States. This convocation drafted the *Declaration of Indian Purpose,* an elaborate policy statement, which, among other things, asked for a reversal of the federal government's termination policies; for increased Indian educational opportunities, more economic development programs, and better health-care-delivery systems; for the abolition of ten BIA area offices; for the protection of Indian water rights; and for presidential reevaluation of federal plans to build the Kinzua Dam. The Indians insisted in the *Declaration:*

"What we ask of America is not charity, not paternalism, even when benevolent. We ask only that the nature of our situation be recognized and made the basis of policy and action."[1] Although the conference has been credited with promoting the development of a new awareness of American Indian concerns, a new national Indian organization—the National Indian Youth Council (NIYC)—and a more radical turn in the formation of Indian political strategy, scholars have totally ignored the meeting's specific impact on eastern Indians.[2]

In 1968, Nancy Lurie, who assisted Tax in his efforts, reflected on the AICC and its influence: "Certainly, it had a profound influence on a number of tribes in offering a model of action and a good deal of moral support for what in 1961 were, as far as the general public is concerned, unpopular and incomprehensible goals."[3] One of these "unpopular and incomprehensible goals," which was pushed by Tax from the beginning, was his aim of bringing eastern Indian concerns to the fore. Besides a conscious effort to bring public attention to the plight of the Seneca Indians, whose lands were being inundated by the Kinzua Dam, the conference organizers focused on Indian communities east of the Mississippi whose primary concern was federal and state recognition.[4] This conscious decision, which went against much of the anthropological, policymaking, and reservation Indian thinking of the time, contributed significantly to increased efforts by the Abenaki, Gay Head Wampanoag, Haliwa, Houma, Lumbee, Mashpee Wampanoag, and Narragansett in seeking federal recognition over the past quarter-century.

In 1960, Tax, after discussions with members of the Schwartzhaupt Foundation, developed a proposal to update the Meriam Report, a comprehensive analysis of American Indian conditions and federal Indian policies undertaken by scholars for the Institute of Government Research and published in 1928. According to Carl Tjerandsen, the executive secretary of the foundation, Tax insisted that, unlike the Meriam Report, the Indians should have the "central role" in producing a document assessing the current scene. Having been initially awarded ten thousand dollars by the Schwartzhaupt Foundation, Tax then approached the leaders of the National Congress of American Indians (NCAI) for support of his idea.[5] At a time of significant Indian land loss, as a result of federal hydroelectric and/or flood control projects and major efforts to terminate federal treaty and trust responsibilities to Indian nations, Tax's proposal received a favorable response from the NCAI leadership. It also endorsed Tax's only stipulation, namely, that any and all Indians have the opportunity to participate in all deliberations.[6]

Tax had long prepared for the inclusion of eastern Indian groups at the AICC. While spending much of his time in the late 1950s as an "action anthropologist" among the Fox in Iowa, he had worked with Robert K. Thomas,

Samuel Stanley, Bruce MacLachlan, and Myron Rosenberg in mapping North American Indian populations. From 1956 to 1961, he revised this map four times and included on it, unlike BIA maps of the period, communities that claimed Indian heritage but which, at that time, were not recognized by federal or state agencies. These Indians included the Haliwa, Houma, Lumbee, Mashpee Wampanoag, Mohegan, Narragansett, Pequot, and Tunica-Biloxi. Later, this revealing map, although criticized by federally recognized Indians and some anthropologists, was distributed at the AICC meetings and subsequently reprinted in one of Lurie's publications.[7]

Tax also was in direct correspondence with Indian-rights advocates, as well as with anthropologists and sociologists, in order to identify and ascertain the needs of these eastern groups. From the beginning, his intention was to get as wide a representation of American Indian people as possible. After being sent three separate reprints from sociologist Brewton Berry about these southern communities, Tax noted on top of one of Berry's articles that it "may prove useful documentation in [the] Eastern Area."[8] Significantly, Tax, unlike Berry and other academics, never referred to these populations as "racial hybrids," "mestizos," "almost white," "triracial isolates," or "marginal groups." Indeed, he and Lurie would frequently refer to these groups as "self-identified Indians."[9] Lurie later expounded upon Tax's thinking, writing about a preliminary AICC planning meeting held in Chicago: "Sol invited 20 people and got a good representation about groupings (org. and unorg. tribes; urban indians, nonfederal recognized; intertribal groups—NCAI, Longhouse, etc. and Native American Church) and good geographic spread."[10] Consequently, nine hundred American Indians from the East received AICC mailings, and seven Indians from this region were appointed to the AICC rules committee of twenty-four members, including Chief W. R. Richardson, the Haliwa leader, and Judge Lacy R. Maynor, a prominent Lumbee and town justice of the Maxton, North Carolina, recorder court.[11]

In order to pursue this "eastern strategy," Tax had to balance diplomatically the interests of competing Indian groups and organizations. He had worked almost from the beginning with the leadership of the National Congress of American Indians (NCAI). Through D'Arcy McNickle, Clarence Wesley, and Helen Peterson, Tax received the NCAI's formal endorsement.[12] Although this endorsement proved useful in the West, many eastern Indians viewed the NCAI as too conservative, too much aligned with the BIA, and too opposed to eastern Indian interests, including federal recognition efforts. Thus, Tax and Lurie, although relying on the skills of McNickle, nevertheless attempted to prevent the AICC from appearing to be merely a carbon copy of a NCAI convention.[13]

Two eastern American Indians played key roles in the planning and development of the AICC: (1) William Rickard (Tuscarora) and (2) Lacy W. Maynor (Lumbee). Rickard, the son of well-respected Chief Clinton Rickard who had aided eastern Indians through the Indian Defense League, had come to public attention in the late 1950s as a prominent activist fighting against Robert Moses and the New York State Power Authority's efforts to expropriate Tuscarora lands.[14] Historian Barbara Graymont has described the qualities of William and Clinton Rickard that made them leaders of the Indian Defense League and eastern Indians:

> William and his father [Clinton] were always very close and in many ways very similar. They were alike in their interest in Indian rights, in their Indian conservatism, and in their personalities. Both were men of brilliance and native genius, easygoing nature, selfless devotion to others, and tenacious actions. Both were deeply religious men but revealed this trait in different ways. Clinton always preferred the church. William, though he had been voluntarily baptized as an adult and had passed through the "Christian degrees" of Masonry, came to be a devoted follower of the Longhouse religion, much preferring it to Christianity.[15]

On January 26, 1961, Tax extended an invitation to William Rickard, explaining the goals and agenda of the AICC meeting. Tax insisted that instead "of having 'experts' plan for communities of people, we have learned that people have to plan for themselves." He continued by indicating that any "plan for American Indians is a bad plan if the Indians who have to live with it do not understand it or do not want it," adding that improvement could not take place "unless the Indian point of view is fully expressed and honored." Tax assured Rickard that he was the coordinator, not the czar, of the meetings, and that he was attempting to bring all Indian viewpoints together. Yet he conceded to Rickard that he had limited knowledge of the diversity of positions: "But who are 'all Indians' and how can such a national discussion be carried through?" Tax then appointed Rickard to the planning committee of "12 or 15" Indian leaders from all over the United States to meet with him at the University of Chicago for four days beginning on February 10.[16] Rickard, as representative of the Iroquois Defense League and the Iroquois Longhouse, was subsequently chosen as a member of the Indian steering committee of the planned Chicago conference and chairman of the eastern regional meeting at Haverford College, leading up to the major convocation in Chicago. Rickard, who checked out all his statements beforehand with the chiefs of the Onondaga Longhouse, realized that the Iroquois were not as open-minded and sympathetic to the aims and aspirations of nonfederally recognized Indian groups as he was. In writing a summary report of an early AICC planning meeting, he feared that the Iroquois might not "work with the East coast Indians, Shinacooks [sic], Naragansetts [sic], etc. I might have to have two meetings, one for each. I hope not."[17] In the end, Rickard nevertheless was able to convince the Iroquois of the importance of participation in the AICC at the regional and national levels.

From the inception of his involvement in the AICC, Rickard was at odds with many of the sentiments expressed by other Indian representatives. After an early planning session in February, Rickard wrote: "I was not at all satisfied the way the Chicago meeting was conducted by the National Congress of American Indians. If their plans is [sic] to be followed, the venture is doomed to failure. They talk of a 'new frontier' but it is the same old muddle that has got our Indian people in such a deplorable state." In typical Iroquois fashion, he added that his aim was to "initiate the True [sic] course for our Indian people at Haverford" and, obviously later, at Chicago.[18] As a result, he suggested that more effort be made to broaden the representation. He recommended that invitations be sent to Indians with nonfederally recognized status, including Mary Red Wing Congdon, a prominent Narragansett, as well as representatives of traditionalist perspectives such as Iroquois Tadodaho George A. Thomas.[19] Rickard's involvement in AICC was no easy task for Tax and Lurie. In February, Lurie wrote McNickle that "Helen Peterson [an NCAI leader] will be just as happy to have Rickard out of the picture," but that Lurie hoped to straighten out any misunderstandings with him in order to avoid later complications in Chicago. Since Rickard had sizable influence over traditionalists, or "Longhouses" (Lurie's words), involved in the AICC process, Lurie worked hard to keep the channels of communication open to Rickard and his followers.[20]

At the February strategy meeting held in Chicago, Rickard was one of thirteen Indians in attendance. Three represented eastern Indians: Rickard, Judge Lacy Maynor (Lumbee), and George Heron (Seneca). Rickard and Heron recounted the troubles that each of their Iroquois nations was facing at the time. Heron described the Kinzua Dam controversy that threatened over 9,000 acres of Seneca lands in Pennsylvania and New York, and Rickard recalled the Tuscarora loss of 556 acres of tribal reservation land to a New York State Power Authority's reservoir and hydroelectric project along the Niagara River. Judge Maynor sadly indicated that his people had no federal recognition, but proudly insisted that they had retained a sense of Indian identity and distinctive community, despite the "racially complicated picture of the Southern states, since colonial times." It was at this meeting and at subsequent ones that an eastern alliance was formed that proved useful at the Chicago convocation six months later. The Maynors impressed Rickard, leading the Tuscarora to praise the judge. Rickard later wrote that the Lumbee did not have a reservation; but they did have the "same status as other people," and "they are sticking together and are not being pushed around to any great extent." In appreciation, Judge Maynor was supportive of Rickard's causes—protecting treaty rights and reaffirming Indian sovereignty—and Rickard believed that "he [Judge Maynor] and his people would help in any way possible."[21]

Tax and Lurie set up regional meetings around the country, leading up to the final conclave in Chicago. One of the coordinators of these meetings explained the reasons for this administrative structure: "Tax thought that [Indian] people ought to get warmed up and think their problems over and get things formulated in advance so that the Chicago experience would be more profitable."[22] Because of this format, Judge Maynor proved to be invaluable in promoting the AICC in the South, especially when a hitch occurred at the last moment over the site of the southeastern regional meeting. When the University of North Carolina at Chapel Hill turned down the AICC's organizers' request to host a regional meeting because the university's administrators found a southern conference on the race issue "too touchy," Tax and Lurie approached Maynor to have Pembroke State College (now Pembroke State University) hold the conference. Lurie also wrote Maynor, asking him to promote the AICC as far away as Alabama and Louisiana in order to get widespread support in Indian communities for the regional and Chicago meetings. Through a committee of thirty-two Lumbees, Maynor and his daughter Helen organized the Pembroke meeting.[23]

The site selection for this southeastern meeting is quite significant. Coming less than three years after the Lumbee won public attention by driving the Ku Klux Klan out of Robeson County, North Carolina, this decision was not merely by chance. The Lumbee, the largest Indian population east of the Mississippi, had founded Pembroke State College, their own institution of higher learning, in the 1880s. Moreover, as highly educated, numerous, and powerful as they were, compared to other nonfederally recognized Indians, the Lumbee offered a protected enclave in the South, during a time of racial tensions, where Indian issues could be discussed. Since one of the goals of the AICC was to develop Indian leadership, the availability of an Indian-founded, Indian-administered college as the host institution is noteworthy. Although no full transcript of the Pembroke meeting has been found, the regional conference held in April focused on educational problems facing American Indians and, in particular, southeastern communities, as well as racial discrimination, media stereotyping, housing problems, and concerns for economic development.[24] Since the Lumbee had sought federal recognition since the 1930s and had come close to achieving it in 1956, one could surmise that this issue also received

The Haverford College regional meeting of the American Indian Chicago Conference, April 1961 (courtesy Dr. Theodore Hetzel).

attention at Pembroke. It is also significant to note that one prominent anthropologist, who attended the meeting, observed that "reservation groups were badly underrepresented" at Pembroke since nonfederally recognized Indian groups were in the vast majority.[25]

A second regional meeting was held at Haverford College and organized by Theodore B. Hetzel, professor of engineering and longtime Indian-rights advocate. In order to prepare for the conference, Hetzel wrote Lurie to inquire about Nanticoke and Lumbee participation and adding names to the AICC mailing list, including state-recognized Pamunkey and Mattaponi chiefs, two Catawbas, and the Indian governors at the Penobscot and Passamaquoddy reservations in Maine. Besides Hetzel, Heron, and Rickard, the Indian committee organizing the Haverford College regional meeting included a Narragansett and a Mohawk-Cherokee married to a Narragansett Indian.[26] As a result of Rickard's influence, the Haverford meeting included federally recognized as well as nonrecognized reservation, and urban Indians. Besides Rickard, his father Clinton, and other Iroquois, the registration list included a "who's who" of off-reservation and/or nonfederally recognized Indians: Lewis Mofsie, Clarence Wood, and Mimi Hines, leaders in the New York City Indian community; Mary Red Wing Congdon and Tall Oak, a future leader of the Red Power movement among the Narragansett of Rhode Island; Gladys Widdiss, the former tribal chair among the Gay Head Wampanoag; Earl Mills, a prominent Mashpee; as well as delegates from the Abenaki, Penobscot, and Shinnecock.[27]

For three full days, the conferees talked about Indian sovereignty and communicated about common problems. William Rickard, who served as the chairman of the meeting held on April 7–11, 1961, once again expressed his concern that Indian sovereignty was being eroded by such actions as those by the New York State Power Authority. Rickard then went on to discuss his spiritual visit to the traditional people of the Hopi Nation. Penobscot Richard Bounding Elk insisted that the United States must provide a "Marshall Plan for Indians." He joined in an appeal with a Mohawk conferee urging President Kennedy to recognize the Six Nations as a sovereign nation just like Italy viewed San Marino. Importantly, at Haverford, Bounding Elk and other Indians insisted that the United States government recognize the federal status of Indians' reservation lands in Maine. Francis McCall, another Penobscot, recounted the prejudice and economic problems faced by Indians in Maine. He maintained that the state was the major problem and that its supervision of Indian affairs was abominable. Later, McCall insisted that the Penobscot were beyond the jurisdiction of Maine's laws since they were foreign nations and that treaties made with these Indians were more than just documents housed in the Maine state house.[28]

Not all of the AICC regional meetings supported the concept of an open convocation with nonfederally recognized Indian communities in attendance. This issue came to a head at the Oklahoma regional meeting held at the University of Oklahoma in the early spring of 1961. Alice Marriott and Carol Rachlin reported to Tax that the meeting focused its attention on the meaning of "self-identified Indians" and that these words produced great concern among the leadership among the Five Civilized Tribes. The two anthropologists, who had been working on behalf of the AICC, were asked to explain the term. When they were unable to do so, the regional meeting, with the support of Marriott and Rachlin, adopted a resolution insisting that "only members of federally-recognized Indian tribes who can so identify themselves in Chicago, be recognized at the June conference." The Oklahoma conferees, fearing the influence of what it claimed were individuals of questionable Indian heritage, also criticized the AICC map for including nonfederally recognized communities and suggested that the "identity of Indian tribes" be "based upon the estimates of a Federal agency, such as the Bureau of Indian Affairs."[29] The attack on so-called self-identified Indians, a code name for Afro-Indians in the minds of some of the leaders of the Five Civilized Tribes, was because of rampant discrimination since, in Rachlin's words, these Indians (leaders of the Five Civilized Tribes at

AICC), "REPRESENT THE OLD SOUTH IN OKLAHOMA."[30] Indian disdain and in-
tolerance of these communities was long-standing and pervasive especially in
Oklahoma and in the South, and was largely based on the white man's taboos
against white and Indian miscegenation with blacks since the age of slavery.

After the regional meetings, the AICC organizers solicited follow-up re-
sponses from those in attendance. One respondent, Richard Gaffney, an Abenaki Indian, emphasized that the AICC should take up "Federal 'recognition'
of the legal existence of certain tribes east of the Mississippi who are on state
reservations or not at all."[31] Helen Attaquin, a Wampanoag from Middleboro,
Massachusetts, suggested that the AICC should encourage a realization that
nonreservation Indians can aid reservation Indians and be "their biggest and
best spokesmen."[32] An Oneida and several Rappahannocks insisted that the
AICC focus on claims to lands lost; one Tuscarora stressed the need to focus
on treaties; while a Houma asked to serve on the education and law committees of AICC.[33] Karen Rickard, William's sister and a founder of NIYC, hoped
that the AICC would promote the preservation of Native arts. Importantly,
she added that the AICC should avoid breaking down into small groups right
away at the approaching Chicago meeting. She concluded by asserting that
what "the Indian needs is unity, which can be done during the first days—then
break up later in the week."[34] Yet, unlike Rickard, Emmanuel Many Deeds, a
Standing Rock Sioux and NCAI member, stressed the need for a committee on
screening that would limit seating at the Chicago conclave to those who could
document their Indian heritage.[35]

In one of the most ambitious endeavors, Zara Ciscoe Brough, a Nipmuck,
from her home at Grafton, Massachusetts, drafted a detailed plan for the complete overhaul of Indian affairs in the United States. She suggested abolish-
ing the BIA and its civil-service structure and establishing an "Indian Board
Committee Government" in the Interior Department, composed of a chairman and four board members selected by the president of the United States.
The Indian Board, funded by the federal government, would allocate funds
to tribal projects through four regional district offices. In each district, there
would be a governor, the Indian district chairman, who would be responsible to both reservation and nonreservation Indians in his/her district. At the
bottom of this new structure would be reservation and nonreservation tribal
committees with proportional representation according to the size of reservation or individual groups. Importantly, nowhere in this elaborate plan were
federally recognized and nonfederally recognized Indians set apart.[36]

Eastern Indians hoped that the AICC would bring a new day to their communities. Despite outright racism expressed against them by other Indians and
warnings about their seating at the Chicago conclave, Brough wrote Tax that

the Indians in Connecticut, Massachusetts, and Rhode Island were "very en-thusiastic about the conference" and were "anxiously awaiting the outcome of the conference."[37] Mary Red Wing Congdon talked up the significance of the AICC among the Mohegans and Narragansetts, attended a strategy meeting at Mashpee, and discussed her findings about the matter with local New England Indian nationalist organizations. In writing Tax, she went so far as to volun-teer her services at Chicago and requested that Tax allow her to address the full convention about "Our Golden Heritage," Indian affairs in general, and the Narragansetts' survival as Indian people.[38]

Tax carefully tried to win acceptance of these groups prior to the Chicago conclave. In a major article written for the *Chicago Sun Times,* Tax wrote:

> IT IS SOMETIMES ARGUED that the crippling effects of governmental paternalism could have been avoided if the government had simply "stayed out of the Indian business." But this has not worked either. There are many Indian communities which are not recognized by the government which face problems as acute as those of the overregulated communities. These "non-reservation" settlements, even when they no longer "own" their land, are identifiable as communities whose members are as attached to their territories as any other Indians, and with pressing problems comparable to others. Their problems cannot be wished away by refusing to recognize them. These are communities without paternal-istic control but also without the needed subsidization to begin to carry out choices they would like to make for their own benefit.[39]

Despite Tax's efforts, internal disputes erupted in Chicago over the partici-pation by these Indians. In fact, the entire week-long convocation in Chicago was marred by intense conflict. According to McNickle:

> Even in the presence of a common danger, however, collaboration was not spontaneously achieved. Indians from traditionalist communities were fearful of finding themselves associated with ideas or actions which might betray their interests. Reservation Indians were especially distrust-ful of their urbanized kinsmen, whom they suspected of scheming to liq-uidate tribal resources and claim their share. In the absence of traditional channels for intertribal communication, the conferees had as their only guiding experience their generations of negotiating with the white man, an experience that had taught extreme wariness and distrust. At several critical moments the conference stood ready to dissolve, but on each such occasion an acceptable base for continuing discussion was found.[40]

McNickle was vague in his description and failed to elaborate on the friction over the nonfederally recognized Indians' role at the Chicago meeting; however, Lurie clarified the nature of this conflict by specifying that nonreservation Indians in general, "and the presence of non-federally recognized tribes, also evoked their [the delegates of federally recognized groups] anxiety." By favoring and establishing a "60%–70%" arrangement, in which the federally recognized communities would have the larger share of votes, these Indians held the power at the Chicago conclave. Moreover, these federally recognized communities further alienated some Indians, but mostly urban and nonfederally recognized groups, by pushing through a resolution allowing them to use their 60 percent as a bloc vote at the convocation![41] Despite these power plays, the voices of Indians east of the Mississippi were not silenced at Chicago. Once again, William Rickard's influence was apparent.

Rickard, who participated and addressed the convocation in Chicago, caused a commotion when he objected to a pamphlet prepared by Sophie Aberle and William Brophy, entitled "A Program for Indian Citizens," which had been distributed prior to the June meeting.[42] Since the Iroquois considered themselves as citizens of their individual Indian nations or of the Iroquois Confederacy, the Tuscarora interpretation of the Aberle–Brophy pamphlet was as government design to assimilate the Indians. In Chicago, after hearing McNickle read the *Declaration of Indian Purpose,* Rickard pointed out that some Indians did not come to an American Indian conference to be told that "ALL INDIANS ARE U.S. CITIZENS." Rickard explained that Iroquois traditionalist views did not recognize the 1924 Indian citizenship act and that there was nothing wrong with the requirements before 1924, when an Indian had to qualify, be educated, and become a citizen of his own free will and accord. Rickard concluded by blaming the NCAI, who "is influenced mainly by white politicians and lobbyists and that they have not worked for the best interests of the Indians," "Indian Bureau politicians," and misguided academics, diplomatically excluding his hosts, Tax and Lurie. Yet after the AICC, the Tuscarora activist later insisted, in Iroquois metaphorical style, that the voice of eastern Indians, "supposedly assimilated, terminated or relocated and are not federally recognized," had, despite efforts to silence them, been heard. They had questioned the dangerous parts of various proposals, "symbolically screaming a warning to other Nations and Tribes of Indians of approaching danger as is the duty of the eagle atop the Iroquois tree of peace." No longer, according to Rickard, could the NCAI ignore the existence of Indian groups and Indian organizations east of the Mississippi.[43]

Rickard later claimed that the AICC was not an open conference and that the convocation had insulted Indians east of the Mississippi:

> We who were from the east were permitted to speak and serve on the various committees, but for the most part, it was only a token courtesy.

Several times in a discussion group I heard the phrase used, "You are not from the federally recognized tribes" when an eastern Indian spoke. You would be allowed to talk. When you finished, they paid no attention to any suggestions you might have made.[44]

Yet Rickard was only partially correct. Although open discrimination against nonfederally recognized Indians was clearly practiced, much to the embarrassment of Tax, Lurie, and many Indians in attendance, Indians east of the Mississippi without federal status achieved some notable results. Without question, the AICC's *Declaration of Indian Purpose* showed no inkling of this internal battle and reflected true concern for these Indian communities:

Mention has not been made in the above categories of the situation of those Indian groups, mostly in the East and the South, for whom no lands were ever reserved under federal law and for whom no federal services have ever been provided. Yet, they remain Indian, and they remain isolated. We say emphatically that the problems of health, education, economic distress and social nonacceptance rest as heavily on all the Indians in these categories as they do on the reservation Indians, and possibly more heavily. Therefore, in all the recommendations herein, it is to be understood that even where non-reservation or off-reservation are not specified, it is our purpose to insist that their needs be taken into account.[45]

Equally astounding, the *Declaration* contained no distinctions in its text about federally recognized and nonrecognized Indians and made no attempt to define *Indian* or *tribe*.[46]

Perhaps more importantly, the AICC gave renewed hope to Indians east of the Mississippi to push for federal recognition. Helen Maynor (Schierbeck), who subsequently became a leading Indian educator, wrote Tax a month after the AICC that "many good things happened at the Chicago Conference." Citing the group discussions and the acquaintances she made, Maynor insisted that "Indian thinking as a national group grew."[47] At a time when federal recognition of Maynor's Lumbee community had recently been denied, she was apparently reacting to the realization that other eastern Indians experienced the same frustrations as well as aspirations. In this vein, Chief Calvin W. McGee, an Alabama Creek, told Nancy Lurie in Chicago that he could not believe there were "so many Indians in the same boat."[48] The AICC, to be sure, had contributed to networking American Indian communities, including those eastern groups who had long aspired for federal recognition. Defended by prominent anthropologists and receiving attention on a national scale for the first time, these Indians went back to their communities more confident about their future and more committed to pushing for recognition of their Indian status. It was no coincidence that two of the Houma delegates, after attending the AICC in Chicago, went back to their community in the Louisiana bayou country and began a major effort to achieve federal recognition.[49]

Perhaps the most extraordinary impact of the AICC on eastern Indians was its effect on the Haliwa of North Carolina. Chief W. R. Richardson, who is still the leader of the Haliwa, had actively participated in the planning sessions leading up to the Chicago meeting. In the process, he became acquainted with William Rickard and his family. This friendship made at Chicago had significant results. Twice between June 1961 and early 1963, William, his father Clinton, and other family members, as well as Chief Elton Greene and Walter Printup of the Tuscarora, visited the Haliwa. On one of these visits, the Tuscarora, after learning of the history and customs of these North Carolina peoples, gave their formal tribal recognition to the Haliwa. Rickard stated the following in an affidavit to Chief Richardson: "It is my observation that the Indians of the Haliwa Indian Community are the direct descendants of remnant groups of Tuscarora, Cherokee, and other Indian tribes and nations occupying their territory many years ago."[50] One year after William Rickard's death in 1964, North Carolina granted the Haliwas state recognition as an Indian community. Since that time, Chief Richardson and the Haliwa have pressed for federal recognition and are currently preparing a petition of status clarification for the Department of the Interior.[51]

On August 15, 1962, thirty-two Indians active in AICC presented the *Declaration of Indian Purpose* to President John F. Kennedy at a special ceremony at the White House. Nine Indians from nonfederally recognized communities attended the ceremony, including two Chickahominy, four Alabama Creeks, one Lumbee, one Narragansett, and one Ottawa. Helen Maynor [Schierbeck] of the Lumbee and Chief Calvin W. McGhee of the Alabama Creek, both of whom had played important roles in the acceptance of the AICC in the South, were there along with Robert Burnette, executive director of the NCAI, to push for improvement of Indian conditions in the United States. After the White House gathering, the Indians met with Vice President Lyndon Johnson, Senator Sam J. Ervin, Jr., and Congressman Ben Riefel, himself of Lakota Indian ancestry and a founder of NCAI, in order to discuss a legislative program suggested by the *Declaration of Indian Purpose*.[52]

The seeds sown at Chicago were generally slow to reach harvest. In 1976, the American Indian Policy Review Committee Task Force 10 covered much of the same ground that Tax and Lurie had initiated a decade and a half earlier, mapping Indian populations east of the Mississippi and identifying their needs.[53]

With the establishment of the Federal Acknowledgment Branch in the Department of the Interior in the late 1970s and increased congressional sensitivity to these Indian communities came federal recognition for the Alabama Creek (Poarch Band), the Narragansett, the Ottawa, the Tunica-Biloxi, the Mashantucket Pequot, and other groups as well as the reinstitution of federal status for all of the Indian nations of Maine.

By allowing a forum for eastern American Indians and their concerns, the AICC stimulated the movement for federal recognition. Tax and his staff should also be credited with helping to instill a new pride, confidence, and direction to the leaders of these long-neglected communities who, for the first time, shared the podium with tribal chiefs and chairmen from around the country. Tax, in an interview in 1982, was correct in his assessment that "we [the AICC] started this movement for federal recognition."[54] The AICC was truly a vast experiment in action anthropology, whose overall significance to eastern Indians is becoming easier to comprehend more than three decades later.

9 WARRIORS WITH ATTACHÉ CASES

In the past decade, popular writers have increasingly concentrated their investigative energies on Native Americans, their contemporary issues and overall concerns; nevertheless, these books almost exclusively focus on the rise of Red Power militancy, the "warriors movement," and other forms of Indian activism, giving the public further misconceptions about the overall nature of Native American existence. In this vein are books by Rex Weyler, *Blood of the Land: The Government and Corporate War against the American Indian Movement* (New York: Everest House, 1982; repr., New York: Vintage Books, 1984); Rick Hornung, *One Nation under the Gun: Inside the Mohawk Civil War* (New York: Pantheon Books, 1991); and two books by the noted novelist Peter Matthiessen — *In the Spirit of Crazy Horse* (New York: Viking Press, 1983) and *Indian Country* (New York: Viking Press, 1984). Although the history of Native American militancy is an important subject, each of these authors portrays Native America in a most limited way, dramatizing the armed confrontational aspects of Indian–white and Indian–Indian relations. To authors such as Matthiessen and Weyler, the heroic figures of Indian country are those Native Americans who risk their lives in challenging the white man or tribal governments imposed by the white man. The readers of these books get the impression that the only "true Indians" are those in mortal combat at Wounded Knee (1973) or at Oka (1990).

When combined with one-minute sound bites on the evening news and Hollywood's version of the recent Indian past such as *Thunderheart* (1992), these simplistic images give the American public, already ignorant of Native Americans, even greater misconceptions about Indian country. Rennard Strickland, the prominent legal scholar of Native American ancestry, has explained this phenomenon: "White society can define, even absorb and tolerate a second Wounded Knee, AIM, and Indian violence. Such conduct is definitionally Indian. What cannot be understood is what the modern Indian is seeking to do. Indians are behaving in a way that the white inventor of the Indian did not imagine; therefore, such conduct is intolerable." Strickland concluded: "It is hard for whites to imagine Indians who identify themselves with native cultural and tribal values as energy entrepreneurs, as doctors, as lawyers, as business executives, as computer programmers, and as government officials on previously all-white school boards and city councils" (Rennard Strickland, "White Memory: Red Images and Contemporary Indian Policy: A Forward," in Raymond Stedman, *Shadows of the Indian: Stereotypes in American Culture* [Norman: University of Oklahoma Press, 1982], pp. xii–xiii).

Today, Native Americans are faced with fighting new versions of the "Indian wars" to ensure their survival as culturally and legally distinct peoples. Most of these conflicts, more often than not, are fought in the federal courts, in the halls of Congress, and at negotiating tables. The origins of these wars are many and include numerous issues of importance to Native American communities: tribal, civil, and criminal jurisdiction; the sanctity of Native American burials; Native American access to and protection of sacred sites; the ceremonial use of peyote by members of the Native American Church; land claims; voting rights and civil liberties; federal recognition; and economic issues including the protection of water rights, tribal exemption from state sales taxes, and gaming.

Warriors with attaché cases—both men and women attorneys—are at the frontlines of these conflicts. In fact, they are the essential warriors along three battle zones—tribal attorneys dealing with the day-to-day legal concerns of modern-day Native American communities; regional legal-services agencies attempting to guarantee civil liberties and equal protection under American law to Native Americans on and off reservations; and national legal-advocacy organizations, especially the Native American Rights Fund (NARF), who lobby on Capitol Hill as well as argue their cases before lofty tribunals, including the United States Supreme Court.

In Shakespeare's *King Henry VI*, Dick the Butcher utters the all-too-familiar refrain to Smith the Weaver and to the rebel Jack Cade: "The first thing we do, let's kill all the lawyers."[1] Dick's words reflect the strong feelings of resentment that Englishmen in the Elizabethan era, as well as modern-day Americans, have about attorneys and their profession; however, to Native Americans, the tribal attorney, regional legal services, and national Indian legal-advocacy groups are essential bulwarks protecting Native Americans and their communities against the often shifting political winds emanating from county seats, state capitals, or Washington, D.C. Because of the unique legal status of American Indian nations and past failures in protecting Indian lands, natural resources, and religious freedom, attorneys who are both Indian and non-Indian are essential figures in shaping modern Native American existence.

Part of my interest in this important subject is motivated by my past archival historical research and by observing attorneys at work on behalf of Native Americans. In fact, nearly every historical project I have worked on over the past twenty years has had contemporary legal implications. For example, in my pursuit of nineteenth-century Iroquois history in the early 1970s, I uncovered documents from the period from 1850 to 1914, related to the origins of the contemporary Seneca-Salamanca lease controversy; twenty years later, I testified as the "expert" historical witness at congressional hearings that attempted to resolve this thorny issue. From my attendance at open tribal-council meetings in the 1970s, to seeing able tribal attorneys furiously preparing for testimony or lobbying on Capitol Hill, to keenly observing the attorneys on the Senate Select Committee, I had the opportunity to understand this important side of the contemporary Native American world.[2]

My interest in this particular subject was also stimulated by the reading of a novel, *The Indian Lawyer,* written by James Welch, the prominent author of Native American ancestry. In it, Sylvester Yellow Calf, the protagonist, is faced with some of the cultural dilemmas of modern Indian existence. Yellow Calf, a former star athlete and a graduate of Stanford Law School, is a partner in the prestigious law firm of Harrington and Lohn in Helena, Montana. Faced with assimilationist pressures and blackmail, he abandons the fast track of corporate law and a run for Congress. Inspired by his great great grandfather's medicine pouch, given to him by his grandmother Mary Bird, he leaves the acquisitive world of Helena and returns to his roots in Browning. In the end, he uses his advocacy skills to help his people, becoming a new warrior in a new West.[3]

Welch's significant novel is only a partial portrait of the legal world of Native America. Although there are cultural dilemmas that Native Americans face, not all have to physically return to their communities to serve their people or indigenous peoples as a whole. Important to note, because of the heated politics that exist in certain Native American communities, lawyers get "burned out," working incredible hours under tremendous pressures. More often than not, they have a short-lived tenure as designated tribal attorneys and are often out when new councils enter office.

Despite the focus of this chapter on Native American attorneys, one should also understand that much of the groundbreaking legal work on behalf of American Indians over the past three decades has been done by non-Indians, some working in well-appointed corporate law offices and others in makeshift storefronts. Some examples are necessary to illustrate this point. In 1974, George Shattuck, a non-Indian, of the major central New York law firm of Bond, Schoeneck and King, won a landmark decision in the United States Supreme Court. In *Oneida Indian Nation of New York State et al. v. the County of Oneida et al.*, the highest court held that the 1790 and 1793 Trade and Inter-course acts were applicable to the original thirteen states, including New York, thus opening up the federal courts to the Oneida as well as to all other Indians seeking to get back land in the original thirteen states.[4] The case's outcome directly led, in the same year, to the court's favorable decision in the Passama-quoddy case argued by Tom Tureen, a non-Indian, and subsequent settlements of land-claims cases in Maine, Massachusetts, Connecticut, and Rhode Island.[5] In 1989, after the initiation of litigation, a battery of non-Indian attorneys representing the Puyallup Indians of Washington won a major land-claims settlement, 162 million dollars, through negotiations with the City of Tacoma. Besides receiving a sizable cash settlement, the Puyallup won title back to some of their long-lost lands, including the city's waterfront.[6]

Attorneys representing Native Americans are not merely part of the corpo-rate scene. In *Windy Boy* v. *Big Horn County* in 1986, Jeff Renz and Laughlin McDonald, two non-Indian American Civil Liberties Union attorneys, suc-cessfully argued in federal courts that an at-large system in county commis-sion and school-board elections in Big Horn County, Montana, "diluted the Indian vote so as to disenfranchise American Indian voters," in clear violation of section 2 of the 1965 federal Voting Rights Act.[7] Legal-services attorneys, mostly non-Indians, have also fought for Native American civil liberties, fed-eral recognition, land claims, improved state and local social services, and educational opportunities. Always underfunded and decimated by cuts during the Reagan–Bush years, these organizations, especially Alaska Legal Services, headed by Judy Bush, do their important work far from the glitter of Wash-ington, D.C., and the public spotlight. Largely as a result of the efforts of Pine Tree Legal Assistance of Maine, headed by Nan Heald, the Micmacs, mostly poor, became a federally recognized "tribe" in 1992, thus becoming eligible for BIA and other federal Indian programs.[8]

Non-Indian attorneys serve Native American communities in other areas. Lawrence Aschenbrenner and Donald Miller, both non-Indians, have done outstanding service for Native American communities as NARF-affiliated at-torneys. Aschenbrenner has long worked on behalf of eastern Indian land claims and has headed NARF's office in Alaska, fighting to protect indigenous rights on the "last American frontier." Miller, who represents the Catawba Indians of South Carolina in their land-claims suit, recently won a federal re-versal for the Alabama-Coushatta, in the Indian nation's quest for their land claim.[9] Non-Indian attorneys such as Pete Taylor, a senior staffer of the United States Select Committee on Indian Affairs, do much of the legal research, write the legislative history on issues to brief the Senate committee's mem-bers, and draft final legislative reports on bills. Taylor works closely with his

Native American colleagues, especially Alan Parker, senior attorney of the Senate Select Committee, to facilitate testimony by visiting Indian delegations and expert witnesses to serve the legislative process.[10]

Although Native American lawyers are not new to the scene, they nevertheless have only begun to appear in significant numbers in Indian country within the last three decades. As a result of the social ferment of the 1960s, the development of Indian legal-issues courses at law schools; the active recruitment of Indian students; the establishment of major Indian legal institutes, such as the one at the University of New Mexico in Albuquerque; and the hopes raised by more favorable federal court decisions in the 1970s, many Native Americans sought out a legal career. Encouraged by elders and politically savvy tribal leaders, they saw law as the new weapon of individual and tribal survival.

These tribal attorneys work in a variety of areas. The Oneida Nation of Indians of Wisconsin is a case in point. Five attorneys of Oneida ancestry have to contend with historic concerns as well as with those largely generated in recent years. These attorneys have worked with NARF in pursuit of Oneida Indian land claims in New York State and have played a significant role in the negotiation process since the mid-1980s. They also have had to contend with tribal economic success generated over the past decade by bingo and casino gaming. These attorneys supervise personnel service contracts for a nation of more than eleven thousand members, whose tribal employment is almost one thousand and whose annual budget is several hundred million dollars a year. When the tribally owned Oneida Rodeway Hotel, now the Oneida Radisson, was constructed in 1986, these attorneys had to supervise contracts; when a new hotel management team replaced the old one, this same process was repeated. Equally important, when the success of Oneida Bingo engendered a backlash in Green Bay and environs to tribal efforts to purchase more land, all within the boundaries of its original sixty-five-thousand-acre Wisconsin reservation, most of which had been lost through allotment policies, tribal attorneys fought off these local efforts.[11]

The backgrounds of tribal attorneys reveal much about these new warriors with attaché cases. Two of the senior attorneys of the Wisconsin Oneida had distinct roads to the legal profession. Francis Skenandore was partly inspired by his uncle, Willie "Fat" Skenandore, who had had no formal legal training, but who had done groundbreaking research on allotment, land claims, and tax issues from the 1920s until his death thirty years later. Gerald Hill was a "participant" in the takeover at Alcatraz Island in 1969 and 1970; his path from disillusionment with some aspects of Red Power politics to his position as tribal attorney was guided and encouraged by his remarkable uncle, the late Norbert Hill, the former tribal chairman of the Oneida Nation of Indians of

Wisconsin. In the recent past, Hill also served as the president of the American Indian Bar Association.[12]

Two Native American lawyers of the Seneca Nation illustrate other aspects about the nature of practicing as tribal attorney. Loretta Crane moved back to Seneca country from Utah to serve her people during several years of the most difficult lease negotiations. From 1988 onward, she was largely responsible for gaining a new lease agreement with the City of Salamanca and other congressional villages and building a tribal consensus on the agreement. A former NARF lawyer, Douglas Endreson, an attorney of Navajo ancestry working for the law firm of Sonofsky, Chambers and Reid in Washington, D.C., under retainer from the Seneca Nation of Indians, then tirelessly lobbied for congressional legislation to compensate the Seneca for past failures to carry out federal trust responsibilities. The two attorneys helped to secure sixty million dollars from the federal and state governments as compensation for the Seneca. As is often true in the highly volatile world of Native American politics, Crane and Endreson were no longer needed once they succeeded, and subsequently their contracts were not renewed. In circumstances a far cry from Welch's novel, Crane moved back to Utah and Endreson practices law, now as a partner, in Sonofsky, Chambers and Reid in Washington, D.C. Thus, the contemporary Native American legal world often does not have neatly wrapped, simple endings.[13]

Because of the familial and tribal political pressures, many Native Americans serve their people for certain intervals and then shift away from these legal pursuits, although their priorities, even then, are seldom far from their homeland. Marguerite Smith, a Shinnecock, demonstrates this phenomenon. While working three hours from her home as a corporate attorney with Union Carbide in Danbury, Connecticut, Smith also served as tribal attorney to the Shinnecock of Southampton, Long Island, throughout much of the 1980s. In 1989, she resigned from her post with Union Carbide to take a position, which she held until recently, as assistant attorney general of New York State in Mineola, Long Island, only an hour from her home in Southampton. In order to avoid any conflict of interest because of her new position, Smith resigned as tribal attorney, allowing Roberta Hunter, another Shinnecock and a recent law school graduate, to take her place. Although it appears that Smith withdrew from tribal responsibilities, she and her family remain active in currently planning a new tribal museum as well as in other tribal concerns. By gaining valuable experience in both corporate and governmental law, Smith can provide this expertise to benefit the Native Americans of Long Island. Unlike the Matthiessen and Weyler image, she is the perfect example that Strickland describes, namely, the Indian, invisible to non-Indians, who identifies with native cultural and tribal values while on occasions serving as a lawyer-government official.[14]

Native Americans also practice law as regional legal-services attorneys throughout the United States. Before being murdered in February of 1988, Julian Pierce, a Lumbee Indian, was among the best of this new generation of legal-services attorneys. Pierce grew up in Hoke County, North Carolina, adjacent to Robeson County, the Lumbee homeland where more than 35 percent of the residents are of Native American ancestry. In the early and middle 1970s, he attended North Carolina Central University and Duke University School of Law. Because of his keen abilities, he was appointed as a counsel to the United States Securities and Exchange Commission, serving two years in Washington, D.C., from 1976 to 1978. Reacting to this experience much like the fictional Sylvester Yellow Calf in Welch's novel *The Indian Lawyer*, Pierce, in 1979, moved back to North Carolina, more specifically to Robeson County, to serve as the first director of Lumbee River Legal Services, representing those—black, white, Indian—too poor to afford legal counsel. He also practiced public-interest law and took on and prosecuted class action suits.[15]

Lumbee River Legal Services was also the leader in pushing for meaningful federal recognition of the Lumbee. In 1956, in a bizarre twist, the Lumbee were federally recognized, but, in the same legislation, were denied access to federal services. The Lumbee received a hopeful sign of a reversal of fortunes when, in 1978, the Branch of Federal Acknowledgment was established in the Bureau of Indian Affairs. Over a six-year period, through Pierce's guidance, Lumbee River Legal Services prepared a federal petition in cooperation with Indian community leaders, historians, and anthropologists. In support of these efforts, Dr. Jack Campisi of Wellesley College undertook archival research and gathered community history through fieldwork. Lumbee River Legal Services also assembled and verified a tribal roll of more than thirty-six thousand Lumbee names by filing extensive family ancestry charts. By 1986, the Lumbee recognition petition was formally submitted to the Branch of Federal Acknowledgment.[16]

Lumbee efforts toward meaningful federal recognition weakened on March 26, 1988, when Julian Pierce was murdered, shotgunned three times at point-blank range through a backdoor kitchen window at his home in Wakulla, North Carolina.[17] His execution-style murder was not surprising to some of those interviewed at the time of his death since he had been threatened many times before. Moreover, Pierce found much wrong upon his return home in 1978. One-fourth of the people of Robeson County were below the poverty line, unemployment was among the state's highest, and per capita income

Julian Pierce, Lumbee attorney (courtesy Lumbee River Legal Services and Dr. Jack Campisi).

was among the lowest. Four or five drug organizations operated in the hard-scrabble rural county of 949 square miles in the south-central part of the state. To the underworld, the county's location, equidistant from New York City and Miami and conveniently situated off Interstate 95, facilitated their operations. Racial tensions were high and the area had a history of Ku Klux Klan activity.[18]

Local Indians as well as African Americans, who totaled over 25 percent of the population, had accused county law-enforcement officials of collaborating with racial hate groups as well as drug dealers. In November 1986, an unarmed Lumbee man was shot to death by Kevin Stone, the sheriff's son, during a routine drug search, after Stone and another law officer had been accused of illegally removing fifty drug cases of cocaine from an evidence-storage locker. Although Stone was never charged, another sheriff's deputy was eventually indicted. By 1987, a coalition called Concerned Citizens for Better Government, composed of Native American, African American, and white members, was formed and began to protest against corruption, violence in the county, and the inequities in the education of the county's minority children. On Easter Day, 1987, fifteen hundred of the county's residents joined in a rally on these issues.[19]

As a result of these actions, the state legislature created a new special judicial district, thereby giving racial minorities a better chance of electing a judge. In early 1988, Pierce declared himself a candidate for Superior Court judge, thus attempting to be the first Native American to be elected to a major judicial office in North Carolina. His opponent in the Democratic primary was Joe Freeman Britt, the local district attorney who had been accused earlier by Pierce's supporters of cooperating with drug dealers and violating the civil liberties of both Native Americans and African Americans. Pierce was seen as the best hope for the county's unrepresented minorities because of his past civil-rights record and his promise of fairer dealings with the Native American and African-American communities.[20]

Tensions ran high in this heated contest. On February 1, 1988, two young Lumbee activists seized control of the *Robesonian,* the daily newspaper in the county seat at Lumberton, holding its staff hostage after accusing the newspaper's editors of biased reporting about the campaign. Less than four weeks later, Pierce's body was found face down in a blood-spattered kitchen at his home. At the time of the murder, the Lumbee attorney was investigating the criminal-justice system in the county, attempting to tie it to drug trafficking. Two Indians—John Anderson Goins, the "hitman," and Sandy Gordon Chavis, the "getaway man"—were soon implicated in Pierce's murder by Sheriff Hubert Stone, Kevin's father. Goins, the alleged trigger man, was a small-time hood, well known for his questionable dealings in the region. Subsequently, Goins was found dead by the sheriff, an alleged suicide by shooting himself through the head in a closet at his father's home; Chavis's arrest soon followed. Later, both the North Carolina State Bureau of Investigation and the state office of the FBI in Raleigh confirmed the sheriff's report, which had "neatly" tied up the loose ends of the case. In it, the sheriff indicated that Goins murdered Pierce because he believed that the Lumbee attorney was responsible for legal warrants restricting Goins's access to see his former girlfriend, Shannon Bullard, whose mother was dating Pierce. Thus, the heinous crime was presented as being the result of a love-crazed, unstable young man's infatuation with a teen-age girl![21] Although few cases are as dramatic as this one except in the movies, Pierce's life and death are most noteworthy, illustrating the courageous work of attorneys involved in legal services on behalf of America's underclass.

The third major area of contemporary Native American involvement in providing legal expertise is at the national level. NARF and its history since its inception are at the center stage of this involvement. Not only has the organization revolutionized the case law affecting Native Americans in this country, but NARF has also been the training ground for young aspiring attorneys, both Indians and non-Indians, seeking to specialize in Native American legal issues.

ounded in 1970 as an eighteen-month pilot project of Califor-
al Services. The Ford Foundation, hoping to create a national
for Indians, built on the success of the ongoing California pro-
me its major financial supporter for its first three years. NARF
arated from the California Indian Legal Services in 1971, soon
growing from a three-attorney pilot project to a major law firm of eighteen
attorneys. NARF moved its headquarters from California to Boulder, Colorado, and later opened a Washington, D.C., office, which primarily focuses on
national legislation affecting Native Americans as well as eastern Indian legal
matters. With the help of a grant from the Carnegie Corporation, NARF established the National Indian Law Library in Washington, D.C., which serves as
the major legal clearinghouse for tribal and legal-services attorneys working
on behalf of Native Americans. In 1984, NARF opened an Anchorage office to
serve the legal needs of Native Alaskans. Although NARF solicits its funding
from individual, corporate, and tribal sources, much of its funding has come
from the Administration of Native Americans (ANA) in the United States Department of Health and Human Services, moneys that have significantly dried
up because of budget cuts during the Reagan–Bush years and the continued
downturn of the American economy. Today, NARF's thirteen-member Board
of Directors, composed entirely of Native Americans, has five major priorities: (1) the preservation of tribal existence; (2) the protection of tribal natural
resources; (3) the promotion of human rights; (4) the accountability of governments to Native Americans; and (5) the development of Indian law.[22]

Even in its initial years, NARF attorneys achieved notable successes in
carrying out these priorities. From 1971 through 1973, NARF attorneys helped
restore the Menominee of Wisconsin to federal tribal status after having been
terminated. Two of their attorneys worked with Ada and Connie Deer and Jim
White and their organization DRUMS in helping to draft the initial Menominee Restoration Bill, spending more than fourteen hundred hours in these
efforts on Capitol Hill. The Menominee were subsequently restored to federal
status. Later, in the 1980s, Ada Deer became the chair of the Board of Directors
of NARF.[23] In 1976, in *Fisher v. Montana,* NARF attorneys won a United States
Supreme Court decision that recognized that tribal courts had exclusive jurisdiction in Indian adoption proceedings in which all parties were tribal members.[24] Importantly, two years later, in a move supported by NARF, the United
States Congress passed the Indian Child Welfare Act, thus setting minimum
standards for the removal of Indian children from their families and establishing standards for adoptive and foster-home placement.[25] Since 1978, especially
in the United States Supreme Court case *Mississippi Band of Choctaw Indians v. Holyfield* (1989), NARF attorneys have given priority to this concern, be-

coming advocates in promoting the stability of Indian families and, at the same time, allowing tribal courts self-determination on this important issue.[26] NARF achieved one of its most heralded victories in 1980. Largely as a result of the efforts of Tom Tureen, a non-Indian working for NARF, Maine Indians—the Penobscot, Passamaquoddy, and Houlton Band of Maliseet—received a settlement award of 27 million dollars, and additional moneys totaling 54.5 million dollars to purchase back 300,000 acres of their traditional lands in Maine.[27]

The career of Arlinda Locklear, who is now in private practice but serves as the Lumbee tribal attorney, illustrates much about NARF and its importance in Indian country.[28] Growing up in North Carolina during the civil-rights revolution, she later attended Duke University School of Law. After graduation, she became a NARF staff attorney in Washington, working mostly on land claims, federal recognition, and jurisdictional issues. In 1984, Locklear, working for NARF, became the first Native American woman to argue a case before the United States Supreme Court. She challenged the state of South Dakota's insistence on criminal jurisdiction over Indians on 1.6 million acres—lands opened up to non-Indians in 1908, under a 1906 "surplus" lands act—which had reduced the boundaries of the Cheyenne River reservation. The United States Supreme Court unanimously decided that Congress, through its allotment policies, had not necessarily revoked the reservation or "disestablished" federal jurisdiction over this territory. This historic case has had legal implications for many western Indian nations since many reservations from Wisconsin westward had been allotted and existed in checkerboard fashion, with whites and Indians interspersed within the original boundaries of older reservations.[29]

The following year, Locklear achieved another stunning legal victory in the United States Supreme Court. Charles F. Wilkinson, the noted legal scholar, has called her "a brilliant oral advocate" who, in the Oneida case, "stood alone at the Bar and marshaled at congeries of law, history, and morality in her struggle to counteract the equities accumulated during the course of 175 years."[30] The NARF attorney achieved a 5 to 4 decision in favor of the Oneida. This case involved fewer than nine hundred acres of the extensive Oneida tribal land claim. The United States Supreme Court held that Oneida and Madison counties, New York, were liable for damages—fair rental value for two years, 1968 and 1969—for unlawful seizure of Indian ancestral lands. Associate Justice Lewis F. Powell, Jr., who wrote the majority opinion, insisted that the Indians' common-law right to sue was firmly established and that Congress did not intend to impose a deadline on the filing of such suits. This effectively nullified the counties' contention that the Indians had not made a timely effort to sue and thus had forfeited their legal rights. The decision thus erased the main argument against the Indians and opened the door for further Oneida ɪ involving their lost lands. The court also suggested that, because of ɴendous economic implications of the case, Congress should help settle w York Indian land claims, as it had done in Connecticut, Maine, and Rhoᴜe Island.[31] As noted previously, NARF attorneys had been directly involved in these earlier land settlements. Moreover, Locklear and other NARF attorneys, including Aschenbrenner, had prepared briefs and testified in 1982 against pending legislation introduced by South Carolina and New York State politicians who had attempted to extinguish Indian rights to sue for land.[32]

Locklear and other NARF staff attorneys, especially Henry Sockbeson, a Penobscot Indian from Maine, have also focused their attention on efforts by certain Native American communities to secure federal recognition. As of mid-1994, partly as a result of NARF legislative efforts or its support of the federal petition route through the Branch of Acknowledgment, the following Native American communities have achieved federal recognition status and are now eligible for federal Indian programs: (1) Grand Traverse Band of Ottawa and Chippewa (Michigan); (2) Jamestown Klallam Tribe (Washington); (3) Tunica-Biloxi Indian Tribe (Louisiana); (4) Death Valley Timbi-Sha Shoshone Band (California); (5) Narragansett Indian Tribe (Rhode Island); (6) Poarch Band of Creeks (Alabama); (7) Wampanoag Tribe of Gay Head (Massachusetts); (8) San Juan Southern Paiute Tribe (Arizona); (9) Cow Creek Band of Umpqua Indians (Oregon); (10) Mashantucket Pequot Tribe (Connecticut); (11) the Micmac Tribe (Maine); and (12) the Mohegan Tribe of Connecticut. Three other petitioners received federal recognition when their "ambiguous" legal status was clarified: (1) Lac View Desert Band of Lake Superior Chippewa Indians (Michigan); (2) the Texas Band of Traditional Kickapoos (Texas), who withdrew its petition after the determination that their community had already been federally recognized; and (3) the Confederated Tribes of Coos, Lower Umpqua, and Siuslaw Indians who were legislatively restored to federal status in 1984. As a part of legislative recognition efforts, several of these Indian communities received federal moneys to purchase land and to start tribal development projects; and some, such as the Mashantucket Pequot, have had resounding economic successes.[33]

Hard-fought NARF victories have also been achieved in the area of human rights, especially concerning the sanctity of Indian remains and the repatriation of burial goods. Through the leadership of two NARF senior staff attorneys—Robert M. Peregoy, a Flathead and part-time appellate court judge of the Confederated Salish and Kootenai, and Walter Echo-Hawk, a Pawnee—this issue has been a major focus of the organization's legal efforts. Many thousands of Native American peoples have been dug up from their graves in the United States and are now held in the nation's universities, museums, state and federal agencies, and tourist attractions. In 1868, the United States Surgeon General ordered the procurement of Indian crania for the Army Medical Museum; over four thousand heads were subsequently taken from Indian graves, burial scaffolds, morgues, hospitals, and POW camps in the name of "scientific research."[34]

NARF work in this area started long before the public outcry of the late 1980s. In the 1982 United States Supreme Court case, *Charrier* v. *Bell,* NARF attorneys argued successfully that artifacts dug from graves in an ancient Tunica-Biloxi Indian burial ground belonged to that Native American community.[35] With the growing concern over this issue, the organization pushed for legislative remedies throughout the 1980s. Largely as a result of their efforts, the Nebraska State Legislature in 1989 passed the Unmarked Human Burial Sites and Skeletal Remains Protection Act of 1989, which specifies that its intent is to "assure that all human burials are accorded equal treatment and respect for human dignity without reference to ethnic origins, cultural backgrounds, or religious affiliations." This precedent-setting law required the return of tribally identifiable dead bodies and associated grave offerings held by public entities in the state, as well as the protection of unmarked burials throughout the state.[36] Over thirty states have followed the Nebraska example in passing laws to protect Indian graves. Moreover, in November 1990, President Bush signed into law the Native American Graves Protection and Repatriation Act (NAGPRA).[37] The new federal law "increases protections for Indian graves located on federal and tribal lands and provides for native control over cultural items obtained from such lands in the future; (2) it outlaws commercial traffic in human remains; (3) it requires all federal agencies and federally funded museums (including universities) to inventory their collections of dead Native Americans and associated funerary objects and repatriate them to culturally affiliated tribes or descendants on request; and (4) it requires all federal agencies and federally funded museums to repatriate Native American sacred objects and cultural patrimony under procedures and standards specified in the act."[38]

Despite the focus of this chapter on the achievements of Native American attorneys, there have also been major setbacks.[39] NARF efforts in support of the Mashpee Tribe of Wampanoags' efforts at federal standing ended in failure in a Boston courtroom in 1978.[40] NARF's initial success in protecting Indian water rights in *Pyramid Lake Paiute Tribe* v. *Morton* (1972) was reversed by the United States Supreme Court in 1983.[41] The legal-advocacy organization has also met a major defeat in guaranteeing First Amendment rights in *Employment Division* v. *Smith,* a United States Supreme Court case in 1990, involving two American Indians in Oregon fired for ingesting peyote, which they deemed was a sacrament, while off duty as participants in a religious ceremony of the

Native American Church.[42] When members of the Yurok, Karok, and Tolowa tribes sought to use the American Indian Religious Freedom Act of 1978 to halt the United States Forest Service from constructing a six-mile road and logging in and around their sacred area, the United States Supreme Court, in *Lyng* v. *Northwest Indian Cemetery Protective Association,* held against NARF's legal position.[43] Moreover, in some quarters of Indian country, NARF's past economic reliance on federal funding has generated suspicions about its claims to be a national nonpartisan legal-advocacy organization. This charge is largely without merit, since NARF attorneys have aggressively pursued a variety of basic legal issues for a wide number of Native American communities. They have rarely shied away from taking on states as well as federal agencies.

Although not recognizable to the American public, "Red Empowerment," the legal struggles to empower Native Americans, has been occurring in Indian country over the past twenty-five years. Both Red Empowerment and Red Power have affected every Native American community in the United States. Both Red Empowerment and Red Power are intertwined since they both grow out of the same sources, namely, the past failures of the American system of law to protect and guarantee Native American human rights. Yet, as we have suggested throughout this chapter, Red Power, however important, tells only a part of a larger history of contemporary Native American existence. New warriors with attaché cases, however obscured from view, are blazing their trails with legal briefs, federal court appeals, and legislative lobbying on behalf of Native Americans. Although some of their recent routes have been blocked, they are nevertheless determined and ready as old-style Indian runners, avoiding traps, to search for new paths through the forest in service to assure their communities' survival and betterment.

NOTES

Preface

1. Daniel J. Boorstin, *Hidden History* (New York: Random House, 1987; paperback reprint, New York: Vintage Books, 1989), p. 11.
2. Michael Kammen, *Mystic Chords of Memory: The Transformation of Tradition in American Culture* (New York: Alfred A. Knopf, 1991), pp. 9, 38, 49–50, 85–87, 184–188, 250–251.
3. Eric Hobsbaum, "Introduction: Inventing Traditions," in: *The Invention of Tradition,* Hobsbaum and Terence Ranger, Eds. (Cambridge, U.K.: Cambridge University Press, 1983), p. 1.
4. Richard Slotkin, *Gunfighter Nation: The Myth of the Frontier in Twentieth-Century America* (New York: Atheneum, 1992), p. 16.

Chapter 1

1. James Axtell, *Beyond 1492: Encounter in Colonial North America* (New York: Oxford University Press, 1992), pp. 260–63.
2. Richard White, "Morality and Mortality," *New Republic* (Jan. 18, 1993): 33–36. White, in his excellent, thought-provoking review of David E. Stannard's *American Holocaust: Columbus and the Conquest of the New World* (1992), correctly observes: "I want to be absolutely clear. Instances of what can only be called genocide *did* occur against particular Indian peoples repeatedly during the long European invasion of America: the actions of white settlers in northern California and southern Oregon, for example, were genocidal in intent and often in consequence. But finding specific instances of genocide does not make the entirety of American Indian policy genocidal" (p. 35). Unfortunately, Stannard is not the only historian to employ these terms too loosely. See two fine studies whose titles create the mental depth charge that Axtell warned about: Russell Thornton, *American Indian Holocaust and Survival: A Population History since 1492* (Norman: University of Oklahoma Press, 1987); and Richard Drinnon, *Keeper of Concentration Camps: Dillon S. Myer and American Racism* (Berkeley: University of California Press, 1987). I should like to thank my colleague David Krikun for bringing White's article to my attention.
3. James A. Clifton, "Alternate Identities and Cultural Frontiers," in *Being and Be-*

coming Indian: Biographical Studies of North American Frontiers, ed. James A. Clifton (Chicago: Dorsey Press, 1989), p. 6.

4. Thornton, *American Indian Holocaust and Survival*, p. 49.

5. John W. De Forest, *History of the Indians of Connecticut: From the Earliest Known Period to 1850* (Hartford, Conn.: W. J. Hamersley, 1851; repr., Hamden, Conn.: Archon Books, Shoe String Press, 1964), pp. 138–39; Hubert H. Bancroft, *Works* (San Francisco: The History Company, 1886–90), 25: 561 passim.

6. The process by which Jews were dehumanized is clearly outlined in Helen Fein, *Accounting for Genocide* (New York: Free Press, 1979), pp. 3–30.

7. Richard Drinnon, *Facing West: The Metaphysics of Indian-Hating and Empires-Building* (Minneapolis: University of Minnesota Press, 1980), pp. 469–552. George Washington wrote to the head of the Indian Committee in Congress, in September 1783, that Indians were like wolves "both being beasts of prey, tho' they differ in shape." J. C. Fitzpatrick, ed., *Writings of George Washington* (Washington, D.C.: U.S.G.P.O., 1931–41), 27: 140. General James Carleton, who forced the Navajo out of Canyon de Chelly on the "Long Walk" and established the horrendous "Bosque Redondo Experiment," justified his actions in this manner: "The races of the Mammoths and Mastadons, and the great sloths, came and passed away: The Red Man in America is passing away." Quoted in Gerald Thompson, *The Army and the Navajo* (Tucson: University of Arizona Press, 1976), p. 158.

8. Leo Kuper, *Genocide: Its Political Use in the Twentieth Century* (New Haven: Yale University Press, 1982), appendix I.

9. Frank Chalk and Kurt Jonassohn, *The History and Sociology of Genocide: Analyses and Case Studies* (New Haven: Yale University Press, 1990), pp. 23–27.

10. See Elie Wiesel, "Shadows in the Camps," *New York Times*, Feb. 25, 1993, p. 19. See "Commission on Human Rights: 'Ethnic Cleansing' Condemned," *UN Chronicle* 29 (December 1992), 22; "War Crimes in the Former Yugoslavia," United States Department of State *Dispatch* 3 (Sept. 28, 1992): 732–35; "Nuremberg in Bosnia," *Time* 140, Dec. 28, 1992, p. 15.

11. For Pequot history, see Laurence M. Hauptman and James Wherry, eds., *The Pequots in Southern New England: The Fall and Rise of an American Indian Nation* (Norman: University of Oklahoma Press, 1990).

12. For analyses of the war, see Francis Jennings, *The Invasion of America: Indians, Colonialism and the Cant of Conquest* (Chapel Hill: University of North Carolina Press, 1975); Neal Salisbury, *Manitou and Providence: Indians, Europeans, and the Making of New England, 1500–1643* (New York: Oxford University Press, 1982); and Alden T. Vaughan, "Pequots and Puritans: The Causes of the War of 1637," *William and Mary Quarterly* 21 (April 1964): 256–69; and Vaughan, *New England Frontier: Puritans and Indians, 1620–1675* (Boston: Little, Brown and Co., 1965; rev. ed., New York: W. W. Norton and Co., 1979). Vaughan has produced three major interpretations of the Pequot War, modifying, revising, and refining his conclusions each time. Recently, Alfred A. Cave has modified some of Jennings's conclusions. See his "The Pequot Invasion of Southern New England: A Reassessment of the Evidence," *New England Quarterly* 27 (March 1989); 27–44; and his "Who Killed John Stone? A Note on the Origins of the Pequot War," *William and Mary Quarterly* 44 (July 1992): 509–21. The four contemporary seventeenth-century accounts of the war written by Lion Gardiner, John Mason, John Underhill, and Philip Vincent are con-

veniently found together in *History of the Pequot War*, ed. Charles Orr (Cleveland: Helman-Taylor Co., 1897).

13. James Kendall Hosmer, ed., *Winthrop's Journal: "History of New England," 1630–1649* (New York: Charles Scribner's Sons, 1908), 1: 222.

14. Kevin A. McBride, "The Historical Archaeology of the Mashantucket Pequots, 1637–1900: A Preliminary Analysis," in Hauptman and Wherry, *Pequots in Southern New England*, p. 104.

15. Ibid., p. 97; Jack Campisi, "The Emergence of the Mashantucket Pequot Tribe, 1637–1975," in Hauptman and Wherry, *Pequots in Southern New England*, pp. 117–18; Salisbury, *Manitou and Providence*, pp. 222–24; Jennings, *Invasion of America*, pp. 220–27; Vaughan, *New England Frontier* (1979 ed.), pp. 144–52. For the enslavement of Pequots and dispersal to Bermuda, see Ethel Boissevain, "Whatever Became of the New England Indians Shipped to Bermuda to Be Sold as Slaves," *Man in the Northeast* 11 (Spring 1981): 103–14. Sherburne F. Cook in "Interracial Warfare and Population Decline among the New England Indians," *Ethnohistory* 20 (Winter 1973): 6–9, insists that 180 Pequot prisoners were distributed as slaves to Indian and non-Indian alike. See also Carolyn T. Foreman, *Indians Abroad, 1493–1938* (Norman: University of Oklahoma Press, 1943), p. 29.

16. Quoted in Alden T. Vaughan, ed., *The Puritan Tradition in America, 1620–1730* (New York: Harper and Row, 1972), p. 66. For the Puritans' perception of the Indians, see the excellent article by William S. Simmons, "Cultural Bias in the New England Puritans' Perception of Indians," *William and Mary Quarterly*, 3d ser., 38 (January 1981): 56–72.

17. Cotton Mather, *Magnalia Christi Americana: or, The Ecclesiastic History of New England* (New York: Russell and Russell, 1967), 2: 558.

18. Chalk and Jonassohn, *History and Sociology of Genocide*, p. 180. For a different view, see Stephen T. Katz, "The Pequot War Reconsidered," *New England Quarterly* 64 (June 1991): 206–24.

19. Elie Wiesel, "Keynote Address," Conference on Group Defamation and Genocide, Hofstra University, April 21, 1988. Wiesel went on to say, paraphrasing the *Talmud:* "Before there is hate, there are words of hate.... Words transcend time and geography. Words said today can hurt people well into the future." The Pequot example shows the wisdom of Wiesel's remarks.

20. Bancroft, *Works*, 25: 561 passim. I should like to thank Dr. Jack Campisi of Wellesley College for allowing me access to his rich research files on the Indians of northern California.

21. Edward D. Castillo, "The Impact of Euro-American Exploration and Settlement," in *Handbook of North American Indians*, vol. 8: *California*, ed. Robert F. Heizer (Washington, D.C.: Smithsonian Institution, 1978), p. 118. Thornton, *American Indian Holocaust and Survival*, pp. 104–13; Alfred L. Kroeber, "The California Indian Population about 1910," in *Ethnographic Interpretations*, 1–6, University of California Publications in American Archaeology and Ethnology, 45 (2) (Berkeley, 1957), pp. 218–25. Sherburne F. Cook, *The Population of the California Indians, 1769–1970* (Berkeley: University of California Press, 1976), pp. 69–71; and his essay, "Historical Demography," in *Handbook of North American Indians*, vol. 8, 91.

22. United States Congress, *Senate Document No. 131: Memorial of the Northern California Indian Association Praying that Lands Be Allotted to the Landless Indians*

of the Northern Part of the State of California, Jan. 21, 1904, 58th Cong., 2d sess. (Washington, D.C., 1904), p. 1.

23. A summary of the depredations can be found in United States Department of the Interior, *Annual Report of the Commission of Indian Affairs for 1862* (Washington, D.C.: U.S.G.P.O., 1862), p. 191. Sherburne Cook *The Conflict between California Indians and White Civilization* (Berkeley: University of California Press, 1976), pp. 255-361; Robert F. Heizer and Alan A. Almquist, *The Other Californians: Prejudice and Discrimination under Spain, Mexico and the United States to 1920* (Berkeley: University of California Press, 1971), pp. 23-91; Robert F. Heizer, ed., *The Destruction of the California Indians* (Santa Barbara, Calif.: Peregrine Smith, 1974); and Heizer, *Ishi, The Last Yahi: A Documentary History* (Berkeley: University of California Press, 1979).

24. Heizer, *Destruction of the California Indians,* pp. vi–ix.

25. J. Y. McDuffie to A. B. Greenwood [Commissioner of Indian Affairs], Sept. 4, 1859, in United States Congress, Senate, *Executive Document No. 46: Report to the Secretary of the Interior, Communicating, in Compliance with a Resolution of the Senate, the Correspondence Between the Indian Office and the Present Superintendents and Agents in California, and J. Ross Browne, Esq.,* 36th Cong., 1st sess. (Dec. 5, 1859–June 25, 1860), Congressional Serial Set 1033, 11, 30.

26. Albert L. Hurtado, *Indian Survival on the California Frontier* (New Haven, Conn.: Yale University Press, 1988), pp. 130, 180–87.

27. *Annual Report of the Commissioner of Indian Affairs for 1862,* p. 459.

28. Lynwood Carranco and Estle Beard, *Genocide and Vendetta: The Round Valley Wars of Northern California* (Norman: University of Oklahoma Press, 1981), p. 94.

29. J. Ross Browne to A. B. Greenwood, Oct. 18, 1859, in United States Congress, House of Representatives, *Ex. Doc. 46,* 36th Cong., 1st sess., Congressional Serial Set 1033, 11, 15.

30. Ibid.

31. Ibid., p. 14. Castillo quotes another report by Browne that describes a massacre at Humboldt of sixty Indian men, women, and children, who "lay weltering in their own blood." Browne said that "girls and boys lay here and there with their throats cut from ear to ear." Castillo, "Impact of Euro-American Exploration and Settlement," p. 108.

32. E. A. Hitchcock to Colonel S. Cooper [Adjutant General of the U.S.], Mar. 31, 1853, in United States Congress, House of Representatives, *Executive Document No. 76: Message from the President of the United States. Transmitting Report in Regard to Indian Affairs on the Pacific,* 34th Cong., 3d ses. (Dec. 1, 1856–March 3, 1857), Congressional Serial Set 906, 9, 78.

33. Castillo, "Impact of Euro-American Exploration and Settlement," pp. 110–12.

34. United States Department of the Interior, *Annual Report of the Commissioner of Indian Affairs for 1861* (Washington, D.C.: U.S.G.P.O., 1861), pp. 639–40.

35. Hurtado, *Indian Survival on the California Frontier,* pp. 144–151; Castillo, "Impact of Euro-American Exploration and Settlement," 110–12.

36. Thomas J. Henley to Captain H. M. Judah, Dec. 29, 1855, found in United States Congress, House of Representatives, *Executive Document No. 76,* 34th Cong., 3d sess., Congressional Serial Set 906, 9, 107–8.

37. Hurtado, *Indian Survival on the California Frontier,* p. 145; Castillo, "Impact of

Euro-American Exploration and Settlement," pp. 110–12. Captain H. M. Judah of the Fourth United States Infantry courageously tried to unseat Henley and expose his corruption. See Judah to Major E. D. Townsend [Assistant Adjutant General], Nov. 2, 1855, and Jan. 21, 1856. Judah blamed the Indian Service for neglecting the starving and peaceful Indians. In response, Henley wrote to Judah and his superior officer General John E. Wool. Henley to Judah, Dec. 29, 1855; Henley to Wool, Jan. 25, 1856, all found in United States Congress, House of Representatives, *Executive Document No. 76*, 34th Cong., 3d sess., Congressional Serial Set 906, 9, pp. 102, 106–8, 110.

38. See references to Captain Judah's appeals in nn. 36 and 37.

39. General John E. Wool to United States Senator [from California] John B. Weller, Oct. 5, 1856, United States Congress, House of Representatives, *Executive Document No. 76*, 34th Cong., 3d sess., Congressional Serial Set 906, 9, p. 141.

40. Hurtado, *Indian Survival on the California Frontier*, p. 147; Castillo, "The Impact of Euro-American Exploration and Settlement," 108.

41. See n. 3.

42. James Brooke, "For an Amazon Tribe, Civilization Brings Mostly Disease and Death," *New York Times*, Dec. 24, 1989, p. 6. The Ache Indians of Paraguay also faced extermination in the 1970s.

43. For the continuing genocide in the Amazon, see "Death in the Rain Forest," *New York Times*, Aug. 27, 1993, p. A28 (editorial); Terence Turner, "Brazil's Guilt in the Amazon Massacre," *New York Times*, Aug. 26, 1993, p. A21 (Op-Ed); James Brooke, "Attack on Brazilian Indians Is Worst Since 1910," *New York Times*, Aug. 21, 1993, A3; James Brooke, "Miners Kill 20 Indians in the Amazon," *New York Times*, Aug. 20, 1993, p. A20.

44. Tim Golden, "Guatemala Indian Wins the Nobel Peace Prize, *New York Times*, Oct. 17, 1992, p. 1. For Rigoberta Menchu's life, see her autobiography: *I, Rigoberta Menchu: An Indian Woman in Guatemala*, Elisabeth Burgos-Debray, ed., Ann Wright, trans. (London: Verso, 1984).

Chapter 2

1. American Psychiatric Association, *Diagnostic and Statistical Manual of Mental Disorders*, 3d ed., rev. (Washington, D.C.: American Psychiatric Association, 1987), pp. 345–46.

2. David Harris Underhill and Francis Jay Underhill, comp., *The Underhill Burying Ground* (New York: Hine Publishing Co., 1926), plate after p. 81.

3. There are several inadequate treatments of Underhill, including Henry C. Shelley, *John Underhill: Captain of New England and New Netherland* (New York: D. Appleton and Co., 1932); and L. Effingham De Forest and Anne Lawrence De Forest, *Captain John Underhill: Gentleman-Soldier of Fortune* (New York: De Forest Publishing Co., 1934). Brief biographies can also be found in the *Dictionary of American Biography* and *Who Was Who in America*.

4. William H. McNeill, *The Pursuit of Power: Technology, Armed Force and Society since A.D. 1000* (Chicago: University of Chicago Press, 1982), p. 126.

5. John E. Ferling, *A Wilderness of Miseries: War and Warriors in Early America* (Westport, Conn.: Greenwood Press, 1980), p. 46; Simmons, "Cultural Bias," 56–72; Adam Hirsch, "The Collision of Military Cultures in Seventeenth Century New

England," *Journal of American History* 74 (March 1988): 1206. Drinnon, *Facing West*, pp. 35–49; Richard Slotkin, *Regeneration through Violence: The Mythology of the American Frontier, 1600–1860* (Middletown, Conn.: Wesleyan University Press, 1973), pp. 69–78. For the Pequots, see Hauptman and Wherry, *Pequots in Southern New England*.

6. For the best scholarly accounts of the war, see this book Chapter 1, footnote 12.

7. John Underhill's account, "Newes from America," as well as Captain John Mason's *Brief History of the Pequot War*, Philip Vincent's *A True Relation of the Late Battell Fought in New England*, and Lion Gardiner's *Relation of the Pequot War* are conveniently found together in Orr, *History of the Pequot War*. These are the four major primary accounts of the Pequot War.

8. Underhill's "Newes from America," in Orr, *History of the Pequot War*, pp. 47–92. See also n. 5.

9. Laurence M. Hauptman, "The Pequot War and Its Legacies," in Hauptman and Wherry, *Pequots in Southern New England*, pp. 69–80.

10. Hirsch, "Collision of Military Cultures," 1205. Ferling, *Wilderness of Miseries*, p. 8.

11. Allen W. Trelease, *Indian Affairs in Colonial New York: The Seventeenth Century* (Ithaca, N.Y.: Cornell University Press, 1960; repr. Port Washington, N.Y.: Ira J. Friedman Division of Kenikat Press, 1971), pp. 60–84.

12. Arnold J. F. Van Laer, trans., and Kenneth Scott and Kenn Stryker-Rodda, eds., *New York Historial Manuscripts: Dutch* (Baltimore: Genealogical Publishing Co., under direction of the Holland Society, 1974), 2: 9–10; 4: 59.

13. Trelease, *Indian Affairs in Colonial New York*, pp. 79–80. "Journal of New Netherland," in *Documentary History of the State of New York*, ed. E. B. O'Callaghan (Albany, N.Y.: Charles Van Benthuysen, 1851), 4: 1–17.

14. "Journal of New Netherland," 17. This account indicates that as many as seven hundred Indians perished. Governor John Winthrop claimed that Underhill was involved in the killing of four hundred Indians in the two attacks. See James Kendall Hosmer, ed., *Winthrop's Journal* (New York: Charles Scribner's Sons, 1908; repr., New York: Barnes and Noble, 1959), 2: 161. It should be pointed out that the use of fire in war was a common strategy in the seventeenth century. The American Psychiatric Association has determined that the setting of fires by youths under fifteen years of age is symptomatic of antisocial personality disorder. Unfortunately, we do not have enough documentation on Underhill's youth to draw any conclusions here. American Psychiatric Association, *Diagnostic and Statistic Manual*, p. 345.

15. Van Laer et al., *New York Historical Manuscripts: Dutch*, 4: 216.

16. Ibid., p. 265.

17. De Forest and De Forest, *Captain John Underhill*, pp. 79–80.

18. Ibid., pp. 85–87; Myron H. Luke, "Captain John Underhill and Long Island," *Nassau County Historical Journal* 24 (Winter 1964): 9–10.

19. See Emery Battis, *Saints and Sectaries: Anne Hutchinson and the Antinomian Crisis in the Massachusetts Bay Colony* (Chapel Hill: University of North Carolina Press, 1962), chap. 17; David D. Hall, ed., *The Antinomian Controversy, 1636–1638: A Documentary History* (Middletown, Conn.: Wesleyan University Press, 1968).

20. Jere R. Daniel, *Colonial New Hampshire: A History* (Millwood, N.Y.: KTO Press, 1981), p. 34.

21. Quoted in Battis, *Saints and Sectaries*, pp. 210–11.

22. Hosmer, *Winthrop's Journal*, 1: 277, n. 1.

23. Ibid., 1: 276–77.

24. Charles Francis Adams, *Three Episodes of Massachusetts History*, rev. ed. (repr., New York: Russell and Russell, 1965), 2: 555.

25. Hosmer, *Winthrop's Journal*, 2: 27–28; Nathaniel Bouton, comp. and ed., *Provincial Papers: Documents and Records Relating to the Province of New Hampshire...* (Concord, N.H.: George E. Jenks, 1867), 1: 110–31.

26. Van Laer et al., *New York Historical Manuscripts: Dutch*, 2: 205–7.

27. Ibid., 4: 219, 307, 336, 352.

28. Oliver A. Rink, *Holland on the Hudson: An Economic and Social History of Dutch New York* (Ithaca, N.Y.: Cornell University Press, 1986), pp. 251–52, 255. See also Edmund B. O'Callaghan, Ed., *Documents Relative to the Colonial History of the State of New York* (Albany, N.Y.: Weed, Parsons, 1858), 2: 151–52.

29. J. Franklin Jameson, ed., *Narratives of New Netherland, 1609–1664* (New York: Charles Scribner's Sons, 1908; repr., New York: Barnes and Noble, 1967), p. 282, n. 2.

Chapter 3

1. Although badly in need of revision, the best biography of James Wilson is still Charles Page Smith, *James Wilson: Founding Father, 1742–1798* (Chapel Hill: Institute of Early American History and Culture, University of North Carolina Press, 1956). See also Geoffrey Seed, *James Wilson* (Millwood, N.Y.: KTO Press, 1978). For the most complete collection of Wilson's published writings, see Robert G. McCloskey, ed., *The Works of James Wilson* (Cambridge, Mass.: Belknap Press of Harvard University Press, 1967), 2 vols., which contains a lengthy introduction on Wilson, his life and writings. Recently, Stephen A. Conrad, Associate Professor of Law at the University of Indiana School of Law, has revived interest in Wilson with his excellent scholarship: "Metaphor and Imagination in James Wilson's Theory of Federal Union," *Law and Social Inquiry* 13 (1988): 1–70; "James Wilson's 'Assimilation of the Common-Law Mind,'" *Northwestern University Law Review* 84 (Fall 1989): 186–219; "Wilson, James," in *The Oxford Companion to the Supreme Court of the United States*, ed. Kermit Hall et al. (New York: Oxford University Press, 1992), pp. 932–33. I have also found the following helpful: George M. Dennison, "Revolutionary Principle: Ideology and the Constitution in the Thought of James Wilson," *Review of Politics* 39 (April 1977): 157–91.

2. Donald A. Grinde, Jr. and Bruce E. Johansen, *Exemplar of Liberty: Native America and the Evolution of Democracy* (Los Angeles: American Indian Studies Center of UCLA, 1991); see also Grinde, "Iroquois Political Theory and the Roots of American Democracy," in *Exiled in the Land of the Free: Democracy, Indian Nations and the U.S. Constitution*, ed. Oren Lyons et al. (Santa Fe, N.M.: Clear Light Publishers, 1992); and Grinde, "The Iroquois and the Nature of American Government," *American Indian Culture and Research Journal* 17 (1993): 153–73. Wilson is curiously not mentioned in earlier studies of supposed Iroquoian influences on the Founding Fathers. See Grinde, *The Iroquois and the Founding of the American Nation* (San Francisco: Indian Historian Press, 1977); and Johansen, *Forgotten Founders: How the American Indian Helped Shape Democracy* (Harvard and Boston, Mass.: Harvard Common Press, 1982). Other academic proponents of this view include Jack

Weatherford, *Indian Givers: How the Indians of the Americas Transformed the World* (New York: Fawcett Columbine, 1988), pp. 133–50; and Gregory Schaaf, *Wampum Belt and Peace Trees: George Morgan, Native Americans, and Revolutionary Diplomacy* (Golden, Colo.: Fulcrum Publishing Co., 1990). For a critique of this view, see Elisabeth Tooker, "The United States Constitution and the Iroquois League," *Ethnohistory* 35 (Fall 1988): 305–66. For a defense of Grinde and Johansen's writings, see Wilbur R. Jacobs, "Commentary: The American Indian Legacy of Freedom and Liberty," *American Indian Culture and Research Journal* 16:4 (1992): 185–93. For the so-called debate, see Bruce E. Johansen's "Commentary" and Elisabeth Tooker's "Rejoinder," in: *Ethnohistory* 37 (Summer 1990): 179–97. There is twice as much popular literature on the subject, which is too voluminous to cite.

3. Grinde and Johansen, *Exemplar for Liberty,* p. xxii.

4. Ibid., p. xxiv.

5. Ibid.

6. Ibid., pp. 131–32, 207–8, 210.

7. See, for example, ibid., pp. 195–96. Grinde, "Iroquois Political Theory," 265, 267, 380, n. 45; and his "Iroquois and the Nature of American Government," 154, 167–68, n. 6.

8. Conrad, "Metaphor and Imagination," 17.

9. Ibid., 6, 16–22, 28. See also Henry F. May, *The Enlightenment in America* (New York: Oxford University Press, 1976), pp. 205–7.

10. Conrad, "Metaphor and Imagination," 6.

11. Ibid., 18.

12. Ibid., 22.

13. Smith, *James Wilson,* pp. 3–61; Milton E. Flower, *John Dickinson: Conservative Revolutionary* (Charlottesville: University Press of Virginia, 1983), p. 61. Wilson was seen as Dickinson's protégé. See John Adams to Abigail Adams, July 23, 1775, in Peter H. Smith, ed., *Letters of Delegates to Congress, 1774–1789* (Washington, D.C.: Library of Congress, 1976), 1: 648–49.

14. McCloskey, *Works of James Wilson,* 2: 715.

15. Ibid., 2: 857–75 (index).

16. Ibid., 1: 100–102; Conrad, "James Wilson's 'Assimilation,'" 186–219; Dennison, "Revolutionary Principle," 179. John V. Jezierski, "Parliament or People: James Wilson and Blackstone on the Nature and Location of Sovereignty," *Journal of the History of Ideas* 32 (January–March 1971): 94–106; Robert G. McCloskey, "James Wilson," in *The Justices of the United States Supreme Court, 1789–1969: Their Lives and Major Opinions,* ed. Leon Friedman and Fred L. Israel (New York: Chelsea House Publishers, 1969), 1: 91–92. Michael Kammen, *Sovereignty and Liberty: Constitutional Discourse in American Culture* (Madison: University of Wisconsin Press, 1988), pp. 73–76.

17. Dennison, "Revolutionary Principle," 159–161. See also n. 16.

18. According to Marquis de Chastellux, Wilson consulted both Montesquieu and Chancellor d'Aguesseau every day. Marquis de Chastellux, *Travels in America in the Years 1780, 1781, and 1782,* ed. and trans. Howard C. Rice (Chapel Hill: University of North Carolina Press, 1963), pp. 143–44. Paul M. Spurlin, *Montesquieu in America, 1760–1801* (Baton Rouge: Louisiana State University Press, 1940), p. 91;

Conrad, "James Wilson's 'Assimilation,' " 204–9. See also Forrest McDonald, *Novus Ordo Seclorum: The Intellectual Origins of the United States Constitution* (Lawrence: University Press of Kansas, 1985), pp. 7, 81–85.

19. Peter S. Onuf, *The Origins of the Federal Republic: Jurisdictional Controversies in the United States, 1775–1787* (Philadelphia: University of Pennsylvania Press, 1983), p. 205.

20. Quoted in ibid.

21. Quoted in ibid., p. 195.

22. Dennison, "Revolutionary Principle," 187. For Wilson's conservatism as well as his associates in Pennsylvania, see Robert L. Brunhouse, *The Counter-Revolution in Pennsylvania, 1776–1790* (Philadelphia: University of Pennsylvania Press, 1942).

23. Smith, *James Wilson*, p. 72.

24. Ibid., pp. 69–72; James Wilson to John Montgomery, Aug. 24, 1775, in Smith, *Letters of Delegates to Congress*, 1: 706.

25. Smith, *James Wilson*, pp. 71–72. Randolph C. Downes insists that Americans did not foment these jealousies. *Council Fires on the Upper Ohio: A Narrative of Indian Affairs in the Upper Ohio Valley until 1795* (Pittsburgh: University of Pittsburgh Press, 1940; repr., 1968), pp. 184–85.

26. Grinde, "Iroquois Political Theory," 389, n. 171.

27. James Wilson to John Montgomery, July 16, 1775, in Smith, *Letters of Delegates to Congress*, 1: 628–30.

28. Worthington C. Ford, ed., *Journals of the Continental Congress* (Washington, D.C.: U.S.G.P.O., 1906), 6: 1078–79.

29. Charles Thompson's Notes of Debates, July 24, 1777, in Smith, *Letters of Delegates to Congress*, 7: 371–72, n. 1.

30. McCloskey, *Works of James Wilson*, 1: 158–59.

31. Seed, *James Wilson*, p. 35.

32. James Wilson, *On the Improvement and Settlement of Lands in the United States* (Philadelphia: Library Company of Philadelphia, 1946).

33. McDonald, *Novus Ordo Seclorum*, p. 220.

34. Fitzsimmons was Morris's partner in his land dealings. For their roles, see Barbara A. Chernow, "Robert Morris: Genesee Land Speculator," *New York History* 58 (April 1977): 195–245. Morris was known as the "greater Eater with a big Belly" to the Iroquois by the 1790s. Anthony F. C. Wallace, *The Death and Rebirth of the Seneca* (New York: Random House, 1969), p. 181. In 1788, Gorham and his partner Oliver Phelps, an experienced speculator, purchased from Massachusetts the preemptive rights to a vast area in Seneca country. Phelps and Gorham subsequently purchased 2,600,000 acres of Indian lands in 1788 and 1789. They not only had to extinguish Indian title, but had to deal with the conflicting claims of competing land companies, which thirsted after reselling these Indian lands at a significantly marked-up price. Robert Morris began purchasing lands from Phelps and Gorham as early as 1790. Barbara Graymont, "New York State Indian Policy after the Revolution," *New York History* 57 (October 1976), 458. Unlike Morris and Wilson, Washington's land-jobbing paid off and he died a wealthy man. He and his friend and attorney, George Clinton, the governor of New York, invested in several thousand acres of Mohawk Valley lands. John C. Fitzpatrick, *George Washington Himself* (Indianapolis: Bobbs-

Merrill, 1933), pp. 428–29; James Flexner, *George Washington and the New Nation* (Boston: Little Brown, 1969), pp. 55–62, 258–65, 301. For Wilson, see the discussion and footnotes that follow.

35. See Grinde and Johansen, *Exemplar of Liberty;* Johansen, *Forgotten Founders;* Grinde, *Iroquois.* George Morgan, one of the "suffering traders" who helped perpetrate the fraud against the Indians at the Treaty of Fort Stanwix (1768), is even presented as their true friend! See Schaaf, *Wampum Belts and Peace Trees.* See n. 39.

36. Laurence M. Hauptman, *Formulating American Indian Policy in New York State, 1970–1986* (Albany: State University of New York Press, 1988), pp. 4–9; Jack Campisi, "From Fort Stanwix to Canandaigua: National Policy, States' Rights and Indian Land," in *Iroquois Land Claims,* ed. Christopher Vecsey and William A. Starna (Syracuse, N.Y.: Syracuse University Press, 1988), pp. 49–65.

37. Reginald Horsman, *The Frontier in the Formative Years, 1783–1815* (New York: Holt, Rinehart and Winston, 1970), pp. 30–31.

38. McDonald, *Novus Ordo Seclorum,* p. 221. I disagree with McDonald's point. See Merrill E. Jensen, *The Articles of Confederation: An Interpretation of the Social-Constitutional History of the American Revolution* (Madison: University of Wisconsin Press, 1940), pp. 198–224; and Jensen's two articles: "The Cession of the Old Northwest," *Mississippi Valley Historical Review* 23 (1936): 27–48; "The Creation of the National Domain," *Mississippi Valley Historical Review* 26 (1939): 323–42; and Onuf, *The Origins of the Federal Republic,* pp. 193–208; and Onuf's "Toward Federalism: Virginia, Congress, and the Western Lands," *William and Mary Quarterly,* 3d ser., 39 (1977): 353–74. Thomas P. Abernethy, *Western Lands and the American Revolution* (Charlottesville: University of Virginia Institute in the Social Sciences, 1937; repr., New York: Russell and Russell, 1959).

39. Ray Allen Billington, "The Fort Stanwix Treaty of 1768," *New York History* 42 (1944): 182–94.

40. Forrest McDonald, *We the People: The Economic Origins of the Constitution* (Chicago: University of Chicago Press, 1958), pp. 28, 57; Charles Beard, *An Economic Interpretation of the Constitution of the United States* (New York: Columbia University Press, 1913; repr., New York: Macmillan, 1939), p. 147; Jacob R. Marcus, *United States Jewry, 1776–1985* (Detroit: Wayne State University Press, 1989), 1: 168–69; McCloskey, *Works of James Wilson,* 1: 18; McCloskey, "James Wilson," 83–86; Smith, *James Wilson,* pp. 73, 99, 134, 136, 202, 305.

41. Smith, *James Wilson,* pp. 129–39.

42. Ibid., pp. 159–68; Jensen, *Articles of Confederation,* 154; Seed, *James Wilson,* pp. 35, 161–63, 175–76; Onuf, *Origins of the Federal Republic,* pp. 78–79; Shaw Livermore, *Early American Land Companies: Their Influence on Corporate Development* (Cambridge, Mass.: Harvard University Press, 1939; repr., New York: Octagon Books, 1966), p. 110.

43. McCloskey, *Works of James Wilson,* 1: 19.

44. Smith, *James Wilson,* pp. 161–62; Lawrence Bothwell, ed., *Broome County Heritage: An Illustrated History* (Woodland Hills, Calif.: Windsor Publications, in cooperation with the Broome County Historical Society, 1983), pp. 20–27; William F. Seward, *Binghamton and Broome County, New York: A History* (New York: Lewis Publishing Company, 1924), 1: 27–28; J. B. Wilkinson, *The Annals of Binghamton and of the Country Connected with It* (Binghamton, N.Y.: Times Association, 1872),

pp. 11–12, 77–78. Marjory H. Hinman, *Onaquaga: Hub of the Border War* (Windsor, N.Y.: privately printed, 1975), pp. 94–99; and Hinman's *The Creation of Broome County, New York* (Windsor, N.Y.: privately printed, 1981), pp. 4–7; Gerald R. Smith, *The Valley of Opportunity: A Pictorial History of the Greater Binghamton Area* (Norfolk, Va.: Donning Company, in cooperation with the Broome County Historical Society, 1988), pp. 21–22. For what befell the Oneida, see Graymont, "New York State Indian Policy," 438–74; and, especially, Jack Campisi, "The Oneida Treaty Period, 1783–1838," in Campisi and Hauptman, eds., *The Oneida Indian Experience: Two Perspectives,* (Syracuse, N.Y.: Syracuse University Press, 1988), pp. 48–64.

45. Paul D. Evans, *The Holland Land Company* (Buffalo, N.Y.: Buffalo Historical Society, 1924), pp. 4–7, 11, 31–37, 87–90, 107–11, 124, 160; Elizabeth K. Henderson, "The Northwestern Lands of Pennsylvania, 1790–1812," *Pennsylvania Magazine of History and Biography* 60 (April 1936): 130–60; William Chazanof, *Joseph Ellicott and the Holland Land Company* (Syracuse, N.Y.: Syracuse University Press, 1970), pp. 16–27; Barbara A. Chernow, "Robert Morris: Land Speculator, 1790–1801" (Ph.D. diss., Columbia University, 1974); and Chernow's article, "Robert Morris: Genesee Land Speculator." Graymont, "New York State Indian Policy"; Wallace, *Death and Rebirth of the Seneca,* pp. 179–83, 214–18; Norman B. Wilkinson, "Robert Morris and the Treaty of Big Tree," *Mississippi Valley Historical Review* 60 (1953): 257–78; Smith, *James Wilson,* pp. 167, 375, 389. The Dutch investors achieved a 5 to 6 percent profit, a significantly higher return than could be realized through government securities in the Netherlands at that time period.

46. May, *Enlightenment in America,* p. 206.

Chapter 4

1. Francis Paul Prucha, "Andrew Jackson's Indian Policy: A Reassessment," *Journal of American History,* LVI (December, 1969), 527–39; and his *The Great Father: The United States Government and the American Indians* (Lincoln, Neb.: University of Nebraska Press, 1984), I, 191–269. The best overall treatment of United States Indian policies during the Age of Jackson still is Ronald N. Satz, *American Indian Policy in the Jacksonian Era* (Lincoln, Neb.: University of Nebraska Press, 1975). For one major case study, see Michael D. Green, *The Politics of Indian Removal: Creek Government and Society in Crisis* (Lincoln, Neb.: University of Nebraska Press, 1982). For the more positive side of missionary involvement, see William G. McLoughlin's excellent *Cherokees and Missionaries, 1789–1839* (New Haven: Yale University Press, 1984). Two other books written by McLoughlin in his trilogy on the Cherokee are also helpful: *Cherokee Renascence in the New Republic* (Princeton, N.J.: Princeton University Press, 1986) and *Champions of the Cherokee: Evan and John B. Jones* (Princeton, N.J.: Princeton University Press, 1990). Unfortunately, there are no similar major detailed historical book-length studies of the Indians of the Northeast in the same period.

2. Robert V. Remini, *Andrew Jackson and the Course of American Democracy, 1833–1845* (New York: Harper & Row, 1984), p. 314.

3. Robert V. Remini, *The Life of Andrew Jackson* (New York: Harper & Row, 1988; paperback edition, New York: Penguin Books, 1990), p. 215.

4. Robert V. Remini, *The Legacy of Andrew Jackson: Essays on Democracy, Indian*

Removal and Slavery (Baton Rouge: Louisiana University Press, 1988), pp. 4–5, 81–82.

5. Robert V. Remini, *The Jacksonian Era* (Arlington Heights, Ill.: Harlan Davidson, Inc., 1989), p. 52.

6. The best analysis of Schermerhorn's career is James W. Van Hoeven, "Salvation and Indian Removal: The Career Biography of Rev. John Freeman Schermerhorn, Indian Commissioner" (unpublished Ph.D. dissertation, Nashville, Tenn.: Vanderbilt University, 1972), pp. 8–9, 104–5.

7. Gary Moulton, ed., *The Papers of Chief John Ross* (Norman, Okla.: University of Oklahoma Press, 1985), I, 573–74.

8. Maris Pierce Speech of July 4, 1838, Maris Pierce Mss., Buffalo and Erie County Historical Society, Buffalo.

9. Van Hoeven, "Salvation and Indian Removal," pp. 98–105.

10. *Ibid.*, p. 105.

11. *Ibid.*, pp. 106–23, 239, 262–64.

12. *Ibid.*, pp. 113–15. See also Francis Paul Prucha, "Thomas L. McKenney and the New York Indian Board," *Mississippi Valley Historical Review* 48 (March, 1962), 635–55.

13. Prucha, "Thomas L. McKenney and the New York Indian Board," 651–52.

14. Van Hoeven, "Salvation and Indian Removal," pp. 118–23. For Schermerhorn's involvement with the Miamis, see Robert A. Trennert, Jr., *Indian Traders on the Middle Borders: The House of Ewing, 1827–1854* (Lincoln, Neb.: University of Nebraska Press, 1981), pp. 45–49; and Bert Anson, *The Miami Indians* (Norman, Okla.: University of Oklahoma Press, 1970), pp. 197–98.

15. Van Hoeven, "Salvation and Indian Removal," pp. 138, 150.

16. For the Second Seminole War see James Covington, *The Seminoles of Florida* (Gainesville, Fla.: University Press of Florida, 1993), pp. 64, 72–109; Edwin C. McReynolds, *The Seminoles* (Norman, Okla.: University of Oklahoma Press, 1957), pp. 118–242; and John K. Mahon, *History of the Second Seminole War, 1835–1842* (Gainesville, Fla.: University of Florida Press, 1967). See also Mahon, "Two Seminole Treaties: Payne's Landing, 1832, and Ft. Gibson, 1833," *Florida Historical Quarterly* 41 (July 1962), 1–21.

17. Van Hoeven, "Salvation and Indian Removal," pp. 138, 150.

18. *Ibid.*, pp. 205–6. See also Gary E. Moulton, *John Ross: Cherokee Chief* (Athens, Ga.: University of Georgia Press, 1978), pp. 67–86. The historian Ralph Gabriel has gone so far as to describe Schermerhorn as "the sanctimonious glove concealing the fist of that uncompromising hater of Indians, Andrew Jackson." Gabriel, *Elias Boudinot, Cherokee, and His America* (Norman, Okla.: University of Oklahoma Press, 1941), p. 145.

19. Moulton, *John Ross*, pp. 67–68.

20. John G. Burnett, "The Cherokee Removal Through the Eyes of a Private Soldier," *Journal of Cherokee Studies* 3 (1978): 180–85.

21. Remini, *Andrew Jackson and the Course of American Democracy*, pp. 295–97.

22. John F. Schermerhorn to Andrew Jackson, Oct. 29, 1836, OIA, M234, Microfilm Reel 583, RG 75, NA; Satz, *American Indian Policy in the Jacksonian Era*, 51–56.

23. Schermerhorn to (Commissioner of Indian Affairs) Herring, May 5, 1836; Schermerhorn to Indian Office, July 12, 1836, Jan. 10, 1837, OIA, M234, Microfilm Reel 583, RG 75, NA.

24. Schermerhorn to Jackson, Oct. 29, 1836, OIA, M234, Microfilm Reel 583, RG 75, NA.

25. Schermerhorn to C. A. Harris (new Commissioner of Indian Affairs), Oct. 27, 1836, OIA, M234, Microfilm Reel 583, RG 75, NA.

26. Report of Exploring Party to the President of the United States, Aug. 5, 1837, OIA, M234, Microfilm Reel 583, RG 75, NA; Report of Exploring Party, Dec. 26, 1837; and "List of Expenses Advanced by Schermerhorn to... Exploring Party Indians," June 14, 1838, OIA, M234, Microfilm Reel 583, RG 75, NA.

27. Report of Exploring Party to the President of the United States, Aug. 5, 1837, OIA, M234, Microfilm Reel 583, RG 75, NA; Report of Exploring Party, Dec. 26, 1837; and "List of Expenses Advanced by Schermerhorn to... Exploring Party Indians," June 14, 1838, OIA, M234, Microfilm Reel 583, RG 75, NA.

28. For Stryker's shady dealings, see Henry S. Manley, "Buying Buffalo from the Indians," *New York History* 27 (July 1947): 313–29.

29. Stryker to Joel R. Poinsett, Sept. 9, 1837, with Report of the Exploring Party to the President of the United States, Aug. 5, 1837, OIA, M234, Microfilm Reel 583, RG 75, NA.

30. Stryker to Poinsett, Sept. 9, 1837; Stryker to C. A. Harris, Oct. 11, Nov. 17 and 27, 1837; Thomas Ludlow Ogden to C. A. Harris, Dec. 4, 1837, OIA, M234, Microfilm Reel 583, RG 75, NA.

31. (Protest of) Seneca Chief (Big Kettle, et al.) to President of the United States, Oct. 16, 1837, OIA, M234, Microfilm Reel 583, RG 75, NA. See also (Protest of) Oneida Chiefs (Moses Schuyler, et al.) to Our Father the President of the United States, Aug. 17, 1837; and (Protest of) Onondaga Chiefs (Captain Frost, Abraham La Fort, et al.) to Great Father, Aug. 11, 1837, OIA, M234, Microfilm Reel 583.

32. Charles J. Kappler, Comp., *Indian Treaties, 1778–1883* (New York, 1970), p. 505 (originally published as *Indian Affairs: Laws and Treaties,* II, Washington, D.C.: U.S.G.P.O. 1903).

33. Van Hoeven, "Salvation and Indian Removal," 264–65.

34. Stryker to Commissioner Harris, Nov. 17, 1837, OIA, M234, Microfilm Reel 583, RG 75, NA.

35. Schermerhorn to Commissioner of Indian Affairs, Nov. 29, 1837, OIA, M234, Microfilm Reel 583, RG 75, NA.

36. Manley, "Buying Buffalo from the Indians," 313–29.

37. Kappler, *Indian Treaties,* pp. 502–16.

38. Manley, "Buying Buffalo from the Indians," 313–29; Jack Campisi, "Consequences of the Kansas Claims to Oneida Tribal Identity." In: *Proceedings* of the First Congress, Canadian Ethnology Society. Jerome H. Barkow, ed., (Canada) National Museum of Man Ethnology Division, Mercury Series Paper 17 (Ottawa, 1974), pp. 35–47. Thomas S. Abler, "Factional Dispute and Party Conflict in the Political System of the Seneca Nation" (unpublished Ph.D. dissertation, Toronto: University of Toronto, 1969), pp. 91–104; and Abler's "Friends, Factions, and the Seneca Revolution of 1848," *Niagara Frontier* 21 (Winter, 1974): 74–79; George Abrams, *The Seneca People* (Phoenix: Indian Tribal Series, 1976), pp. 56–90.

39. Alexis de Tocqueville, *Democracy in America* (1831; Paperback reprint, New York: Vintage), I, 353–54.

Chapter 5

1. For Native Americans in the Civil War, see Annie Heloise Abel, *The American Indian as Slaveholder and Secessionist* (Cleveland: Arthur H. Clark, 1915); *The American Indian as Participant in the Civil War* (Cleveland: Arthur H. Clark, 1919); and *The American Indian Under Reconstruction* (Cleveland: Arthur H. Clark, 1925). These volumes were reprinted in paperback edition in 1992 and 1993 by the University of Nebraska Press. Alvin M. Josephy, Jr., *The Civil War in American West* (New York: Knopf, 1991). Hauptman, *The Iroquois in the Civil War;* and W. McKee Evans, *To Die Game: The Story of the Lowry Band, Indian Guerrillas of Reconstruction* (Baton Rouge, La.: Louisiana State University, 1971); William H. Armstrong, *Warrior in Two Camps: Ely S. Parker, Union General and Seneca Chief* (Syracuse, N.Y.: Syracuse University Press, 1978) Kenny A. Franks, *Stand Watie and the Agony of the Cherokee Nation* (Memphis, Tenn.: Memphis State University Press, 1979); W. David Baird, ed., *A Creek Warrior for the Confederacy: The Autobiography of Chief G. W. Grayson* (Norman, Okla.: University of Oklahoma Press, 1988); E. Stanley Godbold, Jr. and Mattie U. Russell, *Confederate Colonel and Cherokee Chief: The Life of William Holland Thomas* (Knoxville, Tenn.: University of Tennessee Press, 1990); W. Craig Gaines, *The Confederate Cherokees: John Drew's Regiment of Mounted Rifles* (Baton Rouge, La.: Louisiana State University Press, 1989); Edward J. Danziger, Jr., *Indians and Bureaucrats: Administering the Reservation Policy During the Civil War* (Urbana, Ill.: University of Illinois Press, 1974); David A. Nichols, *Lincoln and the Indians: Civil War Policy and Politics* (Columbia, Mo.: University of Missouri Press, 1978). I am currently writing a book on Native Americans in the Civil War, *Between Two Fires: The Tragedy of American Indians in the Civil War* (New York: The Free Press), forthcoming 1995.
2. "Samuel Patterson Entry," Records of the Town of Salamanca, Cattaraugus County, New York, Town Clerk's Registers of Officers, Soldiers, and Seamen, 13774-83, D359/1, Box 6, Records of the Division of Military and Naval Affairs, New York State Archives, Albany.
3. See photographs on p. 52.
4. The Seneca protests can be found in: Seneca Residing at Cattaraugus Petition to Abraham Lincoln, June 4, 1864; and Samuel George to William Dole, July 5, 1864, New York Agency Records, OIA, M234, MR590, RG75, NA. For a detailed analysis of the results, see Hauptman, *The Iroquois and the Civil War,* pp. 108-111, 170-71 n 19-25.
5. H. Craig Miner and William E. Unrau, *The End of Indian Kansas: A Study of Cultural Revolution, 1854-1871* (Lawrence, Kan.: Regents Press of Kansas, 1978; see also Edwin C. McReynolds, *The Seminoles* (Norman, Okla.: University of Oklahoma Press, 1957), pp. 289-330; Covington, *The Seminoles of Florida,* pp. 128-44. Hauptman, *The Iroquois in the Civil War,* p. 13; and my "Samuel George (1795-1873): A Study of Onondaga Conservatism," *New York History* 70 (Jan. 1989): 4-22.
6. Minnie Dobbs Millbrook, "Indian Sharpshooters," in: *Twice Told Tales of Michigan and Her Soldiers in the Civil War,* Michigan Civil War Centennial Observance Commission, ed. (East Lansing, 1966), p. 46.
7. For a published muster roll and history of the unit, see Michigan Adjutant General's

Office, *Record of Service of Michigan Volunteers in the Civil War, 1861–1865* (Kala-mazoo, Mich.: Ihling Bros. & Evard, 1905), XLIV, 1–100; see also James Robertson, Comp., *Michigan Men in the War* (Lansing, Mich.: W.S. George and Co., 1882), pp. 69, 542–53, 748–75.

8. Millbrook, "Indian Sharpshooters," p. 47.

9. For the best secondary accounts on the siege at Petersburg, see Richard Sommers, *Richmond Redeemed: The Siege at Petersburg* (Garden City, N.Y.: Doubleday and Co., 1981); and Noah Andre Trudeau, *The Last Citadel: Petersburg, Virginia, June 1864–April 1865* (Boston: Little, Brown and Co., 1991). For a brief but fine sum-mary of the campaign, see Christopher M. Calkins, "The Petersburg Campaign and Siege," in *The Civil War Battlefield Guide,* Frances H. Kennedy, ed. (Boston: Houghton Mifflin Co., 1990), pp. 251–57. The literature of the Battle of the Crater is immense. For the official War Department inquiry, see United States War De-partment, *The War of the Rebellion: A Compilation of the Official Records of the Union and Confederate Armies* (Washington, D.C.: U.S.G.P.O., 1899), ser. I, vol. XL, Part I. [Hereafter cited as *OR.*] See also Charles H. Houghton, "In the Crater," in *Battles and Leaders of the Civil War,* Clarence C. Buel and Robert U. Johnson, eds. (New York: Century Magazine, 1888; reprint, New York: Thomas Yoseloff, 1956), IV, 561–62; William H. Powell, "The Battle of the Petersburg Crater," in *Battles and Leaders of the Civil War,* IV, 545–60; Henry G. Thomas, "The Colored Troops at Petersburg," in *Battles and Leaders of the Civil War,* IV, 563–67.

10. Millbrook, "Indian Sharpshooters," p. 48.

11. Quoted in George S. Bernard, ed., *War Talks of Confederate Veterans* (Peters-burg, Va.: Fenn & Owen Publishers, 1892), p. 163. For a fine analysis of western Great Lakes religious practices, including attitudes toward and rituals of death, see Christopher Vecsey, *Traditional Ojibwa Religion and Its Historical Changes* (Phila-delphia: American Philosophical Society, 1983).

12. Michigan Adjutant General's Office, Comp., *Record of Service of Michigan Volun-teers...,* XLIV, 1–100.

13. "Chief Silverheels' Capture," *Warren* [Pa.] *Mail,* Aug. 23, 1887, p. 1. James C. Fitz-patrick, "The Ninth Corps," *New York Herald,* June 30, 1864, p. 1. See also Haupt-man, *The Iroquois in the Civil War,* chapter 1.

14. Austin George, Compiled Military Service Record, F Company, 31st U.S.C.T., RG94, NA; Clinton Mountpleasant, Compiled Military Service Record, F Company, 31st U.S.C.T., RG94, NA. Laurence M. Hauptman, "Fifteen Months of Hell and Thirty Years of Misery: A Mashantucket Pequot Indian in the Civil War," paper presented at the Second Mashantucket Pequot History Conference, October 22, 1993 [paper forthcoming as an article].

15. Joseph T. Glathaar, in his splendid book on these units, never mentions the pres-ence of Native American troops. *Forged in Battle: The Civil War Alliance of Black Troops and White Officers* (New York: Free Press, 1990). In Austin George's pension record, an examining surgeon wrote in 1891: "Is a full blood Indian 'Pequot.' No African blood. Lives alone on reservation." Surgeon's Certificate in the Case of George, Austin, Application for Increase, Sept. 16, 1891, Austin George's Civil War Pension Record, Certificate No. 75324, NA.

16. Douglas Summers Brown, *The Catawba Indians: The People of the River* (Columbia,

S.C.: University of South Carolina Press, 1966), pp. 329–30. I should like to thank Dr. James Merrell of Vassar College for giving me this bibliographic reference.

17. *Ibid.* For the Thomas Legion, see Godbold and Russell, *Confederate Colonel and Cherokee Chief.*

18. John R. Finger, *The Eastern Band of Cherokee, 1819–1900* (Knoxville, Tenn.: University of Tennessee Press, 1984), pp. 82–100.

19. Quoted in Brown, *The Catawba Indians,* p. 330.

20. Charles M. Hudson, *The Catawba Nation* (Athens, Ga.: University of Georgia Press, 1970), pp. 66–67, 109–10. For an excellent award-winning analysis of Catawba history, see James H. Merrell, *The Indians New World: Catawbas and Their Neighbors from European Contact Through the Era of Removal* (New York: W. W. Norton, 1989).

21. Hauptman, *The Iroquois in the Civil War,* chapter 1. See also Barbara Graymont, *The Iroquois in the American Revolution* (Syracuse, N.Y.: Syracuse University Press, 1972); Anthony F. C. Wallace, *The Death and Rebirth of the Seneca* (New York: Knopf, 1970); Thomas S. Abler, Ed., *Chainbreaker: The Revolutionary War Memoirs of Governor Blacksnake as Told to Benjamin Williams* (Lincoln, Neb.: University of Nebraska Press, 1989).

22. Hauptman, *The Iroquois in the Civil War,* chapters 2 and 3. *OR,* ser. I, vol. XXXIII, p. 76. New York State Historian [Hugh Hastings], *2nd Annual Report* (Albany, N.Y., 1897), app. F; R. Emmett Fiske, To Whom It May Concern, Jan. 13, 1865, ACP Branch Document File; 1888: Cornelius C. Cusick, Box 1168, Records of the Adjutant General's Office, Record Group 94, National Archives.

23. Ronald N. Satz, "The Mississippi Choctaw: From the Removal Treaty to the Federal Agency," in *After Removal: The Choctaw in Mississippi,* Samuel J. Wells and Roseanna Tubby, eds. (Jackson, Miss.: University Press of Mississippi, 1986), pp. 17–18.

24. Manley, "Buying Buffalo from the Indians," 313–29; and his "Red Jacket's Last Campaign," *New York History* 31 (April 1950): 149–68.

25. Arthur H. DeRosier, Jr., *The Removal of the Choctaw Indians* (Knoxville, Tenn.: University of Tennessee Press, 1970, pp. 174–84. For more on this dispossession, see Mary E. Young, *Redskins, Ruffleshirts and Rednecks: Indian Allotments in Alabama and Mississippi, 1830–1860* (Norman, Okla.: University of Oklahoma Press, 1961), pp. 22–36, 47–72. For more on the Choctaw in this period, see Wells and Tubby, eds., *After Removal: The Choctaws in Mississippi,* pp. 3–93; and Jesse O. McKee and Jon A. Schlenker, *The Choctaws: Cultural Evolution of a Native American Tribe* (Jackson, Miss.: University Press of Mississippi, 1980). John H. Peterson, Jr., "The Mississippi Band of Choctaw Indians: Their Recent History and Current Social Relations" (unpublished Ph.D. dissertation, Athens, Ga.: University of Georgia, 1970), pp. 10–53; and Peterson, Ed., *A Choctaw Sourcebook* (New York: Garland, 1985); and his "Three Efforts at Development Among the Choctaws of Mississippi," in: *Southeastern Indians Since the Removal Era,* Walter L. Williams, Ed. (Athens, Ga.: University of Georgia Press, 1979), p. 146.

26. W.R. Browne to Thomas J. Portis, April 13, 1863; John A. Davis to Major Memminger, April 12, 1863; Special Order No. 112, May 9, 1863; J.N. Pierce to Secretary of War, May 22, 1863 with notation of June 17, 1863; J.L. Carter to Colonel E.E. Ewell, July 28, 1863, War Department Confederate Records: Muster and Pay Rolls,

Box 227, Folder: 1st Choctaw Battalion, Mississippi Cavalry, Pierce, J.W., RG109, NA. OR, ser. II, vol. V, pp. 734, 742, 752–55. A.J. Brown, *History of Newton County, Mississippi, from 1834–1894* (Jackson, Miss.: Clarion-Ledger Co., 1894), p. 96.

27. There is a dearth of secondary literature on these American Indians. For the Pequot, see Hauptman and Wherry, Eds., *The Pequots in Southern New England*. Melville had resided at nearby New London, Connecticut during part of the writing of his classic. The ship in *Moby Dick* was named the "Pequod."

28. Frances M. Caulkins, *History of Norwich, Connecticut: From Its Possession by the Indians, to the Year 1866* (n.p.: p.p., 1866), p. 405n; Barry O'Connell, Ed., *On Our Own Ground: The Complete Writings of William Apes, A Pequot* (Amherst, Mass.: University of Massachusetts Press, 1992), pp. 26–31.

29. *OR*, ser. III, vol. III, pp. 567–68.

30. Jack Campisi, "The Emergence of the Mashantucket Pequot Tribe, 1637–1975," in: *The Pequots in Southern New England*, pp. 131–33; Mohegan Indian Land Distribution. Report of Commissioners on Distribution of Lands of Mohegan Indians, July 2, 1861. Secretary of State Papers, RG6, Box 15, Connecticut State Archives, Hartford.

31. James P. Baughman, *The Mallorys of Mystic: Six Generations in American Maritime Enterprise* (Middletown, Conn.: Wesleyan University Press, 1972), pp. 100–20; Robert O. Decker, *The Whaling City: A History of New London* (Chester, Conn.: The Pequod Press, 1976), p. 121.

32. Ledyard Town Meeting Records, 1862–1864, Connecticut State Archives, Hartford; W.A. Croffut and John M. Morris, *The Military and Civil History of Connecticut During the War of 1861–1865 . . .* (New York: Ledyard Bill, 1868), p. 460. For the transformation of Connecticut into an arsenal for the Union, see Baughman, *The Mallorys of Mystic*, pp. 100–120; John Niven, *Connecticut for the Union: The Role of the State in the Civil War* (New Haven, Conn.: Yale University Press, 1965), pp. 387–95; Carl C. Cutler, *Mystic: The Story of a Small New England Seaport*, Publications of the Marine Historical Association (Mystic, Conn.), II, no. 4 (Dec. 15, 1945), 153–59; Janice L. Trecker, *Preachers, Rebels and Traders: Connecticut, 1818 to 1865* (Chester, Conn.: The Pequod Press, 1975), p. 77.

33. The best scholarly treatments of the Indians of Virginia are Helen C. Rountree, *The Powhatan Indians of Virginia: Their Traditional Culture* (Norman, Okla.: University of Oklahoma Press, 1989), and her *Pocahontas's People: The Powhatan Indians of Virginia Through Four Centuries* (Norman, Okla.: University of Oklahoma Press, 1990). I should like to thank Professor Rountree of Old Dominion University for aiding me in my research on the Virginia Indians in the Civil War.

34. Rountree, *Pocahontas's People*, pp. 188–98; Theodore Stern, "Chickahominy: The Changing Culture of a Virginia Indian Community," *Proceedings* of the American Philosophical Society 94 (1952): 206; James Mooney, "The Powhatan Confederacy: Past and Present," *American Anthropologist* 9 (1907), 145, 147.

35. For one Pamunkey Indian who served as both a land and river pilot for General McClellan's Army of the Potomac during the Peninsula Campaign, see [William] Terrel [Terrell] Bradby [Bradley], Civil War Pension File, Applic. # 12546, certificate No. 19281, Civil War Pension Records, NA. According to Professor Rountree, Indians Terrell Bradby, Sterling Bradby, John W. Langston, and William Langston aided the Union and were dismissed from membership from the Colosse Baptist Church,

a white-dominated congregation that contained a number of Indians and that was strongly Confederate. Terrill Bradby was later accused of killing his brother Sterling during the war. Helen C. Rountree to Laurence M. Hauptman, March 1, 1993, letter in author's possession.

36. Thornton, *The Cherokee: A Population History*, p. 94.

37. Ibid., pp. 90–96; W. Craig Gaines, *The Confederate Cherokees: John Drew's Regiment of Mounted Rifles* (Baton Rouge, La.: Louisiana State University Press, 1989).

38. Moulton, *John Ross, Cherokee Chief*, pp. 166–96; and Moulton, Ed., *The Papers of John Ross*, II, 429–682; Thurman Wilkins, *Cherokee Tragedy: The Ridge Family and the Decimation of a People*, 2nd ed., rev. (Norman, Okla.: University of Oklahoma Press, 1986); Edward Everett Dale and Gaston Litton, Eds., *Cherokee Cavaliers: Forty Years of Cherokee History as Told in the Correspondence of the Ridge-Watie-Boudinot Family* (Norman, Okla.: University of Oklahoma Press, 1939).

39. Thornton, *The Cherokees: A Population History*, pp. 90–93; Arrell M. Gibson, "Native Americans and the Civil War," *American Indian Quarterly* 9 (1985): 391–94. See Franks, *Stand Watie and the Agony of the Cherokee Nation*.

40. Thornton, *The Cherokees: A Population History*, p. 92.

41. The scholarly literature on these horrors are too extensive to cite in their entirety. For concise summaries, see Josephy, *The Civil War in the American West*, pp. 95–154, 283–87; Robert M. Utley, *The Indian Frontier of the American West, 1846–1890* (Albuquerque, N.M.: University of New Mexico Press, 1984), pp. 65–98; Francis Paul Prucha, *The Great Father: The United States Government and the American Indians* (Lincoln, Neb.: University of Nebraska Press, 1984), I, 417–61; Edmund J. Danziger, Jr., *Indians and Bureaucrats: Administering the Reservation Policy During the Civil War* (Urbana, Ill.: University of Illinois Press, 1974), pp. 48–70, 95–164; and David A. Nichols, *Lincoln and the Indians: Civil War Policy and Politics* (Columbia, Mo.: University of Missouri Press, 1978), pp. 65–128, 161–74.

Chapter 6

1. United States Constitution, Article I, Section 2, Clause 3 and Article I, Section 8, Clause 3.

2. 14 Stat. 27 (1868).

3. United States Constitution, Article I, Section 8, Clause 3.

4. Ibid., Article II, Section 2, Clause 2.

5. Stephen L. Pevar, *The Rights of Indians and Tribes* (New York: Bantam Books, 1983), pp. 210–11.

6. *Harrison v. Laveen*, 67 Ariz. 337 (1948).

7. 7 Stat. 156 (1817); 7 Stat. 195 (1819).

8. 7 Stat. 333 (1830).

9. Arthur DeRosier, Jr., *The Removal of the Choctaw Indians* (Knoxville: University of Tennessee Press, 1970), pp. 123–32.

10. James H. Kettner, *The Development of American Citizenship, 1608–1870* (Chapel Hill: University of North Carolina Press, 1978), p. 293.

11. 10 Stat. 1159 (1855); 12 Stat. 1237 (1862).

12. United States Department of the Interior, *Sixtieth Annual Report of the Commissioner of Indian Affairs to the Secretary of the Interior*, pt. 1 (Washington, D.C.: U.S.G.P.O., 1891), p. 21.

13. *Goodell v. Jackson*, 20 Johns. Rep. 693, 712 (N.Y., 1823).

14. *State ex. rel. Marsh v. Managers of Elections for District of York*, 1 Bailey 215, 216 (S.C., 1829).

15. Evans, *To Die Game*, p. 34; Gerald M. Sider, *Lumbee Indian Histories: Race, Ethnicity, and Indian Identity in the Southern United States* (New York: Cambridge University Press, 1993), pp. 19–23; Karen I. Blu, *The Lumbee Problem: The Making of an American Indian People* (London: Cambridge University Press, 1980), pp. 46–50; John Hope Franklin, *The Free Negro in North Carolina, 1790–1860* (Chapel Hill: University of North Carolina Press, 1943), pp. 63–81. For the humiliating treatment perpetrated on Virginia's Indians, see Helen C. Rountree, "The Indians of Virginia: A Third Race in a Biracial State," in Williams, *Southeastern Indians since the Removal Era*, pp. 40–45; and especially her *Pocahontas's People*, pp. 219–35.

16. *Cherokee Nation v. Georgia*, 5 Pet. 1 (U.S., 1831).

17. *Worcester v. Georgia*, 6 Pet. 515 (U.S., 1832).

18. Kettner, *Development of American Citizenship*, p. 299.

19. Ibid., pp. 299–300.

20. Ibid., p. 300.

21. 7 Op. A.G. (1856). In dictum in the infamous Dred Scott case, Chief Justice Roger Taney appears to have challenged Cushing's view. See *Dred Scott v. Sandford*, 19 Howard 393 (1857). R. A. Lee, "Indian Citizenship and the Fourteenth Amendment," *South Dakota History* 4 (1974): 204–6.

22. Felix S. Cohen, *Handbook of Federal Indian Law* (Washington, D.C.: U.S.G.P.O., 1942; repr., Albuquerque: University of New Mexico Press, 1971), pp. 153–54.

23. Vine Deloria, Jr., and Clifford M. Lytle, *American Indians / American Justice* (Austin: University of Texas Press, 1983), pp. 220–25.

24. United States Constitution, Amendment XIV, Section 1.

25. Lee, "Indian Citizenship and the Fourteenth Amendment," 212.

26. United States Congress. *Senate Report No. 268*. 41st Cong., 3d sess., Dec. 14, 1870, ss no. 1443, p. 11.

27. *McKay v. Campbell*, 16 Fed. Cas. No. 161 (D. Or., 1871).

28. 24 Stat. 388 (1887).

29. Ibid. For the exclusion of the Senecas, see L. M. Hauptman, "Senecas and Subdividers: The Resistance to Allotment of Indian Lands in New York, 1887–1906," *Prologue: The Journal of the National Archives* 9 (1977): 105–16; and Hauptman, "Governor Theodore Roosevelt and the Indians of New York State," *Proceedings of the American Philosophical Society* 119 (1975): 1–7.

30. U.S. Congress, Senate, *Congressional Record*, 49th Cong., 1st sess., 1885 (Washington, D.C.: U.S.G.P.O., 1886), 17, pt. 2, 1632.

31. William T. Hagan, *The Indian Rights Association: The Herbert Welsh Years* (Tucson: University of Arizona Press, 1985), pp. 255–60.

32. Francis Paul Prucha, ed., *Americanizing the American Indian: Writings of 'Friends' of the Indian* (Cambridge, Mass.: Harvard University Press, 1973), p. 164.

33. Michael T. Smith, "The History of Indian Citizenship," *Great Plains Journal* 10 (1970): 30–31.

34. *Elk v. Wilkins*, 112 U.S. 94 (1884).

35. Ibid.

36. Ibid.; see Lee, "Indian Citizenship and the Fourteenth Amendment," 215–19.

37. 26 Stat. 81, 99–100 (1890).
38. Jake Whitecrow, "Dual Citizenship," paper delivered at the Ninth Eastern Regional Conference on the Native American, SUNY/New Paltz, May 4, 1980; Deloria and Lytle, *American Indians / American Justice*, p. 223.
39. 34 Stat. 182 (1906).
40. Smith, "History of Indian Citizenship," 33.
41. Hazel W. Hertzberg, *The Search for an American Indian Identity: Modern Pan-Indian Movements* (Syracuse, N.Y.: Syracuse University Press, 1971), p. 184.
42. Quoted in Ibid., p. 187.
43. 41 Stat. 350 (1919).
44. Deloria and Lytle, *American Indians / American Justice*, 221.
45. Laurence M. Hauptman, Iroquois Field Notes, 1971–1987. See Hauptman, *The Iroquois and the New Deal* (Syracuse, N.Y.: Syracuse University Press, 1981), chapter 1; Barbara Graymont, ed., *Fighting Tuscarora: The Autobiography of Chief Clinton Rickard* (Syracuse, N.Y.: Syracuse University Press, 1973), p. 53.
46. 43 Stat. 253 (1924).
47. Ibid.
48. Gary C. Stein, "The Indian Citizenship Act of 1924," *New Mexico Historical Review* 47 (1972): 268.
49. Ibid., p. 266.
50. Ibid., p. 258.
51. Graymont, *Fighting Tuscarora*, p. 53.
52. Laurence M. Hauptman, *Iroquois Struggle for Survival*, (Syracuse: Syracuse University Press, 1986), pp. 5–6.
53. *Ex Parte Green*, 123 F.2d 862 (1941).
54. *United States v. Claus*, 63 F. Supp. 433 (1944); *Albany v. United States*, 152 F.2d 267 (1945).
55. Hauptman, *Iroquois Struggle for Survival*, pp. 6–9.
56. Donald L. Fixico, *Termination and Relocation: Federal Indian Policy, 1945–1960* (Albuquerque: University of New Mexico Press, 1986), pp. 6–8. See also Alison Bernstein, *American Indians and World War II* (Norman: University of Oklahoma Press, 1989).
57. Fixico, *Termination & Relocation*, pp. 45–47.
58. K. W. Johnson, "Sovereignty, Citizenship and the Indian," *Arizona Law Review* 15 (1973): 966, n. 121.
59. Daniel McCool, "Voting Patterns of American Indians in Arizona," *Social Science Journal* 19 (1982): 102.
60. North Dakota Constitution, Section 121, Subdivision 3.
61. McCool, "Voting Patterns of American Indians," 102.
62. *Porter v. Hall*, 271 P. 411 (1928).
63. *Harrison et al. v. Laveen* 67 Ariz. 337 (1948). For Cohen's legal advocacy, see Felix S. Cohen, "Indians Are Citizens," in *The Legal Conscience*, ed. L. K. Cohen (New Haven, Conn.: Yale University Press, 1960), pp. 253–63.
64. See Fixico, *Termination and Relocation*; L. Burt, *Tribalism in Crisis* (Albuquerque: University of New Mexico Press, 1982); and Nicholas Peroff, *Menominee Drums: Tribal Termination and Restoration, 1954–1974* (Norman: University of Oklahoma Press, 1982).

65. Michael L. Lawson, "Federal Water Projects and Indian Lands; The Pick-Sloan Plan, a Case Study," in *The Plains Indians in the Twentieth Century*, ed. Peter Iverson (Norman: University of Oklahoma Press, 1985), pp. 170–73.

66. Hauptman, *Iroquois Struggle for Survival*, pp. 85–178.

67. *Seneca Nation of Indians* v. *Wilbur M. Brucker, et al.*, 262 F.2d 27 (1958).

68. Felix S. Cohen, *Handbook of Federal Indian Law, 1982 Edition* (Charlottesville, Va.: Michie Bobbs-Merrill, 1982), 645–46.

69. 82 Stat. 73 (1968).

70. 88 Stat. 2203 (1975). See Chapter 9 of this book.

71. 92 Stat. 469 (1978); 92 Stat. 3069 (1978).

Chapter 7

1. Mike Wolff, et al., eds., *The Baseball Encyclopedia: The Complete and Official Record of Major League Baseball*, 9th ed., rev. (New York: Macmillan, 1993), p. 1488; Colin G. Calloway, *The Abenaki* (New York: Chelsea House, 1989), p. 81. Paul Brodeur, *Restitution: The Land Claims of the Mashpee, Passamaquoddy, and Penobscot Indians of New England* (Boston: Northeastern University Press, 1985), pp. 132–38. For the history of the Cleveland Indians, see Franklin Lewis, *The Cleveland Indians* (New York: G. P. Putnam, 1949). For Native Americans in professional sports, see Joseph B. Oxendine, *American Indian Sports Heritage* (Champaign, Ill.: Human Kinetics, 1988), pp. 224–32, 243, 249, 251–52, 275, 278. S. I. Thompson, "The American Indian in the Major Leagues," *Baseball Research Journal* 13 (1983): 1–7.

2. Dan Gutman, *Baseball Babylon* (New York: Penguin Books, 1992), pp. 163–64.

3. Calloway, *Abenaki*, p. 81; Oxendine, *American Indian Sports Heritage*, p. 252; Harold Seymour, *Baseball: The Early Years* (New York: Oxford University Press, 1960), p. 332; David Okrent and Steve Wulf, *Baseball Anecdotes* (New York: Harper and Row, 1989), p. 36; Paul Dickson, *The Dickson Baseball Dictionary* (New York: Facts on File, 1989, p. 101; David D. Van Tassel and John J. Graboski, eds., *The Encyclopedia of Cleveland History* (Bloomington: Indiana University Press, 1987), p. 107 (see entry "Sockalexis, Louis Francis 'Chief' "). According to Robert Smith, "Holy Cross … actually set up special classes for ball players, some of whom could not have finished high school with credit." *Baseball in the Afternoon: Tales from a Bygone Era* (New York: Simon and Schuster, 1993), p. 102.

4. *Maine Sunday Telegram*, Aug. 10, 1986, quoted in Dickson, *Dickson Baseball Dictionary*, p. 101.

5. Joseph L. Reichler, comp., *The Great All-Time Baseball Record Book*, rev. ed., updated by Ken Samuelson (New York: Macmillan and Co., 1993), p. 415. Smith, *Baseball in the Afternoon*, p. 102; Van Tassel and Grabowski, *Encyclopedia of Cleveland History*, p. 907; Okrent and Wulf, *Baseball Anecdotes*, p. 36.

6. David Q. Voight, *America through Baseball* (Chicago: Nelson-Hall, 1976), pp. 153–54.

7. David Q. Voight, *American Baseball*, vol. 1: *From Gentleman's Sport to the Commissioner System* (University Park, Pa.: Pennsylvania State University, 1966), p. 262; Okrent and Wulf, *Baseball Anecdotes*, p. 36; Smith, *Baseball in the Afternoon*, p. 103; Van Tassel and Grabowski, *Encyclopedia of Cleveland History*, p. 907.

8. Voight, *America through Baseball*, pp. 153–54; Voight, *American Baseball*, 1: 277; Smith, *Baseball in the Afternoon*, pp. 102–4; Gutman, *Baseball Babylon*, pp. 163–64.

9. Benjamin G. Rader, *American Sports: From the Age of Folk Games to the Age of Spectators* (Englewood Cliffs, N.J.: Prentice-Hall, 1983), pp. 119–20.

10. Voight, *America through Baseball*, pp. 153–54; Voight, *American Baseball*, 1: 277; Okrent and Wulf, *Baseball Anecdotes*, p. 36; Smith, *Baseball in the Afternoon*, pp. 102–3.

11. Brodeur, *Restitution*, p. 132.

12. Van Tassel and Grabowski, eds., *The Encyclopedia of Cleveland History*, pp. 242–243 [entry: "Cleveland Indians"]; p. 273 [entry: "Cleveland Spiders"]; p. 907 [entry: "Sockalexis, Louis Francis 'Chief'"]. Dickson, *Dickson Baseball Dictionary*, p. 101; Calloway, *Abenaki*, p. 81. For more on Sockalexis, see Trina Wellman, *Louis Francis Sockalexis: The Life-story of a Penobscot Indian* (Augusta, Maine: Maine Department of Indian Affairs, 1975).

13. Biographical materials on Silverheels's life are found in the library of the Woodland Cultural Centre, Six Nations Indian Reserve, Brantford, Ontario. The author should like to thank Sheila Staats, the librarian at the Woodland Cultural Centre, for her assistance. For Silverheels's obituary, see "Jay Silverheels, Actor, 62 Dead; Was Tonto in TV 'Lone Ranger,' *New York Times*, Mar. 6, 1980, sec. 4, 19. Other biographical information can be found in: Evelyn Mack Truitt, *Who Was Who on Screen* (New York: Bowker, 1984), pp. 368–69; David Ragan, *Who's Who in Hollywood, 1900–1976* (New Rochelle, N.Y.: Arlington House, 1976), p. 430; Roy Wright, "Silverheels, Jay," in *The Canadian Encyclopedia*, 2d ed. (Edmonton: Hurtig, 1988), vol. 4; *Turtle Quarterly* 2 (Niagara Falls, N.Y., Summer 1988). Wright's article and others suggest that Silverheels was born in 1919. This is unlikely since he would be only fourteen years of age in 1933, at a time when he was already a star in professional lacrosse. Other sources suggest that he was born in 1912, which seems more accurate.

14. Interview with Francis Kettle, July 27, 1977, and June 4, 1978, Cattaraugus Indian Reservation; interview with Arleigh Hill, July 25, 1978, Rochester, N.Y.; interview with Ramona Charles, May 22, 1980, Tonawanda Indian Reservation. "Rochester to Lone Ranger: Tonto Was Iroquois Lacrosse Star Here in 1930s," *Rochester Times-Union*, Feb. 15, 1955, p. 2.

15. See n. 13.

16. Interviews with Francis Kettle, Arleigh Hill, and Ramona Charles; biographical materials on Silverheels's life at the Woodland Indian Centre.

17. Truitt, *Who Was Who on Screen*, pp. 368–69; Ragan, *Who's Who in Hollywood*, p. 430.

18. Alex M. McNeil, *Total Television: A Comprehensive Guide to Programming from 1948 to the Present*, 3d ed. (New York: Penguin Books, 1991), p. 445; Tim Brooks and Earle Marsh, *The Complete Directory of Prime Time Network TV Shows, 1946–Present*, 5th ed. (New York: Ballantine Books, 1992), p. 552.

19. Brooks and Marsh, *The Complete Directory of Prime Time Network TV Shows*, p. 576.

20. Donald L. Kaufmann, "The Indian as Media Hand-me-down," in *The Pretend Indians: Images of Native Americans in the Movies*, ed. Gretchen M. Bataille and Charles L. P. Silet (Ames: Iowa State University Press, 1980), p. 30.

21. Michael T. Marsden and Jack Nachbar, "The Indian in the Movies," in *Handbook of North American Indians*, vol. 4: *History of Indian-White Relations*, ed. Wilcomb E. Washburn (Washington, D.C.: Smithsonian Institution, 1988), p. 612.

22. Raymond William Stedman, *Shadows of the Indian: Stereotypes in American Culture* (Norman: University of Oklahoma Press, 1982), p. 51.

23. Vine Deloria, Jr., *Custer Died for Your Sins: An Indian Manifesto* (Macmillan, 1969; repr., New York: Avon Books, 1970), pp. 199–200.

24. See n. 17.

25. Marsden and Nachbar, "Indian in the Movies," pp. 614–15; John A. Price, "The Stereotyping of North American Indians in Motion Pictures," in Bataille and Silet, *Pretend Indians*, p. 86. For Silverheels's own views, see "Lo! The Image of the Indian!" *Indians Illustrated* 1, no. 6 (July–August 1968): 8–9 (Buena Park, Calif.: Talking Leaves, 1968).

26. See n. 13.

Chapter 8

1. American Indian Chicago Conference, *Declaration of Indian Purpose*, American Indian Chicago Conference Manuscripts, Box 2, File: "The Voice of the American Indian: Declaration of Indian Purpose," (Smithsonian) National Anthropological Archives, Washington, D.C. (hereafter cited as AICC MSS., NAA). More American Indians attended than registered in Chicago. Perhaps as many as eight hundred came to the convocation. Nancy O. Lurie, "The Voice of the American Indian: Report on the American Indian Chicago Conference," *Current Anthropology* 2 (December 1961): 489.

2. Nancy O. Lurie, "An American Indian Renascence?" in *The American Indian Today*, ed. Stuart Levine and Nancy O. Lurie (Baltimore, 1968), pp. 323–24; D'Arcy McNickle, *Native American Tribalism: Indian Survival and Renewals* (New York: Oxford University Press, 1973), p. 117; D'Arcy McNickle, *They Came Here First*, rev. ed. (New York: Octagon Books, 1975), pp. 264–65; Hauptman, *Iroquois Struggle for Survival*, pp. 208–14. The AICC is not mentioned or cited in Frank W. Porter III, ed., *Strategies for Survival: American Indians in the Eastern United States* (Westport, Conn., Greenwood Press, 1986), a recent study of nonfederally recognized Indian communities.

3. Lurie, "American Indian Renascence?," 323.

4. Interview with Sol Tax, Dec. 5, 1982, Indian Rights Association, Centennial Conference, Philadelphia. For the Seneca Indian fight against the Kinzua Dam, see Hauptman, *Iroquois Struggle for Survival*, chaps. 6 and 7.

5. Carl Tjerandsen, *Education for Citizenship: A Foundation's Experience* (Santa Cruz, Calif.: Schwartzhaupt Foundation, 1980), pp. 64–68.

6. Interview with Nancy Lurie, June 20, 1983, Milwaukee Public Museum, Milwaukee. For federal Indian policy in the postwar era, see Donald L. Fixico, *Termination and Relocation*.

7. The map can be found in "Letter to Indians," Dec. 27, 1960, with supplementary documents, Department of Anthropology Records, 1953–1970, Box 1, Folder 9, Special Collections, University of Chicago Library; and in the inside back cover of Levine and Lurie, *American Indian Today*. For criticisms of this map, see Alice Marriott and Carol Rachlin, Apr. 9, 1961, AICC MSS., Box 2, File: "Oklahoma Regional Meeting, NAA."

8. Brewton Berry, "A Study of Certain Racial Hybrids in the Eastern United States," *Ohio State University Graduate School Record* 11 (February 1958); Berry, "Myth of

the Vanishing Indian," *Phylon* (Spring 1960): 51–57; Berry, "The Mestizos of South Carolina," *American Journal of Sociology* 51 (July 1945): 34–41; all found in AICC MSS., Box 15, File: "Brewton Berry," NAA. Berry later developed this theme in *Almost White: A Study of Certain Racial Hybrids in the Eastern United States* (New York: Macmillan, 1963).

9. Lurie and Tax had to grapple seriously with defining Indian identity because of Indian–white and Indian–black miscegenation, and they discussed whether "we are being too liberal in our definition of Indian." See Nancy O. Lurie to Sol Tax, Jan. 10, 1961, AICC MSS., Box 8, File: "N.O.L., Jan.–Feb., 1961," NAA. In contrast, see Berry, *Almost White,* and his "Marginal Groups," in Trigger, *Handbook of North American Indians,* 15: 290–95; Calvin L. Beale, "American Triracial Isolates," *Eugenics Quarterly* 4 (1957): 187–96; Vernon Parenton and Roland Pellegrin, "The Sabines: A Study of Racial Hybrids in a Louisiana Coastal Parish," *Social Forces* 29 (1950): 148–58. In 1972, the *American Anthropologist* had a special section on these communities, edited by B. Eugene Griessman, labeling them "American Isolates."

10. Nancy O. Lurie to Walter Taylor, Mar. 2, 1961, AICC MSS., Box 10, File: "Walter Taylor," NAA.

11. AICC Roster of Committees, June 1961, AICC MSS., Box 3, NAA; AICC *Progress Report* no. 4, Apr. 26, 1961, found in Department of Anthropology Records, 1953–1970, Box 1, Folder 9, Special Collections, University of Chicago Library.

12. See AICC MSS., Box 1, File: "Historical Beginnings of AICC," NAA; Lurie, "Voice of the American Indian," 482–83.

13. Lurie, "Voice of the American Indian," 483; interview with Nancy O. Lurie.

14. Hauptman, *Iroquois Struggle for Survival,* chap. 9.

15. Graymont, *Fighting Tuscarora,* p. xxviii.

16. Sol Tax to William Rickard, Jan. 26, 1961, AICC MSS., Box 10, File: "William Rickard," NAA.

17. William Rickard, "Meeting of Indian Leaders" (report), February 1961, AICC MSS., Box 10, File: "William Rickard," NAA.

18. William Rickard to Sol Tax, February 1961, AICC MSS., Box 10, File: "William Rickard," NAA.

19. William Rickard's List of Indian Invitees, AICC MSS., Box 2, File: "AICC East Regional Meeting," NAA.

20. Nancy O. Lurie to D'Arcy McNickle, Feb. 22, 1961, AICC MSS., Box 9, File: "D'Arcy McNickle," NAA.

21. Rickard Report, February 1961.

22. Interview of Theodore B. Hetzel, Jan. 17, 1984, Kennett Square, Pa.

23. Nancy O. Lurie to Judge Lacy Maynor, Mar. 16, 1961; Judge Lacy Maynor to Nancy O. Lurie, Mar. 7, 1961, AICC MSS., Box 8, File: "MA," NAA.

24. American Indian Chicago Conference, *Progress Report* No. 5, May 26, 1961, found in Department of Anthropology Records, 1953–1970, Box 1, Folder 9, Special Collections, University of Chicago Library.

25. William C. Sturtevant, Reply to Questionnaire, April 1961, AICC MSS., Box 2, File: "Yellow Suggestion Sheets," NAA.

26. Theodore B. Hetzel to Sol Tax, with attached list, Mar. 1, 1961, AICC MSS., Box 7, File: "Ted Hetzel," NAA.

27. Registration List, American Indian Haverford Conference, April 1961, AICC MSS., Box 2, File: "East Regional Meeting," NAA.

28. Anita de Frey (Sunbird) Report on American Indian Chicago Conference Preliminary Eastern Seaboard Conference at Haverford College, Haverford, Pennsylvania, Apr. 8–11, 1961; and her Further Report on Preliminary Eastern Seaboard Conference at Haverford College, Haverford, Pennsylvania, Apr. 8–11, 1961, AICC MSS., Box 2, File: "East Regional Meeting," NAA. For two distinct non-Indian reactions to the Haverford meeting, see Theodore B. Hetzel (positive reaction) to Sol Tax, Nancy Lurie, and D'Arcy McNickle, Apr. 10, 1961, AICC MSS., Box 7, File: "Ted Hetzel," NAA; Frederica de Laguna (negative reaction) to Sol Tax, Apr. 11, 1961, AICC MSS., Box 8, File: "N.O.L., April–May, 1961," NAA.

29. Marriott and Rachlin to Tax, Apr. 9, 1961. See also AICC *Progress Report* No. 4.

30. Carol Rachlin to Sol Tax, Mar. 14, 1961, AICC MSS., Box 2, File: "Oklahoma Regional Meeting," NAA.

31. Richard M. Gaffney Reply to Questionnaire, April 1961, AICC MSS., Box 2, File: "Yellow Suggestion Sheets," NAA.

32. Helen Attaquin, Reply to Questionnaire, April 1961, AICC MSS., Box 2, File: "Yellow Suggestion Sheets," NAA.

33. Replies of the following Rappahannocks: Orlean and Floyd Byrd, Merritt Fortune, and James, Otto, Samuel, Vivian, and W. H. Nelson; Cleo La Pearl (Oneida); and Mrs. Noali Hatard (Houma), April 1961, AICC MSS., Box 2, File: "Yellow Suggestion Sheets," NAA.

34. Karen Rickard, Reply to Questionnaire, April 1961, AICC MSS., Box 2, File: "Yellow Suggestion Sheets," NAA.

35. Emmanuel Many Deeds, Reply to Questionnaire, April 1961, AICC MSS., Box 2, File: "Yellow Suggestion Sheets," NAA.

36. AICC, *Progress Report* No. 5, May 26, 1961. Sol Tax to Zara Ciscoe Brough, May 11, 1961; Brough to Tax, Apr. 26, 1961, AICC MSS., Box 5, File: "Bod-Bz," NAA.

37. Zara Ciscoe Brough to Sol Tax, June 1961, AICC MSS., Box 5, File: "Bod-Bz," NAA.

38. (Princess) Mary Red Wing Congdon (Mrs. Daniel Congdon), June 2, 1961, AICC MSS., Box 10, File: "R," NAA. Red Wing, a member of the Indian Defense League and friend of the Rickard family for thirty years, had initially feared that the AICC was government controlled; however, she became one of the greatest supporters of the AICC and served as the secretary of the regional meeting at Haverford. Mary Red Wing Congdon, Reply to Questionnaire, AICC MSS., Box 2, File: "Yellow Suggestions Sheets," NAA; Mary Red Wing Congdon to Sol Tax, Apr. 28, 1961, AICC MSS., Box 10, File: "R," NAA; Mary Red Wing Congdon to Sol Tax, Box 5, File: "C general file," NAA.

39. Sol Tax, "What the Indians Want," *Chicago Sun-Times,* June 11, 1961.

40. McNickle, *Native American Tribalism,* p. 117.

41. Lurie, "Voice of the American Indian," 495. News coverage of the conference failed to pick up this tension. See the *New York Times,* June 13, 1961, p. 6; June 15, 1961, p. 20; June 16, 1961, p. 34; June 19, 1961, p. 24; June 20, 1961, p. 16; June 22, 1961, p. 12.

42. This issue had arisen as early as April 1961. Sol Tax to Richard Schifter, Apr. 24, 1961, AICC MSS., Box 10, File: "S," NAA. The pamphlet can be found in AICC MSS., Box 4, File: "A," NAA.

43. William Rickard, Report of American Indian Chicago Conference, University of Chicago, Chicago, Ill., June 13–20, 1961, AICC MSS., Box 10, File: "R," NAA. Besides his objection to the NCAI's position on citizenship, Rickard's war with the

NCAI was of a long-standing nature. He believed that the NCAI was too much influenced by the BIA and had not done enough for the Tuscaroras in their fight against the New York State Power Authority. For Rickard's views of the NCAI, see Rickard Report, Feb., 1961; William Rickard to Sol Tax, March 6, 8, and 23, 1961, Rickard to Nancy Lurie, Feb. 16, 1961, AICC MSS., Box 10, File: "Rickard," NAA.

44. Ibid. Rickard, Report ... February, 1961.
45. AICC *Declaration of Indian Purpose.*
46. Ibid.
47. Helen D. Maynor to Sol Tax, July 13, 1961, AICC MSS., Box 8, File: "MA," NAA.
48. Nancy O. Lurie, personal communication, July 7, 1985.
49. Jack Campisi, Houma Field Notes, 1983–1985.
50. William Rickard to W. R. Richardson, Apr. 8, 1983; Resolution from Haliwa Indian Tribe to Tuscarora Tribal Council, n.d.; Rickard to Richardson, July 5, 1962. Letters presented to Jack Campisi by Chief W. R. Richardson.
51. Jack Campisi, Haliwa Field Notes, 1983–1985.
52. AICC, *Progress Report,* Dec. 1, 1962.
53. American Indian Policy Review Commission, *Final Report: Report on Terminated and Nonfederally Recognized Indians, Task Force 10* (Washington, D.C.: U.S.G.P.O., 1976).
54. Tax interview, Dec. 5, 1982.

Chapter 9

1. William Shakespeare, *King Henry VI,* Part II, Act IV, scene 2, line 75.
2. United States Congress, Senate, Select Committee on Indian Affairs, *Hearings on S. 2895: Renegotiation of Seneca Nation Leases,* Sept. 18, 1990, 101st Congress, 2d sess. (Washington, D.C.: U.S.G.P.O., 1991), pp. 19–21, 57–64. For a brief summary of the history of this controversy, see Laurence M. Hauptman, "Compensatory Justice: The Seneca Nation Settlement Act," *National Forum* 71 (Spring 1991): 31–33. See also my other writings on the subject: Hauptman, "The Historical Background to the Present-Day Seneca Nation-Salamanca Lease Controversy," in: Vecsey and Starna, *Iroquois Land Claims,* pp. 101–22; Hauptman, *Iroquois Struggle for Survival,* chaps. 2–4; and Hauptman, *Iroquois in the Civil War,* chap. 9.
3. James Welch, *The Indian Lawyer* (New York: W. W. Norton, 1990).
4. 414 U.S. 661. For Shattuck's analysis of the case, see his memoir—George C. Shattuck, *The Oneida Land Claims: A Legal History* (Syracuse, N.Y.: Syracuse University Press, 1991). See also Hauptman, *Iroquois Struggle for Survival,* chap. 10.
5. Jack Campisi, "The Trade and Intercourse Acts: Land Claims on the Eastern Seaboard," in *Irredeemable America: The Indians' Estate and Land Claims,* ed. Imre Sutton (Albuquerque: University of New Mexico Press, 1985), pp. 337–62; and Campisi, "The New England Tribes and Their Quest for Justice," in Hauptman and Wherry, *Pequots in Southern New England,* pp. 179–93.
6. Thomas Egan, "Indian Tribe Agrees to Drop Claim to Tacoma Land for $162 Million," *New York Times,* Aug. 29, 1988, p. 1a.
7. Orlan Svingen, "Jim Crow, Indian Style," *American Indian Quarterly* 11 (Fall 1987): 275–86.
8. Interview with Jack Campisi, Apr. 9, 1993. Campisi is a leading applied anthropologist who has worked with both of these legal-service agencies.
9. For Miller's work, see Lynn Riddle, "South Carolina Settling Catawba Claim," *New*

York Times, Nov. 15, 1992; "Catawba Tribe Approves Settlement with South Carolina," *NARF Legal Review* 18 (Winter/Spring 1993), 1–12. For Aschenbrenner's work, see, for example, United States Congress, Senate, Select Committee on Indian Affairs: *Hearings on S. 2084: Ancient Indian Land Claims,* June 23, 1982, 97th Congress, 2d sess. (Washington, D.C.: U.S.G.P.O., 1982), pp. 150 passim.

10. I observed the smooth workings of the United States Senate Select Committee on Indian Affairs while serving as an "expert witness" on the Seneca-Salamanca lease controversy. See n. 2.

11. I was a consultant for the Oneida Nation of Indians of Wisconsin, involved in helping to organize historical conferences. Many of the observations presented here are from my Oneida fieldnotes made from 1978 to 1990. For more on the Wisconsin Oneida, see Campisi and Hauptman, *Oneida Indian Experience.*

12. Francis Skenandore, "William Skenandore," in Campisi and Hauptman, *Oneida Indian Experience,* pp. 126–30; interviews with Norbert Hill, Sr., Oct. 17, 1978, July 28, 1982, Oneida, Wisc.; Gerald Hill, p.c., June 4, 1985, Oneonta, N.Y.

13. *Senate Hearings on S. 2895,* pp. 33–40. Laurence M. Hauptman, Seneca Field Notes, 1987-1992.

14. Marguerite Smith, p.c., SUNY College at New Paltz, New Paltz, N.Y.; Laurence M. Hauptman, Shinnecock Field Notes, 1988–1991.

15. Sider, *Lumbee Indian Histories,* pp. xxiv, 271, 291; "Supporters Link Death of Indian to Candidacy," *New York Times,* Mar. 28, 1988, p. 12.

16. Sider, *Lumbee Indian Histories,* pp. xxiv, 271, 291. In May 1982, I coordinated a conference at SUNY New Paltz on federal recognition, which was attended by staff members of the Lumbee River Legal Services. Jack Campisi, p.c., Apr. 9, 1993. For the serendipitous nature of the federal recognition process, see Campisi, "New England Tribes," pp. 179–83; and Sider, *Lumbee Indian Histories,* pp. 19–23, 271, 291.

17. "Indian Politician Killed in Carolina," *New York Times,* Mar. 27, 1988, sec. 1, 25; "Indian Candidate for N.C. Judge Murdered," *Miami Herald,* Mar. 27, 1988, p. 41.

18. Monte Plott, "Friend Says Slain Indian Was Probing Corruption," *Palm Beach Post* (Florida), Mar. 29, 1988; Mab Segrest, "Robeson County's 'Third World Ills,' " *Christian Century* 104 (May 11, 1988): 468–69; "There's Trouble in Robeson County," *U.S. News and World Report* 104 (May 2, 1988): 24–25. For the tense race history in the county and KKK activity, see Evans, *To Die Game,* pp. 254–56. Blu, *Lumbee Problem,* pp. 124–26, 156–60.

19. Segrest, "Robeson County's 'Third World Ills,' " 468–69.

20. Ibid. See also Ronald Smothers, "Steps Taken to Ease Tension in Carolina County," *New York Times,* April 10, 1988, sec. 1, 26.

21. Fred Grimm, "Indian Leader's Death Blamed on Petty Quarrel, Not Racism," *Miami Herald,* Mar. 30, 1988, p. 2–A. "Indian Held in Candidate's Death; Sheriff Rules Out Political Motive," *New York Times,* Mar. 30, 1988, sec. 1, 20; "Prosecutor in Killing of Indian," *New York Times,* Apr. 1, 1988, sec. 1, 26.

22. Susan Sanders and Debbie Thomas, "Native American Rights Fund: Our First 20 Years," *Clearinghouse Review* 26 (1992): 49–56; Jack Campisi, "Native American Rights Fund," in Armand S. LaPotin, ed., *Native American Voluntary Organizations* (Westport, Conn.: Greenwood Press, 1983), pp. 130–31. I have also consulted the NARF *Announcements,* its *Law Review,* and its *Annual Reports* over the past twenty years.

23. Nicholas C. Peroff, *Menominee Drums: Tribal Termination and Restoration, 1954–*

1974 (Norman: University of Oklahoma Press, 1982), pp. 201, 201, n. 3, 225. See also Native American Rights Fund, *Announcements,* 2 (October–December, 1973).

24. *Fisher v. Montana,* 424 U.S. 382 (1976).

25. Indian Child Welfare Act of 1978, 25 U.S.C. 1901 et seq.

26. *Mississippi Band of Choctaw Indians v. Holyfield,* 490 U.S. 30 (1989).

27. William T. Hagan, "To Correct Certain Evils: The Indian Land Claims Cases," in *Iroquois Land Claims,* ed. Christopher Vecsey and William A. Starna (Syracuse, N.Y.: Syracuse University Press, 1988), pp. 24–25; Campisi, "Trade and Intercourse Acts," 337–62; Brodeur, *Restitution,* pp. 127–31.

28. I have known Arlinda Locklear since 1985, and have discussed her work on behalf of Oneida and other Native Americans with her on at least five separate occasions. Besides being an exceptional attorney, she brings to her work a rich sense of history. See her writings: "The Oneida Land Claims: A Legal Overview," in Vecsey and Starna, *Iroquois Land Claims,* pp. 141–54; and her "The Allotment of the Oneida Reservation and Its Legal Ramification," in: Campisi and Hauptman, *Oneida Indian Experience,* pp. 83–93.

29. *Solem v. Bartlett,* 465 U.S. 463 (1984).

30. Charles F. Wilkinson, *American Indians, Time and the Law* (New Haven, Conn.: Yale University Press, 1987), p. 41.

31. *County of Oneida v. Oneida Indian Nation,* 470 U.S. 226 (1985). See n. 29. Locklear, who was eight and a half months pregnant at the time, argued her points for three hours.

32. U.S. Congress, Senate, Select Committee on Indian Affairs, *Hearings on S. 2084: Ancient Indian Land Claims,* pp. 110–12, 150 passim.

33. All except the recently recognized (1992) Micmac and the Mohegan are listed in United States Congress, Senate, Select Committee on Indian Affairs, *Hearings on S. 1315: Indian Federal Recognition Administrative Procedures Act of 1991,* Oct. 22, 1991, 102d Congress, 1st sess. (Washington, D.C.: U.S.G.P.O., 1992), p. 94. For Sockbeson's testimony, see pp. 58–62 of this hearing. Sanders and Thomas, "Native American Rights Fund," 52. For the Pequot revival, see Hauptman and Wherry, *Pequots in Southern New England.*

34. United States Congress, Senate, *Hearings on S. 1021 and S. 1980: Native America Grave and Burial Protection Act (Repatriation): Native American Repatriation of Cultural Patrimony Act: And Heard Museum Report,* May 14, 1990, 101st Congress, 2d sess. (Washington, D.C.: U.S.G.P.O., 1990), pp. 12–13.

35. *Charrier v. Bell,* 547 F. Supp. 580 (M.D. La. 1982).

36. Robert M. Peregoy, "Nebraska's Landmark Repatriation Law: A Study of Cross-Cultural Conflict and Resolution," *American Indian Culture and Research Journal* (1992): 139–96. The entire issue of this journal is devoted to the "Repatriation of American Indian Remains."

37. Native American Graves Protection and Repatriation Act, 25 U.S.C. 3001 et seq.

38. Walter R. Echo-Hawk, "Preface" to special issue on "Repatriation of American Indian Remains," *American Indian Culture and Research Journal* 16:2 (1992): 3. See Echo-Hawk's testimony, cited in n. 34, and his article, written with Roger C. Echo-Hawk, "Repatriation, Reburial and Religious Rights," in Christopher Vecsey, ed., *Handbook of American Indian Religious Freedom* (New York: Crossroad Publishing Company, 1991), pp. 63–80. One of the nations affected most by this issue has been the Echo-Hawk's own Pawnee community.

39. See Jack Campisi, *The Mashpee Indians: Tribe on Trial* (Syracuse, N.Y.: Syracuse University Press, 1991), esp. pp. 19, 153–54; and Brodeur, *Restitution*, pp. 41, 59–60.

40. Rennard Strickland, "Indian Law and the Miner's Canary: The Signs of Poison Gas," *Cleveland State Law Review* 43 (1991): 483–504.

41. *Pyramid Lake Paiute* v. *Morton*, 354 F. Supp. 252 (D.D.C. 1973), *cert denied*, 420 U.S. 962 (1983); *Nevada* v. *United States*, 463 U.S. 110 (1983).

42. *Employment Division* v. *Smith*.

43. *Lyng* v. *Northwest Indian Cemetery Protective Association*, 108 S. Ct. 1913 (1988).

INDEX